BUILT [illegible]

“*Built Without a Bluepri* [illegible] call to action. Ashley Mills shows [illegible]ity, and ambition can break cycles and build legac[illegible] his journey is proof that where you start doesn’t define how far you can go. It’s an inspiring reminder of why representation, opportunity, and belief matter.”

- RIC LEWIS

Founder of The Black Heart Foundation,
Chair of The Crown Estate, Executive Chairman and CIO of Tristan Capital Partners, and The Powerlist 2019’s Most Powerful Black Briton.

"Ashley’s story touched me, inspired me, and taught me the meaning of true resilience - and how being different can be a superpower. His journey resonated with me on a deeply personal level. This memoir is a celebration of what's possible when hardship is transformed into leadership, adversity into strength, and when absence of a blueprint becomes the very blueprint that breaks the cycle."

- MUSTAFA SHAMSELDIN

SVP PepsiCo, Forbes Top 50 Storyteller.

“A deeply moving and powerful story - a testament to grit, identity, and breaking cycles. This book carries both heart and tenacity. Ashley’s story challenges stereotypes and offers a new, powerful yet relatable way of building resilience, leadership, and belonging.”

DR. SELINA NERI – CEO
Dean, and co-founder of the Institute for Future Readiness;
Thinkers50 Radar 2025.

“Ashley’s story moved me deeply. *Built Without a Blueprint* is a testament to resilience, love and the power of breaking cycles. It reminds us that even in absence we can build strength, even in struggle we can find joy & even in difference we can create belonging. This is more than a book it’s a lifeline for anyone who has felt unseen. The book is a rare and powerful combination of raw emotion and vital business wisdom, a must read for business leaders who need to be reminded that their story is their greatest strength”.

- RAKI PHILIPS
Regional President, Accor; CEO &
Middle East Businessperson of the Year 2023.

"We live in stories, they shape us and give our lives meaning and purpose. Ashley’s book is not only an unforgettable memoir of hard-won and insightful lessons mined from his own life, but it’s also an invitation to reflect on your identity story, to mine your own life lessons and craft your own blueprint in service of others. Highly recommended.”

- STEVEN D’SOUZA
Bestselling Author of *Made in Britain* and *Shadows at Work.*

"By facing the pain and shame of growing up without a father in an all-white world, Ashley has courageously transformed that pain into a strong, resilient leader personality who, I have no doubt, will become a unique role model for the many wounded individuals who, by reading this book, will now be given the chance to emulate him."

- GARY R. HAYES
Jungian Psychoanalyst, Faculty Member at the International School of Analytical Psychology, Zürich.

"*Built Without a Blueprint* is more than a memoir - it's an invitation to see adversity not as limitation, but as the foundation for leadership without borders. It showcases resilience as the ability to withstand, adapt, and bounce back from adversity through a positive attitude and strong social connections."

- JOHNY ZAKHEM
Group Chief Financial Officer and Business Officer, Raffles & Fairmont Hotels.

"*Built Without a Blueprint* is a beautiful example of the treasures we can find when we search our own stories for the wisdom they hold. Ashley Mills shows us that the best tools for narrative exploration are honesty, curiosity, courage, and a willingness to be surprised. He has given us a wonderful gift, and a guide for anyone who wants to use the stories of their past to elevate their future. Thank you Ashley!"

- MICHAEL STANFORD, Managing Director, Summit Leadership & author of *Leadership Transition: How Leaders Turn Chaos Into Growth.*

"*Built Without a Blueprint* is Ashley Mills' moving story of resilience and self-discovery, transformed into universal lessons on identity and leadership. Blending lived experience with thoughtful reflection, it speaks to scholars, professionals, and readers alike, offering inspiration and insight for anyone seeking to chart their own path."

- DR. YUSAF H. AKBAR

Professor of Management and Strategy, Central European University, Vienna, Austria, Academic Leader & Expert in Strategy and International Business.

"Ashley's career and life story are powerful examples of what can be achieved through determination, curiosity, and purposeful leadership. His ability to transform challenges into opportunities and to inspire those around him has always set him apart. I have no doubt that the insights and experiences he shares will motivate readers to pursue their goals with renewed focus and confidence."

- IULIANA ISARESCU

Chief People Officer, Piaget, Richemont Group.

“As someone who knows what it means to push through limits, on the track and in life - I found *Built Without a Blueprint* deeply moving and powerfully relevant. Ashley Mills’ story is a testament to resilience, identity, and the strength found in forging your own path. His journey from absence to leadership mirrors the grit and determination it takes to succeed against the odds. This book isn’t just inspiring; it’s a practical and relevant guide for anyone striving to break cycles and build something lasting.”

- MARK RICHARDSON OLY
Olympian, former World Champion 4x400m,
and Senior Client Partner & EMEA Practice Lead at Korn Ferry.

Ashley Mills is a leadership advisor, writer, and speaker with over 25 years' experience in executive search and organisational leadership, including more than a decade as a Senior Partner at Korn Ferry, the world's leading executive search and leadership advisory firm. Born to a single mother in a working-class Yorkshire town, he built a global career spanning London, Paris, Geneva, Zurich, and Dubai. Holding an Executive MBA with a specialisation in Occupational Psychology, Ashley combines behavioural insight with practical leadership experience. Through *Built Without a Blueprint*, he shares his journey of overcoming fatherlessness and breaking cycles, inspiring others to lead, live, and build legacy on their own terms.

Note on Terminology:

Throughout this book I use the term “mixed race”. It was the language of my childhood, my community, and how I understood my identity growing up.

I recognise that language evolves, and today many prefer terms like “dual heritage” or “mixed parentage”, reflecting the truth that there is no such thing as a “pure race”. I honour that evolution. Still, I have chosen to use the words that shaped me, to remain true to the era and experiences I am describing.

ASHLEY MILLS

BUILT WITHOUT A BLUEPRINT

tributary

Published in Great Britain in 2025 by Tributary, an imprint of
Foreshore Publishing Limited
86-90 Paul Street London EC2A 4NE
www.foreshorepublishing.com

ISBN 978-1-9192526-2-9
A CIP catalogue record for this book is available from the British Library.

Typeset in Minion Pro.
Minion was originally created and released in 1990 by Adobe Systems. Designed by Robert Slimbach, it is inspired by late Renaissance-era type and intended for body text and extended reading. Minion Pro is an update of the original family.

Typeset by Richard Powell.
Printed and bound in Great Britain by 4Edge Ltd, Essex.

Contents

Foreword

From Me to You

If you're holding this book in your hands, I want to say something straight away:

This story, my story, is also yours. Maybe you grew up feeling different. Like you didn't quite belong anywhere. Maybe you've walked into rooms where no one looked like you, or spoken in meetings where your voice trembled, not from fear but from the weight of having to prove yourself one more time.

I know that feeling.

For most of my life, I moved through worlds without a map. One foot in working-class Yorkshire. The other in elite management and boardrooms across different continents. I became fluent in adaptation, code-switching, survival. But underneath it all, I was still searching, for identity, for belonging, for a place to call home. This book is the truth of that journey.

It's about growing up mixed-race in a town that wasn't built for difference. It's about danger, shame and the ache of a father who was never there. It's about chasing success across countries and continents and realising, at the height of it all, that none of it means anything if you can't live it as your whole self. It's about breaking cycles. About healing. About becoming the role model I never had, not just for my daughter but for anyone who needs to see someone like them rise, stumble, rebuild and rise again.

I wrote this for people like us. For the ones who grew up between cultures, between classes, between expectations. For those who felt too much of one thing and not enough of another. For anyone who's ever had to build a sense of self from scratch, without a blueprint. Inside, you'll find stories that are raw. Some joyful. Others that nearly broke me. But each one gave me something, strength, insight, a scar I now carry with pride. And maybe, just maybe, they'll help build something in you too.

Because our differences are not our weakness. They're our foundation. And legacy isn't just about what we earn or achieve. It's about what we heal, what we teach and what we pass on.

So if you've ever felt like an outsider, this book is for you. And if you've ever questioned whether you belong, let me tell you now: You do. You always did. And you don't have to build alone anymore. Let's do this, together.

Ashley, September 2025.

Kintsugi

Kintsugi (金継ぎ): *noun*

Literally "gold joinery."
The Japanese art of repairing broken pottery with veins of gold, honouring the cracks rather than hiding them.
It reminds us that what is fractured can be made whole again, and often more beautiful for having been broken.

PART I:

THE EARLY FOUNDATIONS – BUILT FROM ABSENCE

1

SHADOWS IN THE STREETS

I remember the cold first, biting straight through my jumper and into my cheeks. Morley's skies always felt low, grey and heavy, as though holding something back. Even on days when the sun broke through, it never seemed to stay long enough to truly warm us. Cold. Quiet. Uneasy. But it wasn't just the weather that chilled me.

I was maybe eight or nine when I first recognised that sound, boots. Heavy ones. Slow and deliberate, echoing off cracked pavements behind me like a warning. Doc Martens. Steel-capped. You heard them before you saw them and you were meant to.

Even now, decades later, if I close my eyes and listen carefully, I can still feel them, not just in my ears but deep in my chest. A message, clear and unmistakable: "We see you. You don't belong here."

Morley was a hard town built on mills, manual labour and no-nonsense Yorkshire grit. People wore hardship like a badge, shoulders squared against life. There was pride in that struggle but also suspicion. Tight-knit communities took care of their own, if you looked like their own. And me? I didn't.

I was one of the only kids of colour in the area. A mixed-race boy with a redheaded white mum and no father in sight. A walking question mark in a place that didn't like questions. The unwritten rule was simple: know your place. Don't step out of line. Keep your head down. Blend in, if you can. But I couldn't. Not even if I tried.

In the 1980s, Morley had a reputation. It was known, quietly but widely, for having one of the largest memberships of the British National Party (BNP) in the country. The BNP wasn't just a far-right political fringe group; it was a presence. A threat. It seeped into the cracks of the town like damp. You could feel it in the looks, in the whispers, in the silence that followed you into shops. This wasn't about politics. It was about fear. Control. Difference.

The town centre wasn't far from our house but every walk there felt like threading a needle. You stayed alert. Crumbling brick walls. Boarded-up shops. Graffiti, some harmless, others laced with warning. "NF" sprayed in thick white letters. Union Jacks paired with swastikas. A jagged BNP logo drawn by someone indifferent to the eyes of children.

Yet even then, as a kid, I remember thinking: if I could hear their boots, at least I knew which direction to run.

I couldn't blend in. My skin gave me away before I opened my mouth.

But it wasn't just about race. Yorkshire in the 1980s was a place under siege, battered both from within and beyond. The miners' strikes had torn through communities just like ours. Pits were closing. Work was disappearing. Families that had scraped by for generations suddenly had nothing left to scrape. You could feel it in the clipped voices of the men on the corners, the tension in the working men's clubs, the weary looks passed between neighbours who once shared everything but were now barely hanging on themselves.

Thatcher's Britain didn't land gently up north. It hit like a hammer.

Morley was changing.

Families from India, Pakistan, Bangladesh, who had filled jobs nobody else wanted, were now raising second-generation kids like me. New faces in an old town that wasn't ready for us.

The BNP didn't rise in a vacuum. It rose out of fear. Fear of change. Fear of difference. Fear that the only thing people in Morley had left, their identity, was slipping away. And for some, the only way to fight that fear was to turn it outward.

Some adjusted. Many resisted. Yet, quietly, some families stood firm.

The Rhouds' shop was a few minutes' walk away, just down the busy Middleton Road. A small off-license crammed floor-to-ceiling with everything from penny sweets to tins of beans. The air always held the gentle aroma of spices, a reminder there was a bigger world beyond Morley's grey streets. To some in our neighbourhood, it was a target. Kids hurled insults casually, windows shattered overnight, graffiti appeared regularly.

Yet each morning, Mr and Mrs Rhoud reopened, faces composed, quiet dignity in every movement. Once, after a particularly nasty exchange, I caught Mrs Rhoud's eye. Her tired smile spoke volumes. Even as a kid, I realised my struggles were part of something much larger. Courage, I learned, doesn't always shout; it endures silently, rebuilding each day.

Not all dangers came in plain sight. Around that same time, a girl named Sarah Harper lived just minutes away. In 1986, when she was ten, four years older than me, she left home one chilly evening to buy bread and crisps. A simple errand. She was never seen alive again.

Sarah's disappearance changed everything. Posters appeared overnight, parents whispered anxiously, suddenly afraid for their children. Mum's easy confidence tightened, replaced by a quiet panic she tried to hide. Instructions became strict, where to play, who to stay close to.

When Sarah's body was found, Morley shattered. Trust evaporated. The grief wasn't just her family's, it blanketed our community, heavy and suffocating. Childhood freedoms, walking to school, playing outside until streetlamps flickered on, felt fragile.

Yet even as fear lingered in the background, we were kids, determined to carve out pockets of joy wherever we could.

Most days, I spent outside with James and Ryan Shorte, my next-door neighbours, who were more like brothers than mates. The three of us moved as a unit, exploring, daring, surviving.

We tore up and down the street on our bikes, first battered Raleigh Burners and BMXs, then mountain bikes with bald tyres and dodgy brakes. If not racing through ginnels, we hammered tennis balls at brick walls with battered cricket bats or pretended to be Tony Yeboah, volleying goals into nets made from wheelie bins and fence panels.

We weren't angels. We'd lob stones at derelict mills, ghosts of Yorkshire's textile past and run when windows shattered. Not out of malice. Just boredom, adrenaline, curiosity.

But fun never felt far from fear.

There were running battles with older kids, rougher, harder. Sometimes fists and fury. Sometimes skinheads in bomber jackets, faces twisted in hate.

They'd call out the filthiest, vilest words you could imagine, words no child should ever hear, let alone have hurled at them.

"Go back to where you came from!"

"Paki bastard!"

"Nigger! Black c*nt!"

And yet, this was normal. Not right. But normal.

We learned how to run. How to read danger. How to clock when the energy of the street shifted, when what had been banter one second could turn into something darker the next.

It wasn't always older lads. Sometimes it was kids our age, probably younger brothers of BNP lads. Mouthy. Angry. Acting out what they'd heard at home. They'd chase us down in packs, spitting hate through laughter, mocking our skin with monkey chants, their voices high-pitched and taunting, echoing through parks like some warped playground game. I remember the sting of rocks on my arms, the blur of panic as we sprinted away. But I also remember what I refused to do. I refused to cry. Refused to hang my head. Chin up, eyes forward, bloodied but unbroken.

We ran because we had to. Fought when cornered. But bruises faded faster than the doubts they left behind.

At night, alone, I'd sit on the edge of my bed, heart thudding beneath grazed knuckles. Outside, the street went still again but inside, a quiet voice asked: Did I deserve it? Was something wrong with me, or them?

"What did they mean by go back home? I was home. Morley was the only home I'd ever known."

Those doubts planted seeds that grew louder over time. I didn't know what to call it back then, just a flicker of wrongness, like I didn't belong. Later, I'd learn the name: imposter syndrome. We didn't speak of doubts. We had banter. Grit. "Just crack on, lad."

So I did.

But if I could speak to that boy now, the one sat on the edge of his bed, hands stinging, questions swirling, this is what I'd say:

You. You were fast.

Fast to spot danger. Fast to laugh it off. Fast to run.

Even when you weren't sprinting, you were running, from looks, from questions, from the echo of your own name when it didn't feel like it belonged.

You didn't have the language for it then, but you knew. That cold flicker when someone spat a word your way. That sharp breath when you realised you were the only one. You weren't broken. You weren't wrong.

You were surviving.

And no one told you that survival was its own kind of brilliance.

You made maps out of instinct. Built armour from nothing. So if you're still that boy some days, looking over your shoulder, wondering if you're safe, wondering if you belong, let me tell you something:

You do.

You always did.

I didn't know any of that yet. Not consciously. But my body did. And so, like most kids who feel different, I adapted.

In class, I picked up another survival trick.

Copying.

The accent. The jokes. The little phrases other kids used, the ones that got laughs or nods. I learned when to speak up and when to stay quiet. It wasn't a plan. It just happened. Blending in wasn't about being liked. It was about not giving anyone another reason to single you out.

But when words couldn't shield me, I found other ways to win.

Running faster. Kicking harder. Being better. In the playground, on the football pitch, even in games of tag or British Bulldogs, I turned every insult into fuel. If I couldn't hide, I'd outpace them. Outplay them. Outfight them. Prove them wrong.

It worked. Most of the time. Teachers praised me. Even some of the same lads who threw slurs would slap my back when we won together. Over time, classmates started to see what I brought, even if they never said it out loud.

But looking back now, I see the shadow side of that survival trick. The proving never stopped. Even when the playground became boardrooms. Even when the bullies wore suits.

But through it all, through the scraps, bruises and busted bikes, something kept us going. Something louder than fear. Joy.

And I smiled through it all. That's what people remember, the cheeky grin, the twinkle in my eye, even when everything around me said I shouldn't.

Because Morley, for all its flaws, made me.

It taught me how to take hits and get back up.

It showed me how to read people fast, how to spot threat but also how to win trust.

It gave me my first taste of loyalty, of brotherhood, of the kind of friends who'd swing a punch for you one minute and share their last packet of crisps the next.

It gave me edge. And joy. And laughter.

And it taught me how to survive.

Even when the world told me I didn't belong, I found ways to carve out space, to make room for myself, my voice, my future.

I thought those instincts would always serve me. I didn't yet know they carried a cost.

It all started there.

On those cracked pavements.

On that street where I learned to run, to fight, to laugh and to dream.

Those early survival tricks, running, blending, proving, pushed me forward. They helped me climb. But they left shadows, too. Shadows I'd spend years learning to understand.

What I built from those streets would one day lift me far beyond them. But the boy who first learned to fight and dream there? He never fully let them go.

The Blueprint – An Invitation to the Reader

Throughout this book, you'll notice something after each chapter: **The Blueprint.**

When you grow up without a guide, no father, no mentor, no map, you have to build your life from scratch. No one shows you where to place the beams or how to lay the foundation. You learn through trial, instinct and survival. You improvise until it works. And eventually, you realise: what you're building isn't just for you, it's for others too.

For much of my life, I had no plan to follow. No instructions. But I pieced one together in real time, on the streets of Yorkshire, in the silence of fatherlessness and in the unspoken rules of elite rooms I was never meant to enter.

These Blueprint sections are the tools I drew from that journey. They aren't theory. They're lived truths, crafted from scars, street smarts and self-discovery. If you've ever had to figure it out alone… if you've ever questioned your worth in rooms that weren't built for you… if you're building something from nothing, this is for you.

You don't need a perfect map to build something lasting. You just need the courage to lay one brick at a time.

Let's get to work.

The Blueprint – Chapter 1: Thriving When No One Is Coming to Save You

Key Truth

"I wasn't just running, I was smiling through the storm."

Quote

"You may encounter many defeats, but you must not be defeated." - Maya Angelou

---

Theme: Survival Without a Guide

Growing up in Morley, survival wasn't theoretical, it was a daily mission. The streets didn't just teach me about danger; they became my first classroom. When you grow up without a guide, no father to pass on the rules, no mentor to clear the path, you learn early that no one is coming to save you. Whether you faced threats because of your race, your class, your gender, or simply because you didn't fit the mold, this reality is familiar. This is for those who've walked alone, who've navigated between cultures or social classes feeling like outsiders, who've carried invisible battles while the world assumed they were fine. These are the lessons I built from that foundation.

---

1. Resilience is muscle, not magic

No blueprint? No problem. Your resilience didn't arrive fully formed, it was built step by step, in every rejection, every fight, every moment you kept going when it would've been easier to quit. This isn't magic, it's hard-earned muscle. And you'll carry it with you into boardrooms, relationships and moments of legacy.

Why This Matters:
We glorify resilience but rarely name its price. People from stability often ask, "How did you become so strong?" The real answer? You had no other choice. Resilience is built in the grind, not gifted from above. But once it's there, it becomes the foundation under every risk you take. How can I use my unique lens to challenge norms and widen the table for others? Resilience also supports leadership endurance, the ability to navigate pressure, uncertainty and continued responsibility with emotional control.

My Reality:
Each time I got up from a fall, a fight, or a racial slur thrown like a stone, I was unknowingly laying foundations for a different kind of future, one where my ability to absorb pressure became quiet power. At the time, it felt like surviving. Only later did I realise, I was conditioning for life. For boardrooms. For heartbreak. For fatherhood.

Lived Lesson:

When older kids chased me, throwing stones and shouting hateful words, I learned to swallow fear and turn pain into determination. Each time I ran faster, stood taller or returned to school unbroken, I was unknowingly training for bigger stages where resilience would be my greatest asset. Eventually, that resilience allowed me to lead calmly through crises, not because I was unaffected but because I was trained in storm weather.

Make it Real:

Pick one past hardship you rarely speak about. Write down what it taught you. Not just the pain, focus on what skill or strength it developed. Speak it aloud. Let it be evidence.

Reflection Prompts:

- Where do I downplay my own resilience to seem "well-adjusted"?
- How might owning my survival story help someone else trust their own strength?
- What leadership challenges do I now handle with muscle I didn't even know I had?

---

2. Difference is your edge, not your weakness

As one of the only kids of colour in a white, working-class town, my difference felt like a target but it also became my superpower. Outsiders learn to read rooms faster, anticipate reactions and adapt on the fly. Your difference gives you perspective, agility and a sharpness others may lack. Protect it.

Why This Matters:
Difference trains you in nuance. In listening beyond words. In navigating rooms others take for granted. If you've ever felt like you didn't belong, here's the truth: it's not that you don't fit the room. It's that the room was built without your shape in mind. Your difference isn't what holds you back, it's what makes you vital. And later, that same difference often becomes cultural fluency, inclusive leadership and the ability to bridge worlds.

My Reality:
As the only mixed-race kid in my neighbourhood, I learned early that blending wasn't possible, so I made standing out count. I sharpened my ability to quickly understand different perspectives and adapt in tense situations. This instinct later opened doors I never imagined possible. I didn't know then that my difference wasn't just something to overcome, it was something to harness.

Lived Lesson:

At school, I eventually noticed how teachers interacted differently with certain kids, subtle changes in tone and body language. Reading these shifts allowed me to speak up at just the right moments or stay quiet when tension was rising. I learned to use that awareness as a strength, even when I wasn't sure of my place. Later in life, this became cross-cultural agility, giving me an edge in leading diverse teams and building trust across boundaries.

Make it Real:

List three specific gifts your difference has given you, insights, resilience, empathy. Then write one way you'll honour each of them this month. Whether it's how you show up at work, parent your children, or tell your story, lead with your difference.

Reflection Prompts:

- Where have I hidden my difference to feel safe and what has that cost me?
- What part of me sees the world differently and how might that be a leadership strength?
- How can I use my lens to redraw the map for others still finding their way?

---

3. Trust the wisdom in your gut

When you grow up without a map, no father, no blueprint, your body becomes the first compass. Instinct replaces instruction. That subtle shift in energy. The quiet unease in a room. The cold on the back of your neck that isn't about the weather. This isn't paranoia, it's inherited wisdom. Survival sharpened it. Silence shaped it. And now, it's a superpower.

Why This Matters:
People who've had consistent guidance often rely on systems, advice, or rules. But if you were raised navigating uncertainty, of culture, identity or safety, you develop an internal radar others don't. It's how we sensed danger before it appeared, spotted disrespect before it was spoken. As we grow, that gut wisdom doesn't just keep us safe, it helps us lead with edge and presence. This early vigilance can develop into an intuitive leadership trait, pattern recognition, emotional attunement and a sixth sense for what others miss.

My Reality:
I vividly remember one evening walking back from the park, still flushed from a game of headers and volleys. The sun had dipped but the lamp posts weren't on yet. Nothing was visibly wrong but a sudden chill, a tightening in my chest, told me to stop. Moments later, a group of older lads appeared, skinheads, known troublemakers, exactly where I would have

been. My instincts saved me, again. Not with logic. With the kind of sixth sense only the streets can teach.

Lived Lesson:

It wasn't just in danger. I learned to read tension in classrooms too, when a teacher's tone shifted or a mate was about to snap. Over time, that radar moved into boardrooms. Into relationships. Into fatherhood. That gut? It's not guesswork. It's data. Years later, that same awareness helped me sense shifts in mood in high-stakes meetings, anticipate client reactions, and show up with clarity. Gut instinct became both my early defence and later, my strategic edge.

Make it Real:

Start a "gut journal." For one week, track moments when your instincts speak, whether through unease, alertness, or calm. Write down what happened, how you responded, and what the outcome was. Learn to trust the voice beneath the noise.

Reflection Prompts:

- Where has my gut already saved me, not just from danger but from doubt?
- What would change if I treated my instincts as intelligence, not interference?
- How can I use intuitive awareness to lead, support, or guide more effectively?

---

4. Humour is a survival strategy

For those who've lived between two worlds, racially, culturally, socially, humour often becomes both a shield and a bridge. It lightens tension, disarms hostility and reminds you (and others) of your humanity. For me, humour was survival in the streets and later, a leadership tool in rooms where I once felt like an outsider.

Why This Matters:

Humour can be misread as avoidance, but in truth, it's a sign of agility. It's how we make pain palatable. It's how we turn awkwardness into connection. Used with intention, humour builds psychological safety, letting others breathe, belong and bring more of themselves into the room. Leaders with humour often navigate complexity with warmth and ease, using connection as strategy.

My Reality:

I learned early that a quick joke could shift a room. With skinheads chasing me or older kids at school mocking me, humour let me disarm without conflict. It wasn't about hiding pain, it was about surviving it. Later, that same humour walked me into rooms I wasn't "meant" to be in and kept me there.

Lived Lesson:

Whenever tension rose after football or rugby matches,

especially if slurs were shouted, a cheeky remark or self-deprecating joke quickly diffused anger. Those smiles, even grudging ones, disarmed aggression, giving me space and safety to slip away unharmed and respected. That same instinct later helped me manage conflict at work with calmness and connection, often lowering the temperature in tough conversations.

Make it Real:
Think of three scenarios where you might feel exposed or out of place this month. Choose one anecdote, memory, or line that brings levity without losing truth. Have it ready, not as defence, but as bridge.

Reflection Prompts:

- When have I used humour to connect, not just to deflect?
- How can I use laughter more intentionally, as a tool, not just a shield?

---

5. When no one shows you the way, build your own

If you grew up without a guide, you might think you're "behind." You're not. That gap, the father who never showed, the mentor who never arrived, is your construction site. It forces you to lead yourself, to master self-direction. And later, that self-leadership will turn into the kind of mentorship and legacy that changes lives.

Why This Matters:

Growing up without guidance creates two paths: bitterness or leadership. The second path is harder, but transformational. The key is not waiting to feel "ready." You're ready the moment you decide to own your narrative and pass it on. Self-leadership built in absence becomes the anchor for others, in families, teams and communities.

My Reality:

Growing up without a father or mentor felt like stumbling through a maze blindfolded. I noticed the quiet confidence that came from having someone to look up to. Yet that absence forced me to carve out my own path, rely on instincts, and develop self-direction far beyond my years. Without realising, I was training myself to become the mentor and role model I'd desperately wished for.

Lived Lesson:

Watching other boys learn things hand-in-hand with their dads used to leave a sharp ache. I'd see them getting tips on football technique, bike repairs or how to handle themselves. I envied them. But I also observed. And taught myself. Each small, silent win became a brick in the foundation of my confidence. Self-taught didn't mean less, it meant earned.

Years later, that instinct turned into mentoring others who had also grown up navigating without a map.

Make it Real:

Write a letter to your younger self. Not about what was missing but about what you built despite it. Then, think of someone younger who might be walking that same path. Share one insight, one story, or one act of encouragement with them this week.

Reflection Prompts:

- Where in my life am I still waiting for guidance I might now be ready to give?
- What parts of my story show I've been a leader all along, even before I had the title?
- Who might be watching me now, needing a blueprint I'm ready to offer?

What the Streets Left Me:

I didn't know it then but every lesson the streets of Morley taught me would echo throughout my life, in classrooms, in boardrooms and eventually, in conversations with my daughter.

Learning to survive without a blueprint doesn't mean you're behind. It means you've already begun building something most people can't see.

But survival is just the first layer. The real work begins when the danger fades, when you start learning how to live, lead and love without always being on high alert.

That transition started at home. Because behind every young survivor trying to make sense of a hostile world, there's a network, however messy, however imperfect, that helps them keep hold of who they are. For me, that scaffolding was built by my mother, my grandparents and the surrogate families who helped me stay tethered to hope and identity.

Thriving means not just carrying the armour but learning when and how, to set it down.

And that's what I'd begin to learn next.

2

THE MAVERICK AND THE ANCHORS

Even the fiercest winds need a harbour, a place where the weight of the world can be set down, even if just for a moment of calm.

For me, beneath Morley's grey skies and hard pavements, that harbour took the shape of three people: my Mother, my Grandfather and my Grandmother. Each, in their own imperfect way, helped me make sense of a world that was confusing, unkind and full of contradictions. They steadied my spirit. They shaped my sense of self.

By then, I knew Morley's streets intimately, the ginnels where danger could be waiting, the shopfronts where glances could turn cold without warning. But home was different. Home had its own language, its own rhythm. While the town outside bristled with suspicion and change, inside those four walls I found something else: warmth, humour and the small rituals that stitched a family together.

Morley might have taught me how to keep my guard up but my family taught me where to lower it. The town's sharp edges shaped my instincts for survival. But inside our home and in the homes that welcomed me as one of their own, I began learning something just as vital: how to hope, how to dream and how to love imperfectly but fiercely.

My Mother: The maverick with fire in her veins

My Mother could light up a room with nothing but a laugh. A flash of her red hair, a glint in her eye and even the dullest corners of Morley came alive. She was magnetic. Bold. Unapologetic.

While others quietly accepted their lot, my Mother's eyes were already set beyond Morley's borders. The town might have had its grip on her body but it never claimed her spirit.

I'd catch her sitting by the window, *Vogue* or *Tatler* in hand, glossy pages perched atop a stack of unpaid bills. Her eyes lingered not on what was but what could be, grand homes, women wrapped in Prada, men in Savile Row suits. To her, they weren't just images. They were possibilities.

She was a fighter. Fierce and at times, reckless in her convictions. Her temper could flare like a matchstick but so too could her affection. Bear hugs that squeezed the breath out of me. Kisses on the crown of my head that lingered, like she was willing love into my bones.

It wasn't just her laughter that lit up a room, though it was warm, rich and unforgettable. Her beauty already did that for her. Objectively, my mother was - and still is - striking. High cheekbones that framed her face like sculpture. Almond-shaped eyes that sparkled with mischief and depth. Full, natural lips that knew when to smirk and when to smile. And skin so luminous it looked lit from within. There was a cinematic glamour to her, especially in those years. A kind of 80s radiance. If you knew *Dynasty*, you'll know what I mean, she could've been the red-headed Joan Collins, in her prime, only with better curls and more soul. But beyond looks, it was her energy that drew people in. Playful. Quick-witted. The life and heart of any gathering. You couldn't help but notice her. She was unforgettable.

But life with my mum wasn't always safe, or easy. Her longing for companionship, for romance, sometimes led us down dangerous paths.

One of those moments still lives in me, sharp and breathless. I was five years old. Sitting in a classroom, colouring in a worksheet while the teacher read aloud. The door opened and in walked Manny, my Mother's then-boyfriend. He wasn't family. He wasn't supposed to be there. But no one stopped him.

He walked straight up to me, slipped a drawstring gym bag over my head and lifted me, just lifted me, out of my seat like I was his to take. No warning. No words. Just silence, shock and the rustle of chairs scraping back as children froze. The teacher shouted but he didn't stop.

He took me home. Then he called my Mother at work.

When she arrived, panicked, breathless, he savagely beat her with a wooden kitchen stool until the neighbours burst through the door and called the police. Manny was arrested. Sectioned. Removed.

Even then, I didn't know that her fiercest act of protection had come years earlier, in silence, behind closed doors, when she'd refused to let me go.

After he was gone, something inside me stayed unsettled. I'd wake some nights in a sweat, heart racing, my small fists clenched beneath the blankets. I didn't have the words for it then but I'd learned something adults rarely admit out loud.

Safety was fragile.

It could be here one moment and ripped away the next.

My mum tried to carry on, smiles at the breakfast table, quick jokes when she packed my lunch. But her eyes gave her away. And I imagine mine did too.

For a while, I was afraid to close doors. Afraid of loud footsteps. Afraid of being surprised. But more than fear, I felt something heavier.

A question.

Where was everyone when it happened?

Even at five, the seed was planted: when things go wrong, you might be alone.

That idea stayed with me long after the bruises faded.

I still remember the cotton bag over my head. The helplessness. The silence of it all. The heat in my cheeks, not just fear but shame. The kind you can't explain. The kind you carry.

But I also remember my mum. Bloodied. Fierce. Refusing to let that moment break her.

And somewhere deep inside, even as a child, a quiet vow began to form: No one would ever make me feel that helpless again.

And still, through it all, there she was.

Bloodied, bruised but unbowed.

My Mother wasn't perfect. Far from it. But she was mine. And she fought, relentlessly, to give me more than what life had handed her. Even as life tested her in ways I was too young to see, she made sure mine had pieces worth holding on to.

Her resilience wasn't a wall. It was scaffolding, holding her up even when the weight seemed unbearable.

But my mother's fiercest act of love didn't come with a roar. It came with a whisper, a change of heart when the world expected otherwise.

During her pregnancy, her own parents warned her: "You're throwing your life away." Young. Unmarried. And carrying a mixed-race baby. In their eyes, it was a path filled with shame and hardship. Eventually, she agreed. She signed the adoption papers with The Children's Society. A family had been chosen. Everything was arranged.

When she gave birth at Dewsbury Hospital, she did it alone. No father at her side. No partner. No crib waiting back home. I was taken away to a separate ward, already halfway into another life.

But two days later, the nurses asked if she wanted to see me. And when she held me for the first time, no name picked, no plan in place, something shifted.

She looked down at this tiny face and felt, not logic or reassurance, but love. The kind that overrules fear. The kind that rewrites futures.

She asked for me back.

And just like that, she changed everything.

The other family never got a child. And my mother, unprepared and uncertain, brought me home anyway.

That wasn't just the beginning of my life. It was the beginning of *our* fight.

Looking back, I realise how much of her fire lives in me. That hunger. That defiance. That refusal to let the world define my worth.

She made sure I went to Queen Elizabeth Grammar School, a place neither of us could quite believe I got into. She didn't always have the means but she always found a way.

But even then, it wasn't just about getting in. It was about showing her I could rise. Every exam, every effort, it wasn't just for me. I wanted her to feel it had all been worth it. That her fire hadn't burned in vain.

Every future certificate, every small win felt like a down payment on a future I hoped would lift us both. I would never have said it aloud but deep down I wanted her to see it. To believe it. That I wasn't just surviving, I was building something we could both be proud of.

If Morley taught me how to survive, my mother taught me how to dream beyond survival.

My Grandfather: The street philosopher in a flat cap

Just 400 metres down the road from our house lived my grandparents - Grandma and Grandad - in a classic two-up, two-down terraced house. Solid, modest and always spotless. Working-class to the core. But theirs had something special: it faced south, overlooking acres of green fields that stretched toward the horizon. On the rare days when Yorkshire gifted us sunshine, their little garden would bask in it like a freshly washed line of clothes, swaying gently in the glow, grateful for the break in the clouds.

Leslie Mills, my Grandad, wasn't a man of big speeches or dramatic life lessons. But he was a man of rituals. Quiet. Steady. Unshakeable.

But through his rituals, the bookies' runs, the bacon butties, flat cap always sat just right, not too proud, not too scruffy, he passed on wisdom all the same.

He went to the bookies *every* day. Rain or shine, wind or snow, it didn't matter. A folded newspaper under his arm, a nod to Ernie, their neighbour and off he'd go. Sometimes he'd place a ten-pence bet. Sometimes fifty. But it was never about the money. It was about rhythm. Ritual. The pulse of his day.

To the outside world, he looked every inch the classic Yorkshireman: fish and chips on a Friday, treating bread and dripping like it was a delicacy and an encyclopaedic hatred of Manchester United. He'd never dream of ordering from the chippy without asking for *scraps*, the greasy golden batter bits at the bottom of the fryer that many overlooked but he treated like treasure.

My Grandad never held down a single profession in his life. He was a jack of all trades and master of none. Postman one year, milkman the next. He did stints in building, bits of labouring and many stretches of being "between jobs" before that phrase had an official ring to it. He grafted when he had to but never let work define him. Life, for him, was more about living than climbing ladders.

In his younger years, he fancied himself a kind of northern Frank Sinatra, sharp dresser, lover of music and never one to miss a night of dancing on a Sunday with my Grandma. He smoked forty a day until two heart attacks forced him to quit at fifty-five. But the twinkle in his eye and the cheek in his grin never left him.

His love for me didn't arrive all at once. When my mum told him she was pregnant, with a mixed-race baby, from a Black man, with no father in the picture, both he and my grandma advised her to give me up for adoption. They feared what it would mean for her future. For our family. For me.

But by the time I was four, their love for me was undeniable. Solid. Fierce. Unshakeable.

We'd walk the fields for hours opposite my grand-parents' house, picking rhubarb for my grandma to stew. He'd bowl a cricket ball underarm to me in the park, show me how to bat properly. He wasn't a cook but he taught me how to flip pancakes on Shrove Tuesday and his bacon and egg sandwiches with Worcestershire sauce were legendary.

His humour was dry and sharp, not cruel but cutting in a way that made you laugh and think at the same time. It was his armour. His way of saying, *"Aye, life's hard but you don't have to let it break you."*

Through all the banter and bravado, I saw the quiet love he had for my Grandmother. They bickered like clockwork, classic old northern couple but beneath it was loyalty. A tenderness that lived between cups of tea and Sunday roasts.

He showed me what resilience looked like when it wore a flat cap and carried the scent of salt and vinegar from the chippy. He didn't *speak* love, he lived it.

And in that, he anchored me.

My Grandmother: Grace in a pearl cardigan

If my Grandad was the laughter and lessons told sideways through jokes, Edith Mary Mills - my Grandma - was the foundation beneath us.

Mary or Mrs Mills, as she was known, wasn't loud. She didn't need to be.

Her presence shaped our family with the quiet authority of someone who understood that true strength often speaks in actions, not words.

She carried herself with quiet dignity.

Whenever I struggled, whether with school, with feeling out of place, or when occasionally I'd lose my temper, she had this fantastic ability to always ground me. She regularly reminded me:

"Shoulders back. Chin high. Walk like you belong anywhere."

It wasn't just advice. It became a ritual. A steady act of defiance against the feeling that I didn't fit. My Grandma was fantastic like that. Usually making me feel better by the time I left their house, compared to when I arrived.

My Grandmother was tough, though. Despite her warmth and her silk-like hands and skin, if she saw you crossing a line she deemed unacceptable, you'd know about it. No shouting, no theatrics. Just that look, calm but razor-sharp, able to cut through chaos like a blade.

She helped raise me with a quiet authority, supporting my mum by instilling Victorian values, manners, modesty and discipline. She believed in doing things properly, in earning your place rather than expecting one. Her four brothers, all gone before I was born, had served in the police and the RAF and that same sense of duty ran through her like steel.

She worked in accounting at Rowntree's chocolate factory (now Cadbury's / Mondelez) for thirty years, steady hands on ledgers, balancing not just numbers but lives. And at home, she ran everything else. The bills, the routines, the emotional centre of the family. She wasn't loud about it. She didn't need to be. Her presence carried weight.

After she retired, every day, she would sit in her armchair in the living room with a cup of tea and a crossword. *"Seven across, means cheeky but clever,"* she'd call out. *"Just like you."*

My Grandmother's love for me was constant. I couldn't wait to arrive at their house after school. We'd play dominoes for hours. Checkers, snakes and ladders, rummy. Her laughter, warm and whole and unstoppable, could light up a room better than any bulb. That laughter still lives in me.

Sometimes, I'd stay over at Grandma and Grandad's, sleeping upstairs in the converted loft. It was always freezing but it felt like my second bedroom. The walls were lined with old cupboards filled with family letters, faded photographs, ornaments from another era and a handful of books, *Dickens*, *Robinson Crusoe*, even the *Bible*. There was *A.A. Milne*,

Rudyard Kipling and the *Brontë sisters* too. Stories of faraway lands, quiet struggles and stubborn hearts. We weren't especially religious or literary but those books sat there like quiet companions, echoes of something gentler, dreamier, tucked inside a home built on grit.

It wasn't grand but it was warm in its own way. Just down the road, just for me. And it was mine.

That house held stories, not just in its books and letters but in the people who lived there. My Grandma, for instance, in her prime was very glamorous. Always immaculately dressed, red hair curled just so. A resemblance to Rita Hayworth. I often wondered how someone so elegant ended up in Morley. Maybe she did too. But she'd fallen for my Grandad, a charming rogue with a pint in one hand and a wink in the other. And somehow, they made it work.

She taught me something priceless: softness and strength aren't opposites. They're just different forms of courage, worn in different ways.

And thanks to her, even when the world tried to tell me I didn't belong, I had a ritual:

Shoulders back. Chin high. Walk like you belong anywhere.

The Shortes and The Whitings: Mirrors of belonging

Even with the strength my family gave me, my Mother's fire, my Grandad's quiet wisdom, my Grandma's steadfast grace, there were still gaps.

Spaces I couldn't yet name.

Questions that whispered when the house grew quiet at night.

What does it feel like to have a father's steady hand on your shoulder?

What does stability really look like, not just survival?

Those unspoken needs were answered, in part, by two other families who didn't have to claim me but did.

The Shortes and the Whitings offered not just care but belonging.

The Shortes lived next door. To others, they were neighbours. To me, they were kin, the only other mixed-race family I knew in Morley. Their presence felt like an unspoken lifeline.

James, the eldest of two boys at the time (eventually three, with Adam), was nearly four years younger than me. His brother Ryan, two years younger, was never far behind. They weren't just friends. They were my absolute brothers from another mother. I loved them like that then and I love them like that now. And when Adam came along, ten years younger than James, it felt like the Shorte bond simply grew longer and deeper.

Allison brought a softness to the storm, a calm, nurturing presence that made the chaos feel safe. How she kept that household running, with all those boys and all that energy, I'll never quite understand. But her care gave the house its heart. Honest, decent and hard-working, she had a warmth that wrapped around you like a second skin. I wasn't just "Ashley from next door." I was hers, in all but name.

She was, without question, a second mother to me.

Irvine Shorte, their father, became the closest thing I had to a dad.

He was the biggest, strongest and hardest Black man I'd ever met in my life – and still to this day!

He wasn't just a neighbour's dad. And he wasn't just a mentor.

He never made a fuss about it but back then in his own dependable way, he showed up, filling the space that had always been empty.

I realise now, I looked at Irvine the way other boys looked at their fathers. Not just for protection but for cues. How to walk into a room. How to be listened to without raising your voice. How to laugh big, live bold and still hold your ground.

I watched how people responded to him, how James and Ryan leaned into his orbit, drawn in by that steady gravity. I did too. Admiration, intimidation, imitation, they all came at once.

Maybe I didn't have the language for it then but in my younger years part of me hoped I could grow up to be a man like that.

And for a long time, before I ever met my own father, Irvine was the closest I came to understanding what black fatherhood could look like, loud, present, proud and full of life.

We used to joke he was Deebo from the film *Friday*, the same actor who played the gentle giant in *The Green Mile*. But Irvine wasn't gentle. He was magnetic, hilarious like Eddie Murphy and carried himself with a pride and confidence that turned heads wherever he went.

You felt him before he spoke. Especially when it came to discipline. Step out of line and the correction was swift. Black parenting in the 80s and 90s came with a different weight, looking back, sometimes harsh, even brutal. But back then, it was seen as love through authority, protection through fear. And while James and Ryan bore so much more of the brunt than I did, I wasn't spared.

And while it's easy to judge that era by today's standards, back then, it was seen as structure. A way to prepare you for a world that wouldn't go easy on you. In their eyes, to be soft on your child was to leave them unprotected. Harsh discipline wasn't cruelty, it was armour. The world would hit harder, they believed, so they got in the first blow. Not out of malice but out of a desperate, generational instinct to toughen us up for survival.

But beneath the power and presence, there was something else. A steadiness. A strength that didn't waver. For me, growing up without a father, he filled a gap I didn't yet know how to name. He wasn't just someone who showed me how to stick up for myself or taught me how to hold my ground, he made those lessons feel like early lessons in becoming. Through his presence, I saw that fatherhood wasn't just about instruction. It was about rhythm, pride and being seen.

Dinner at the Shortes' was laughter and noise, warmth, Caribbean spices and portions generous enough to feed both hunger and spirit. The house always smelled like something good was cooking, jerk chicken, rice and peas, chicken kievs, chips and beans... or whatever was bubbling on the stove. Conversations overlapped, kids talking over adults, Luther Vandross, Aswad and Soul II Soul playing in the background. A house that wore its heart on its sleeve.

Then there were the Whitings.

A Yorkshire family who reflected the steady confidence of those edging into upper-middle class, without ever needing to declare it.

Daniel and Katie felt like siblings. Their house was a second home.

Dinner at the Whitings' was calm, still full of warmth and laughter but tidier somehow. Plates set just so. Conversations polite but lively. Plans for the weekend, homework routines, hobbies.

Everything had a place. Including me.

Their parents offered a stability that fascinated me. It was aspirational, the nuclear family structure, the sense of order, the quiet certainties.

David Whiting, their father, was handsome and eloquent, with a refined Yorkshire accent that made even casual conversation sound thoughtful. On Sunday afternoons, he'd retreat to the second living room, a calm refuge from the bustle of family life, where he'd watch Formula 1, sip something modest and often doze off mid-race, undisturbed and content.

Jean Whiting was the heartbeat of the home.

Beautiful, full of life and never short on sparkle, she lit up every room she entered. She wasn't shy of a martini or two but her generosity ran deep, especially with the children, who always felt seen, safe and special in her presence. Her laugh was infectious and her energy gave their house its glow, turning it into a haven without ever trying too hard.

Both homes were completely different.

One was all sound and spice.

The other, warmth and structure.

But both offered me something priceless: models of family. Each distinct. Each teaching me something invaluable.

At the Shortes', I learned cultural pride, loud resilience and the power of claiming space unapologetically.

At the Whitings', I learned the quiet strength of consistency, structure and aspiration, the small rituals that add up to stability.

It wasn't just food or conversation. It was identity in action.

Each family filled in pieces my fractured home life couldn't always provide.

Each, in their own way, helped me patch together a sense of belonging.

Without realising it, I was already navigating between worlds, adjusting, adapting, reading the room.

Skills that would become my strength.

And later, a silent burden.

The quiet architects of my future

As I sit here now, reflecting on those early years, I realise how intricately these relationships wove the fabric of who I would become.

My mother's fire lit the path ahead, but it also burned within me. I didn't just witness her fight, I carried it. And long before I understood legacy, I walked through life with one quiet hope: that she would feel it had all been worth it.

Her boldest act, though, came not in defiance but in stillness, holding me for the first time in that hospital, choosing love over fear. A silent decision that changed both our lives, and one I've only recently begun to grasp in full.

My Grandparents taught me that strength often wears quiet clothes, small rituals, silent sacrifice, unwavering care.

The Shortes and the Whitings filled in missing pieces of identity, showing me that belonging could be found in borrowed spaces and shared traditions.

And Irvine, proud and present, never tried to fix the absence. He simply stood in it. And sometimes, that's what a boy needs most.

I didn't see it then but all of them were shaping something in me, laying a foundation for a life I hadn't yet imagined. A life where I could stretch beyond survival, without letting go of where I began.

But it wasn't just the grown-ups who shaped me.

James and Ryan, my neighbours, my first best friends, and eventually Adam too, played a quieter, often overlooked role in the man I would become. We were all mixed-race boys growing up on a street that didn't always know what to make of us. At the time, we didn't name it. We didn't need to. Our bond was instinctive, built not on language, but on belonging. I didn't have brothers by blood but I had them by fire.

I wanted to be their older brother, not by age but by presence. I felt responsible for them. Protective. And in our endless races across the cracked tarmac of the yard, the muddy football pitches and eventually the athletic tracks, something bigger was being built. They wanted to beat me. I couldn't stand to lose. That rivalry, sharp, playful and full of banter, pulled something out of me I didn't yet have words for: drive, leadership, resilience. It wasn't just about winning, it was about showing them what was possible. And in trying to be their guide, I sharpened my own edge.

Those boys lit a fuse in me. Their fire became the mirror for my own. Looking back, I see now that it wasn't just competition. It was training. For life, for leadership, for the hunger to prove myself in a world that offered few templates for boys like us. And today, my love for them remains. It's shaped differently now, carried in memory not mischief but it runs deep. On reflection, I have more to thank them for than I ever realised. They didn't just shape my childhood. They shaped my compass.

And through them all, my friends, my surrogate families, my grandparents and Irvine, I saw pieces of her too. My mother's ambition in the hunger. Her tenderness in the quiet moments. Her fire in every dream I began to believe might one day be mine.

They were my foundation stones, each leaving their own imprint. The laughter, the discipline, the pride, the pain. All of it lived inside me.

In their own imperfect ways, they handed me the tools I'd one day need to build a life beyond Morley, even if none of us could quite see it yet.

But even with that fire, stepping beyond Morley would test everything they had given me.

Just as I was beginning to feel rooted, the knock came, a scholarship of sorts. Actually, it was a means-tested bursary, awarded not for status or legacy but for potential and need. These were rare, given quietly to a handful of kids who had something in them and not much around them. Fortunately, I was one of those kids. A door had opened, into a world of legacy, wealth and unspoken rules. One foot still in Morley, the other stepping into ancient corridors not built for boys like me. The path ahead was unfamiliar, unmapped. But thanks to the love that raised me, messy, flawed, unwavering - I didn't arrive empty-handed.

The Blueprint – Chapter 2: Finding Your Anchors Without a Map

Key Truth

"The anchors that steady you aren't always the ones you're born to, they're the ones who show up."

Quote

"My mother was my first country, the first place I ever lived." - Nayyirah Waheed

---

Theme: Role Models in Imperfect Places

Not everyone grows up with a father, a stable home, or a clear model for who they could become.

Some of us built identity from fragments, borrowing strength from a neighbour's laugh, a teacher's belief, a friend's family dinner.

There were no tidy lessons. Just flickers of guidance stitched together in the dark.

We found father figures in the unlikeliest of places, on rugby sidelines, at dinner tables that weren't ours, in men who weren't bound to us by blood but showed up like they were.

Because not all fathers are biological and not all maps are printed.

Some are drawn in silence, in sacrifice, in presence that didn't have to be offered but was.

This Blueprint is for anyone who learned how to grow up without a manual.
For those who discovered that mentorship doesn't always come from one perfect source, but from the many imperfect hands that reached out when you needed them most.
It's for the ones who built a sense of self from borrowed bricks and still stand strong.

---

1. Your origins don't need to be ideal to be powerful

We don't choose our beginning but we do choose what to carry forward.
If you grew up in instability or pain, it's easy to believe your foundation is flawed. But those same experiences can teach endurance, empathy and fire. You weren't meant to stay in survival mode forever. What once felt like damage may have been preparation.

Why This Matters:
We're told greatness begins with strong foundations. But some of the fiercest leaders are shaped by fractured ones.
If you've had to navigate trauma, silence or chaos, you're not broken, you're battle-tested. These early adaptations often become leadership superpowers: the ability to stay calm under

pressure, read danger before it escalates, and lead with presence when others spiral.

They also build something quieter but vital: the instinct to scan the room, to sense tone, to protect. These aren't just coping mechanisms, they're deep competencies formed in the absence of safety.

Your beginning doesn't disqualify you. It deepens your capacity to lead, relate and respond to adversity with clarity.

My Reality:
At five years old, I was taken from school by someone who had no right. That moment, raw, confusing, terrifying, didn't just scar me. It revealed my mother's strength. Bloodied, bruised but unbroken, she came for me and in that moment, something shifted: I saw that even in fear, love could roar.

Lived Lesson:
I vividly recall the confusion and fear when Manny entered my classroom and took me away without a word, pulling a drawstring gym bag over my head.

What I didn't realise then was that this moment also planted something in me: a deep instinct to protect, to act quickly under pressure, and to spot danger before it escalates.

Years later, in teams and leadership rooms, that same instinct has guided me. When others freeze, I move. It's not just reaction, it's lived vigilance. And it's helped me lead in high-stakes spaces with calm, clarity and conviction.

Make it Real:

Think back to one hard moment from your early life. Instead of focusing on what was missing, ask: what strength did I gain? Write that strength down as a badge, not of shame but of survival.

Then ask yourself: How might that strength show up today, in the way I lead, relate, coach or parent?

Reflection Prompts:

- What early experience shaped how I see strength?
- How can I honour the pain without being defined by it?
- How does that experience shape how I lead under pressure or offer safety to others?

---

2. Imperfect love is still love

Not all love is soft. Some love arrives late. Some arrives loud, broken, or barely formed.

But if someone showed up, even clumsily, that love counts. You don't have to rewrite history to honour what you were given. Even flawed love can leave behind fuel for the future.

Why This Matters:
It's tempting to reject what didn't feel perfect. But by dismissing imperfect love, we also dismiss its lessons. You can carry gratitude and grief in the same hand. You can acknowledge the storm and still say: I was loved.

And in leadership, whether in families, teams or communities, understanding this truth helps us lead with compassion instead of perfectionism. Imperfect love often gives rise to emotional attunement, self-awareness and the ability to hold space for others who feel unseen or messy themselves.

My Reality:
My mum wasn't always easy to understand. Her temper could flare. Her decisions weren't always safe. But underneath all of it, I saw something relentless. A fire. Her love was fierce, protective and ambitious. A belief in better, even when everything around us shouted otherwise.

Lived Lesson:
I remember her sitting by the window, flicking through fashion magazines she couldn't afford, her mind somewhere bigger. Those images were part escapism but they were also ambition. She saw something beyond Morley and in doing so, taught me how to dream beyond my postcode. Even when she wasn't watching, I was performing for her. Trying to turn struggle into something golden. That instinct, to find beauty inside pressure, became part of how I operate professionally, too.

I learned early to read between the lines, to stay driven amidst difficulty and to lead not from resentment but from aspiration. And just like she once searched for light inside limitations, I learned to do the same, in strategy, in people and in myself.

Make it Real:

Recall a messy but meaningful moment of love from your childhood. What did it teach you about hope, ambition or emotional resilience?

Now ask: *How might that lesson still shape how I drive forward, care for others or lead under pressure?*

Write a short thank-you note, real or symbolic, to the person who gave it.

Reflection Prompts:

- Have I confused inconsistency with indifference?
- What flawed love helped shape the best in me?
- Where might my capacity to care, push or envision more come from early experiences of imperfect love?

---

3. Wholeness begins at home – honouring both your roots and your raising

You're not made to choose between ancestry and upbringing. You're meant to carry both with grace. You're not just where

you come from, you're also who raised you.
Heritage and home may not always align but both leave their mark.
Wholeness isn't about picking a side.
It's about holding both with pride and letting them shape the full story of you.

Why This Matters:
Complexity can be a compass. You get to carry the values of your bloodline and the wisdom of your lived experience.
You're not half of anything.
You're the full sum of everything you've inherited, survived and chosen.

In leadership, this kind of dual-rooted awareness builds range. Those who can hold contrast, between cultures, generations or value systems, often lead with greater nuance, empathy and adaptability.

They don't fracture under contradiction. They gain insight from it.

My Reality:
My grandmother's quiet discipline and Victorian values gave me structure.
My grandfather's wit and street-smart wisdom gave me resilience and a sense of humour that could weather anything.
They were white, working-class and full of Yorkshire grit.

The Shortes brought me spice, story and sound.
Two worlds. Two cultures. One heart that knew how to hold them both.
I didn't have to choose. I was built to carry both.

Lived Lesson:
Before heading out, my mother would straighten my shirt and remind me to "walk tall." She never said why. But I knew. Out there, the world might question who I was. But inside those walls, her walls, I was already someone. There was no room to falter. Only to carry myself like I belonged.

Later in life, that grounding became a kind of code-switching with soul, the ability to adapt while staying anchored. Not hiding who I was but translating it with fluency.

I didn't always know how to bring both my roots and my raising into the room.
For years, I softened parts of myself to belong.
But over time, I learned that what made me different didn't need managing, it needed honouring. And when I finally did, I didn't just fit in.
I changed the space.

Make it Real:
Create a "roots map." On the left, write what you've inherited from your ancestry, values, struggles, strengths.
On the right, list what you've learned from your environment, habits, lessons, ways of thinking. Then circle the traits you're

most proud of. That's your foundation. Own it. Now ask: How does holding both show up in the way you lead, relate, or navigate conflict?

Reflection Prompts:

- What dual roots do I carry that give me an edge?
- How can I honour both where I'm from and who I've become?
- Where might the tension between heritage and experience be offering me insight, empathy, or leadership range?

---

4. Fluent in contradiction – how mixed identity becomes a superpower

When you grow up between cultures, languages, or class codes, it can feel like you're constantly translating, shifting tone, posture, even identity to fit. But over time, that translation becomes fluency. Not in hiding but in leading.

Why This Matters:

Being mixed, by race, class, culture, or lived experience, gives you a way of seeing the world that others may never access. You read the room. Feel the tension. Navigate the grey. That's not a burden. That's leadership.

People who live at intersections often develop social agility, emotional intelligence and the ability to build bridges. It becomes second nature to sense when something's off, to shift gears in real time, to connect across difference.
What once felt like fragmentation becomes a kind of superpower: pattern recognition, adaptability and cross-cultural fluency.

My Reality:
I moved between worlds from day one. White grandparents. Black "uncles" from the Shorte family. Northern streets. Quiet living rooms and loud ones. For years, I felt like I had to shrink or split depending on the room. Then I realised: I wasn't broken, I was fluent.

Lived Lesson:
At school, I bounced between groups. I knew how to crack jokes with the misfits, be diplomatic with the popular kids and defend the ones who got picked on. I didn't fully belong anywhere and yet, I could speak to everyone. That wasn't a weakness. That was agility.

Later in life, that same fluency helped me navigate boardrooms, multicultural teams and complex social dynamics. It taught me to see nuance, defuse tension and connect across silos. What once felt like changing masks became the art of meeting people where they are.

Make it Real:

Sketch out the "worlds" you move between, cultural, professional, social. Then name one trait each has gifted you. That's your unique operating system. Now ask: Where does that agility show up in your leadership, parenting or relationships?

Reflection Prompts:

- Where have I tried to simplify myself to be understood?
- What would it feel like to show up carrying all of me, not just the easy parts?
- How can I turn the pressure to adapt into a skill for connecting, translating and leading?

---

5. You don't have to repeat their story to honour it

Some of us try to succeed not just for ourselves but for those who carried us.
For the parent who gave everything but never had enough. For the ancestor whose strength was survival.
But over time, that sense of duty can become a quiet weight.

This lesson is about releasing the guilt that sometimes comes with growth and recognising that legacy isn't about reliving someone else's struggle.

It's about transforming it.
You can honour your roots without being bound by them.
You can build a different life not in betrayal but in tribute.

Why This Matters:
Sometimes we feel like leaving our past behind means betraying it. But legacy doesn't have to mean imitation. You can honour someone's fight by building something freer with what they gave you.

This shift often marks a pivotal moment in leadership growth: moving from obligation to authorship. Many high performers, especially those from underrepresented or working-class backgrounds, carry an invisible pressure to justify their success.
But true leadership requires space for vision, not just repayment. When we release the need to replicate, we create room to *reimagine.*

My Reality:
My mum survived on grit, not guidance. She fought hard but life rarely gave her softness or space. For years, I tried to carry her fight on my back to prove her pain hadn't been in vain. But eventually, I had to find my own rhythm. My own version of strength.

Lived Lesson:

Getting into grammar school was a milestone. But it wasn't just about me. It was about her. I wanted to be the one who broke the pattern. Who turned the fight into flight.

What I didn't realise then was that progress didn't have to mean suffering.
It could also mean softness. Joy. Freedom.

In leadership, that meant letting go of the belief that only pressure produced value.
And learning instead that ease, permission and emotional space could be just as powerful.

Make it Real:

Think of someone whose life shaped you. What part of their struggle are you still carrying and which parts might you now choose to let go? Now ask: How can I honour their impact not by repeating their hardship, but by turning it into something freer?

Reflection Prompts:

- Can I create a new path while still honouring the one they walked?
- Where might guilt or obligation be limiting how I show up as a leader or parent?

- How can I reframe legacy as transformation, not repetition?

What Family Left Me:

Even without a father, I was never truly without guidance. Resilience came wrapped in roast dinners, domino games, forehead kisses, bear hugs and the unspoken loyalty of those who stayed. Through trauma, laughter and borrowed traditions, I found not just survival but direction.

These early architects of my life, my fiery mother, my quiet grandparents, the Shortes, the Whitings, didn't hand me a map. But they gave me tools. And slowly, I learned how to read the compass of my own becoming.

And Irvine, part protector, part presence, was a different kind of guide. Not perfect but powerful. He gave shape to something I'd longed for without realising: what fatherhood might feel like.

All of them, in their own flawed and beautiful ways, helped lay the foundations I would one day build upon. Not with answers but with effort. Not with clarity but with care.

3

BROADENING HORIZONS

The bursary - my scholarship of sorts - came as a ticket to another world, one I didn't fully understand at first but quickly learned to navigate. I was eight years old at the time.

Queen Elizabeth Grammar School, a 400-year-old institution steeped in tradition, was nothing like the rough, working-class streets of Morley. It was an elite academic powerhouse where excellence was expected, not just hoped for. Many of the teachers had studied at Oxford or Cambridge and their pupils were being groomed to follow the same path. The sons of managing directors of industrial companies, former mill and textile owners and professionals whose last names carried weight in Yorkshire's circles filled its halls.

The school itself felt ancient: polished wood panels, towering shelves of leather-bound books and portraits of alumni who'd gone on to run banks, courts and even shape UK law and society. Tradition wasn't just a backdrop. It was a language. Uniforms crisp. Manners exact. The house system bred competition and loyalty in equal measure, while unwritten codes, how to speak, how to carry yourself, marked insiders from those still learning the rules.

QEGS had produced an extraordinary blend of leaders over the centuries, rugby icons like Mike Harrison, who captained England and Mike Tindall, who won a World Cup and married into the Royal Family; pioneering medics, legal minds and business leaders; even Richard Henry Lee, a founding father of the United States and signer of the Declaration of Independence. Despite their different paths, all shared something distinctly Yorkshire: a relentless work ethic and quiet resilience.

Every headmaster over the school's 400-year history, without exception, had been educated at Oxford or Cambridge. That continuity wasn't just tradition. It was a statement. Leadership here was expected to meet the highest standards and those standards shaped everyone who walked the halls. I still remember when we celebrated that 400th anniversary. Queen Elizabeth II herself came to visit. Even as a boy, I understood the weight of that moment.

For boys like me, the expectations were heavy but so was the potential prize: a seat at tables few from Morley ever reached.

Yet, I never thought of myself as "different." The other boys didn't know about the bursary and for a long time, neither did I. My mum never mentioned it. To her, this wasn't charity or financial aid. It was strategy. A ticket to a better future and she'd worked relentlessly to make it happen.

Still, even if I didn't carry the label of "bursary / scholarship kid" in the eyes of others, the reality quietly shaped my experience. The scholarship, though a privilege, also placed me in a position where I had to constantly prove myself, not just academically but socially, as the outsider in a world that wasn't built for me. There were moments, subtle glances at parents' evening when my mum always arrived on her own, teachers assuming I couldn't afford the optional ski trip, the way certain boys talked about their second homes in Spain or the Alps, or their summer plans, that reminded me I didn't quite fit the mould. Yet, those very challenges sharpened me, teaching me how to move in spaces where I wasn't expected to thrive. I learned how to blend, how to adapt and ultimately, how to stand out on my own terms.

I stood out but not always in ways the school expected or encouraged.

For most of my time at Queen Elizabeth Grammar School, I was one of only two boys of Afro-Caribbean heritage in the entire school. Later, when I was around fifteen or sixteen, two younger Black boys joined, several years below me and I saw firsthand how hard it was for them. They were often in fights, picked on, pushed to the margins. They gravitated toward me during breaks or after school, not always with grand requests but quiet questions. Sometimes they just needed to be seen. I gave advice where I could and always made sure they knew I had their back.

But that solidarity wasn't limited by race.

Without fully realising it, I often found myself standing up for others who carried their own forms of otherness. Tariq, whose parents were Jewish with close family ties to Israel, navigated the same elite corridors with quiet dignity. Our conversations were brief, often just nods across the room but those small exchanges spoke volumes about belonging without words.

Then there was Bhaskar, the grandson of Indian immigrants, whose father had carved out a successful career in medicine. He was relentlessly picked on, not for anything he did but simply for being brown and smart. I didn't hesitate to back him when things got rough. Years later, over a beer in central London, he told me how much it had meant that I'd stood up for him back then. At the time, I hadn't thought much of it. Defending those who needed it simply felt natural.

The margins may have separated us from the mainstream but they connected us to each other.

But while I looked out for others, another side of me was also taking shape.

For all my loyalty and seriousness when it counted, I was cheeky, restless, quick with a grin and never far from mischief.

I wasn't a bad lad, not really. But I was constantly pushing boundaries, always ready with a one-liner that got me into as much trouble as it did laughter. I must've spent more Tuesday afternoons in detention than I did at home. One hour after school, every week, like clockwork. Rack up three detentions and you earned the dreaded Saturday session: nine till midday.

Not brutal because of the hours but because it meant missing my beloved rugby matches.

The irony? I was a key player in the rugby team at the same time. Teachers would catch me on a Monday in assembly, shaking their heads as they handed out match reports full of praise, knowing full well I'd be back in detention forty-eight hours later.

My school reports read like copy-and-paste jobs: "If only Ashley could apply as much focus and effort to his English/Maths/Physics/ *(INSERT SUBJECT...)* as he does to his sport, he would be an exceptional student." Always the same refrain. Could do better. Needs to concentrate. Shows potential but lacks focus. My mum must have read the phrase "Could do better" a hundred times.

And that was where it all shifted.

For all my antics in the classroom, on the sports field I was different, disciplined, driven and determined to lead.

Sport wasn't just an outlet. It was my proving ground.

Rugby. Cricket. Athletics. Basketball.

Sport was my passport to belonging.

I was fast, faster than most. I could tackle hard, hit clean and run like hell. On the rugby pitch, where physicality ruled, I thrived. On the cricket field, where precision and patience were king, I held my own. In athletics, my speed set me apart. And on the basketball court, I wasn't the tallest but my agility and hunger gave me an edge when it counted.

I was a natural all-around sportsman and that versatility became one of my greatest strengths, not just in sport but in life. There wasn't a day I wasn't out there: in the playground, the gym, on the pitch, or staying late for after-school practice. I didn't just play sport, I lived and breathed it.

In the locker room, stripped of blazers and ties, we were equals. No one cared if your dad drove a Jaguar or a battered Ford Escort. After a muddy win, the roar of "Come on, lads!" and the stinging slap on my back from teammates felt like currency, proof that I belonged.

By the age of 10, I was captaining the cricket team and by 11, I led the rugby team out onto the field. There was pride in that, real pride. Teachers singled me out during assemblies, coaches asked me to help settle younger boys. It was here, on the sports field, that I first tasted leadership and learned it could transcend the social markers that otherwise set us apart.

One of my proudest moments came when I was selected to represent Yorkshire for cricket. Pulling on that white rose emblem stitched onto my jumper, standing in a line with lads from other schools, some from even more privileged backgrounds, is a feeling I still remember vividly. Yorkshire is steeped in sporting history; to wear its colours was a badge of honour and respect, one that even the wealthiest couldn't buy. It was earned through grit, skill and heart.

But even then, a quiet tension lingered beneath the pride. Yorkshire County Cricket Club, one of England's most storied institutions and home to many former England captains, was fiercely "traditional." Until that very year, 1992, it had only ever selected players born within the county. That summer, Sachin Tendulkar became their first non-white overseas signing, a moment that signalled change but didn't sit comfortably with everyone.

Even as a boy, I could sense it, the smiles that didn't quite reach the eyes, the unease in certain rooms. The institution I was so proud to represent also carried the weight of long-standing, often unspoken exclusion.

Looking back, I realise that even in that moment of triumph, I was stepping into a space that hadn't been designed for people like me. But like Tendulkar, though on a much, ***much*** smaller stage, I was quietly claiming space, carving out room in places that hadn't made room before. There was pride in that quiet rebellion. But also a heaviness I didn't yet have language for.

It felt, for a while, like I had cracked the code, figured out how to exist in two worlds. At school, I adapted, learning the unspoken rules of boys who had been quietly groomed for success. At home, in Morley, I still had to keep my head down, stay aware, move fast when necessary.

But even as I thrived in sport, there were quieter battles taking shape beneath the surface.

At QEGS, being tough wasn't just about physical strength. It was emotional armour, never showing vulnerability, never admitting fear. Lads didn't talk about feelings or doubts. We bantered. We competed. We won. That was the language of belonging.

For someone like me, that pressure felt doubly heavy. I wasn't just trying to prove my strength as a leader or sportsman. I was carrying the unspoken weight of not confirming racial stereotypes, the fear that any show of weakness might reinforce the very assumptions I was already fighting to dismantle.

The expectation was clear: be faster, be stronger, be sharper. Outperform. Outlast. But never let them see the cracks.

That kind of vigilance takes a toll.

Even as I racked up victories and earned respect on the field, whether scoring hat-tricks in rugby or a century in cricket, I felt the toll of recalibrating myself in every setting, my stance, my humour, even my pain responses were shaped to fit the room. I had to be unbreakable. Or at least, appear to be.

But of course, no one stays unbreakable forever.

As adolescence took hold, the cracks began to show, not through failure but through the quiet pull of other identities taking shape.

I started leaning more into basketball, hip-hop and how I carried myself. My dress sense changed, baggier trousers, big NBA or NFL jumpers and whatever trainers we could manage. I used to stare at the brand-new Jordans the other lads wore, longing for a pair of my own. We couldn't afford them but that didn't stop me trying to carry the look with what I had. Pride can make even the simplest outfit feel sharp. My haircuts became sharper too, more defined. I'd always loved sport but basketball brought with it an entire cultural identity I felt drawn to. It was the early '90s, MTV was booming, Snoop Dogg and Biggie were on the rise and for the first time, I saw versions of Blackness that felt powerful, expressive, cool.

But embracing that identity added another layer to the balancing act, what empowered me in one world sometimes raised eyebrows, or quiet resistance, in the other.

I didn't have the words for it yet but I was beginning to ask bigger questions about who I was, where I belonged and what it meant to be a mixed-race kid navigating elite spaces. In some ways, the shift helped me blend in, this was the cultural zeitgeist and most of the lads were swept up in it too. But where it was a passing phase for many, it felt more personal to me. It wasn't just a trend. It was something closer to truth.

Still, I didn't let any of that show too much. I smiled. I cracked jokes. I kept moving forward.

Until around the age of 16, it seemed like sport had allowed me to cut through race, as if my ability was all that mattered. But as I grew older, I started noticing a shift.

I remember one afternoon in the Sixth Form common room, chatting about the weekend's rugby match. One of the lads joked about "smashing the big Black bastard" on the other team.

Another chimed in, "Yeah, that nigger," before turning to me, half-laughing, half-serious and adding, "Don't worry, mate, you're not like the rest of them."

It was meant as reassurance but it landed like a punch to the gut. The implication was clear, my acceptance was conditional. I was "different" because I'd captained their teams, scored tries, worn the school colours. But in the wider world, I was still the 'other'.

Race had always been there, but now it was on the surface too, in banter, in arguments, in how people looked at you. I could feel a shift in the air, an awareness that my position in this world wasn't as simple as just being a sportsman or a friend.

I remained positive, smiling, pushing forward as I always had. But beneath the surface, I now recognised a pattern, there were invisible boundaries in every space I moved through. Even among those who respected me, there were limits. Quiet lines I wasn't meant to cross.

Sport had bought me a seat at the table but it hadn't rewritten the rules.

What I didn't fully realise yet was that my life was becoming a constant negotiation between worlds, learning to navigate, to read the room and reshape my edges, to survive where I didn't fully belong.

But that constant negotiation was about to collide with something far more dangerous, my own recklessness.

One decision.

One moment.

And if not for the grace of a man who could have ended it all, I wouldn't be here to tell this story.

A sliding doors moment, *When recklessness met grace*

In the final year of school, while leading sports teams during the week, I was also working weekends at one of the busiest bars in Wakefield, *the Diner*, a buzzing place with a nightclub, *Foundation*, attached, popular with all the local crowds. I did everything: glass-collecting, flyering, cloakroom shifts, low-level promotions. I worked there with Dan Whiting and a few other lads from school too. And after a late shift one weekend, a group of us ended up at a staff party.

The drinks were flowing, the music still pulsing in our ears from hours behind the bar and when supplies started to run low, someone suggested carrying on at my mate Simon's house, twenty minutes away. Taxis were scarce at 2 a.m. and we were mostly skint. That's when someone said it: "Anyone want to drive?"

Without thinking, without *truly* thinking, I said, "Yeah, go on then."

I didn't have a licence. I was still learning. And I *might* have been over the limit. But none of that registered. Not really. The bravado of youth, the buzz of the night, the casual "fuck it" attitude, we just climbed in and set off in this tiny, boxy '80s

Mini, music loud, windows down, three of us, Simon, Vanessa and myself packed inside, laughing and shouting into the wind.

The road to Simon's was mostly quiet but as we approached his place, I saw it, a long, straight stretch leading up to his house, with a speed ramp in the middle and, crucially, our headmaster's house just before it.

I stopped at the bottom of the road.

"Floor it," someone said, grinning.

And I did.

We roared up the road, engine screaming, music thumping. Just before the bump, I lifted my foot slightly, bottling it at the last second. We caught a bit of air but nothing dramatic. Laughter filled the car, until Simon turned to me, smirking: "Ah, come on, shame you didn't keep your foot down. Why did you bottle it?"

Challenge accepted.

I slammed it into reverse.

This time we were flying *backwards* down the road, hurtling toward the ramp with no control, no sense. I barely had a grip on the wheel. We hit the speed bump at a slight angle and everything exploded.

The car left the ground.

The sound of metal cracking against concrete. A jolt. Screams. Then darkness.

We'd veered off the road, up onto the pavement and slammed into a telegraph pole just before the car could tumble down a ten-foot slope into a full car park. The pole buckled. Cables tore free from houses, including my headmaster's. The back window blew out, the front seat with Simon in it snapped clean off and we sat there in stunned silence, glass in our hair, smoke curling from the bonnet.

I thought I'd killed someone.

For a moment, everything stopped. My chest was thumping. Ears ringing. I couldn't move. Couldn't breathe. Then, slowly, the adrenaline kicked in. We checked each other, cuts, bruises, blood, yes but miraculously, we were alive.

Vanessa, the girl whose car it was, was screaming. I was frozen, sick with fear, thinking of the licence I didn't have, the booze I'd drunk, the damage done.

We drove the wrecked car half a mile away and hid it in a field to assess the damage: smashed window, dented roof, no backlights, ruined passenger seat. It looked like it had been dragged backwards through a scrapyard.

There were only bad options.

Leave it? Report it stolen? Try and cover our tracks? Vanessa wasn't having any of it. She made me drive her all the way home, thirty minutes through the city centre at 3 a.m., in a car with no lights, broken glass, mangled frame, my hands shaking on the wheel, terrified every second that the police would pull us over. I've never felt so vulnerable, so exposed.

Somehow, we made it to her house without being stopped.

Simon and I crawled into his place around 5 a.m., bloodied, broken and completely rattled. We thought maybe we'd got away with it.

Until 7 a.m., when his mum burst in.

"Simon. Ashley. I want to know *everything* that happened with the crashed car on the street last night and the telephone wires that have been ripped out of every house on this road."

We were done.

She laid into us, rightly so and the next week at school, I was summoned by the headmaster.

His wife had seen everything. She'd looked out the window after being woken by the crash. She saw three people in the car. One of them fit my description exactly.

Sitting across from the headmaster, fear and shame surged together. I wasn't just scared of punishment. I was scared of what the moment revealed, that beneath the confident lad who prided himself on trying to do the right thing, leadership and resilience, was a reckless stranger I didn't recognise.

I thought of my mum. My grandparents. The sacrifices they'd made. The pride they felt when I walked onto a rugby pitch or led a team. And now, all of that stood on the brink of collapse because of one stupid decision.

The silence stretched. My chest tightened.

That wasn't just fear. It was the weight of something deeper, that this mistake might confirm what the quiet voices of doubt had always whispered. That I didn't belong in these elite spaces.

That despite all my adapting, leading and trying to prove myself, I was just another mixed-race kid destined to screw it all up.

I could barely breathe.

Then he spoke.

But something happened I didn't expect.

He let me go.

He told me he should report me. Told me this could derail everything. And then, after what felt like a lifetime, he said he believed I had more to offer than one reckless night. He said he'd be watching me closely and that I'd have to work twice as hard to regain his trust but he wasn't going to end my future before it had begun.

The headmaster never brought it up again. He didn't need to. His silence wasn't forgetfulness, it was a choice. A lesson. And one I carried for years.

To this day, I don't fully understand why he made that choice. Maybe he knew what the consequences would be for a young, mixed-race lad already walking a fine line. Maybe he saw something in me worth salvaging.

All I know is this: that one act of grace changed everything. If he hadn't looked the other way, if he hadn't offered me that second chance, I might have ended up on the other side of the tracks. That moment was a fork in the road. And by some miracle, I was allowed to keep walking the better path.

That reckless night didn't just break the rules. It shattered the illusion that I could keep living between two worlds without consequence. Grace gave me a second chance and I've carried the weight of it ever since.

The Blueprint – Chapter 3: Walking Between Two Worlds

Key Truth

"I don't have to fit in to belong, I was born to stand out."

Quote

"Education is the most powerful weapon which you can use to change the world." - Nelson Mandela

---

Theme: Belonging Without Losing Yourself

Winning a bursary – my scholarship of sorts - to an elite grammar school at age eight put me squarely between two identities: the grit of working-class Yorkshire and the polished privilege of many of the boys at QEGS.

I didn't have a father to teach me how to navigate these two worlds or how to carry my roots while operating in spaces that weren't made for me.

For those of us who've ever felt like outsiders, who've crossed social, racial, or cultural divides with no blueprint, this is for you.

The lessons I learned at QEGS and the near-miss that almost undid everything, will help you master the art of belonging without losing who you are.

---

1. Belonging is earned but self-belief comes first

You don't wait for someone to invite you in, especially in spaces that weren't designed with you in mind. If you come from the margins, no one hands you a roadmap.
Belonging doesn't begin with welcome signs. It begins with a quiet, defiant decision: I'm allowed to be here. Every time you walk into a room and hold your ground, that belief grows. And over time, others adjust to your presence, not the other way around.

Why This Matters:
When you grow up without access or lineage, it's easy to internalise the lie that belonging must be granted. But real belonging, lasting belonging, begins with your own conviction. Self-belief becomes your first passport into spaces that seem closed. And that early defiance, rooted in identity, not arrogance, often becomes the foundation for confident leadership, boundary-setting and relational courage.

My Reality:
I didn't fit the mould. I came from Morley, not money. My mum came alone to parents' evening. But I showed up, competed, led and kept rising. I learned to carry myself with confidence, even when it felt like the room hadn't decided whether I belonged. That inner conviction became the foundation for how I moved through every space that followed.

Lived Lesson:
I captained the cricket team at ten and led the rugby side at eleven. No one asked about my postcode. The pitch was the one place I didn't have to explain myself, presence spoke louder than background. Years later, I led cross-border teams across continents not just with expertise but with a sense of internal grounding that started in those childhood convictions.

Make it Real:
Write your own statement: "I belong in ___ because ___." Say it aloud. Then move through your week with the posture of someone who believes it.

Reflection Prompts:

- Where do I still shrink, despite having earned my place?
- What inner permission am I still waiting for?
- How would my leadership change if I moved from self-doubt to self-rooting?

---

2. Your 'otherness' is a form of intelligence

Being different can feel like a disadvantage. But when you've lived on the margins, you develop a sixth sense, one that reads the room before the room speaks.

That's not just survival. It's intelligence. Cultural fluency. Emotional awareness. Tactical adaptation. Your otherness doesn't just protect you, it equips you.

Why This Matters:

Too often, we treat difference as something to overcome. But the reality is, that difference may have given you gifts others don't possess, pattern recognition, adaptability, conflict diffusion and code-switching: the instinctive ability to shift language, tone or behaviour depending on who's in the room. That's not a liability. That's leadership. That lived adaptability often becomes one of the most sought-after skills in complex environments: reading nuance, holding multiple perspectives and staying grounded amidst difference.

My Reality:

As one of only two Black boys in a school of 800, I learned to spot changes in tone before they turned into tension. I could sense when inclusion was performative and when it was real. Those instincts later became tools, not just for defence but for diplomacy.

Lived Lesson:

Years later, I would find myself in rooms where tension wasn't always spoken but always present. And that sixth sense helped me defuse conflict before it started, build alliances others missed and hold space in ways that made people feel seen. My difference gave me more than resilience. It gave me range.

Make it Real:

Think of a moment when your otherness gave you insight others missed. That's your intelligence. Own it. Develop it. Lead from it.

Reflection Prompts:

- Where have I been taught to camouflage and where is that skill actually my advantage?
- How might I honour my difference as a source of wisdom, not just survival?
- Where could my cultural fluency be a hidden strength I've yet to fully claim?

---

3. Strength cuts through social boundaries

In elite environments, class, race and pedigree often draw quiet lines. But real strength, whether physical, intellectual, or emotional, has a way of cutting through them.
And when you show up consistently with that strength, people take notice, even if they don't want to.

Why This Matters:

When you're not born into legacy or wealth, your talent becomes your bridge. But talent alone isn't enough. It's the repetition of showing up, delivering and leading that transforms strength into credibility. And eventually, that credibility becomes influence, the kind that opens doors for others too.

My Reality:

Sport became my arena. I didn't have old money but I had fast feet and sharper instincts. Pulling on the Yorkshire kit didn't erase my difference but it forced people to respect it. I belonged because I was hard to ignore.

Lived Lesson:

On muddy pitches and in tense dressing rooms, no one cared what my background was if I could outplay, out-lead and outlast. Respect came not from pedigree but from presence, courage and consistency. That kind of respect, earned in pressure, became the foundation for leading diverse teams where influence wasn't given, it was built.

Make it Real:

Name the one strength you carry into every environment. Now ask: how can I sharpen it, not to impress others but to ground myself more deeply in it?

Reflection Prompts:

- Which of my strengths earns trust across boundaries?
- How can I use that to make space for someone else?
- What does it look like to lead from credibility, not just credentials?

4. Lead before you're ready

Waiting to feel "ready" is often a trap. Especially when you come from underrepresented or marginalised places, you may never feel fully prepared.
Leadership isn't about being perfect. It's about showing up with courage and integrity, even when your hands are shaking.

Why This Matters:
If you wait for permission, you'll miss your moment. Leadership often starts in the quiet corners, where someone needs protecting, advocating for, or simply seeing. When you learn to lead early, without applause, you build conviction that can carry you through far more public tests later.

My Reality:
At QEGS I led early, sports teams, schoolmates, younger boys looking for protection. I didn't always feel ready but I showed up. That decision, to stand when no one asked me to, shaped my belief in my own capacity.

Lived Lesson:
When two younger Black boys joined the school and found themselves the target of casual racism and bullying, they started sitting next to me occasionally at lunch. Not because I said anything but because I was there. That visibility was leadership before I even had the language for it.

Make it Real:

Think of a moment when you could step up this week. It doesn't have to be loud. It has to be real.

Reflection Prompts:

- Where am I waiting for someone else to lead, when I could be stepping up?
- What kind of example would my younger self have needed to see?
- How can I lead today through presence, not just performance?

---

5. Know when acceptance is conditional

Sometimes the applause is fake. When acceptance is conditional the invitation comes with strings. You're celebrated but only because you play the part.
This is the trickiest form of exclusion, where you're allowed "in," but only on someone else's terms.
If you've ever had to wonder, Would they still value me if I spoke up? If I stopped blending in, then this lesson is for you.
Conditional acceptance is not the same as respect. And you deserve more than proximity. You deserve wholeness.

Why This Matters:

Some praise comes with strings attached. If your inclusion is based on not "acting too Black," "too working class," or "too different," then it's not acceptance, it's control. True belonging never asks you to amputate parts of yourself. Knowing this becomes a vital leadership trait, being able to recognise when you're compromising authenticity for acceptance, and helping others avoid the same trap.

My Reality:

One afternoon in the common room, a boy said, "You're alright though, not like the others." He thought it was a compliment. But I felt the sting. That wasn't inclusion, it was separation dressed as praise. And I realised: I was accepted but only on terms that made others comfortable.

Lived Lesson:

Even as team captain, there were lines I wasn't meant to cross. When I challenged them, by how I dressed, what I said, who I stood up for, the temperature changed. But I would eventually choose discomfort over dilution. That choice became the cornerstone of how I later led teams where people didn't have to shrink to belong.

Make it Real:

Think of a place where your acceptance has come at the cost of your authenticity. What boundary needs resetting?

Reflection Prompts:

- Where have I bent myself to stay included?
- What would it look like to bring my full self into that space?
- Where in leadership or life have I mistaken proximity for respect?

---

6. One mistake doesn't have to define you but it might

When you grow up without safety nets, the stakes are higher. One poor decision can close doors forever and often, there's no second chance.
That's what makes grace so powerful when it appears. It's rare. It's undeserved. And it demands a response.
If you've been given that lifeline, don't waste it. Let it anchor you in accountability, not shame. Let it become the moment you turn the page and write a better story.

Why This Matters:
When you grow up without privilege, your margin for error is thin. A single mistake can confirm every stereotype or close every door. But sometimes, grace appears. And when it does, you owe it the best of yourself. Knowing this creates leaders who lead with humility, who spot potential in others not because it's earned yet, but because it's possible.

My Reality:

That car crash at sixteen should've been the end. The headmaster lived on that same street. He could've expelled me, or worse. But he didn't. He looked me in the eye, saw something still salvageable and gave me a choice. That grace shook me. It still does.

Lived Lesson:

The headmaster didn't excuse it but he didn't destroy me either. He held the line, looked me in the eye and gave me the space to choose who I wanted to become. That moment has followed me into every near-miss since. And today, I try to hold space for others in the same way: firm, honest but full of possibility.

Make it Real:

If you've ever been given a second chance, write down what you learned. Make a vow: never waste the opportunities others had to fight harder for.

Reflection Prompts:

- What would it look like to truly honour the grace I've been given?
- What shame am I still carrying for mistakes that no longer define me?
- Where can I now extend grace to someone else, without losing accountability?

What School Left Me:

Walking between two worlds, Yorkshire's grit and the polished halls of privilege, taught me that identity isn't something you adjust for each room. It's something you carry with quiet confidence, through every mistake and every moment of belonging.

The sports fields gave me status. The common rooms revealed the limits of conditional acceptance. But it was that crash and the mercy that followed, that cracked me wide open. It showed me how easily everything could be lost and how powerful it is when someone believes in you anyway.

You don't need to abandon your roots to rise. You're allowed to be both humble and proud. Scarred and strong. The street and the private school.

But know this: even if you've learned to navigate the line between two worlds, life will always test whether you can walk it without falling. And if you do fall, get back up. That's where the real blueprint begins.

Next stop: Birmingham.

PART II:

NO BLUEPRINT, JUST GRIT

4

THE BIRMINGHAM HUSTLE

Birmingham – A Taste of Freedom and Reality

I left Wakefield with schoolboy energy and half a plan.

Birmingham was different.

Morley had been overwhelmingly white, my grammar school privileged and selective but here, cultures clashed and coexisted: Indian, Pakistani, Caribbean, African, Irish. The city buzzed with an energy I'd never felt before.

I didn't know it then but Birmingham would come to hold deeper significance in my story, connected to my past in ways I wouldn't uncover for years.

Birmingham itself was changing too.

This was the era of Cool Britannia and New Labour optimism. Tony Blair's government promised social mobility and cities like Birmingham, once symbols of post-industrial decline, were reinventing themselves.

Birmingham, like much of Britain then, was caught between the old and the new, where the factories had closed but the dreams hadn't. New music scenes were emerging. The Bullring redevelopment was reshaping the skyline. There was a sense that the old divisions, class, race, regionalism, were starting to blur, even if only at the edges.

For a lad from a small Yorkshire town, Birmingham felt like the future and a battleground. It was Britain in transition and so was I.

Yet while the city felt alive, university life hit differently. At eighteen, I arrived with the excitement of freedom, the thrill of a new city, a new chapter. I was the first in my family to go to university, carrying the weight of that pride and the pressure of that unknown.

But that excitement quickly faded as the realities of student life hit. I'd grown up in a working-class household. Money was never something that came easily. And now, in Birmingham, I was on my own.

Rent, food, books, every penny mattered.

Like many people from a working-class background at University, I worked part-time to stay afloat, late-night shifts in cocktail bars and clubs, juggling work with lectures, trying to balance it all. Baker's, Henry's, Via Vita's, various spots around town.

I learned to move behind the bar with flair and confidence, spinning bottles, mixing drinks, reading a room in seconds. It was fast-paced, social and for a lad like me, buzzing with charm, mischief and cheap aftershave it gave me a stage. A sort of budget Tom Cruise in *Cocktail*, minus the hair and Hollywood smile. It also opened up a new chapter in my relationship with women.

Bernadette was my first proper girlfriend in Birmingham, kind, grounded, full of heart. We met at university, when I was a fresher and she was in the final year of her degree, two lives moving at different speeds but something between us clicked straight away. There was no performance, no chase, just an easy connection that felt both surprising and familiar.

In a time of motion and mischief, she brought calm. She loved without complication, believing in the best version of me, even when I couldn't see it myself. For a while, we carved out a little bubble against the chaos. We shared real moments, laughter, comfort, connection and she became close with my family, folding into our world with warmth and ease. I sometimes reflected on that chapter, not with regret, but with a quiet recognition: had I been further along in my growth, things might have turned out differently. Even years later, I'd remember Bernadette's quiet belief in me, not as a lost love but as a reminder that sometimes others see your potential before you do.

Still, even that kind of love couldn't steady what was still unsettled in me.

I was still chasing something I couldn't name.

If the first year at university had been a whirlwind of discovery, freedom, music, girls, the second year was where the cracks began to show.

I'd arrived in Birmingham wide-eyed and open-hearted, still carrying the energy and innocence of school days behind me. But without the structure of sport, the guidance of school, or the presence of a father figure to anchor me, I started drifting.

My lectures became optional. My priorities scrambled.

I was living life like I'd won the lottery of freedom, when in truth, I was spiralling into chaos.

My bank account was constantly overdrawn. Rent was due. And I knew, deep down, I wasn't going to make it through uni. Not like this.

So I dropped out.

Not in a blaze of rebellion. Not with some grand plan. Just quietly, almost shamefully.

One day I was a student with a timetable. The next, I was another young lad in Birmingham trying to figure it out without a map.

And that's when the city began to change shape around me.

The Edge of Darkness

That year, I moved into a vast four-storey Victorian house in Edgbaston, a postcode with polished pockets but also shadowy corners.

Gillott Road was one of them. Known locally for its ladies of the night, this particular stretch had a reputation. The place was cheap, chaotic and slowly slipping into something closer to uninhabitable. You could feel the decay in the walls. Hear it in the pipes. Smell it when the wind blew the wrong way.

One evening, I opened the oven and found a rat staring back at me.

We laughed. Then gagged. And just got on with it.

The house became party central.

Wild BBQs, thumping garage, house music and hip-hop echoing down the stairwell, people we barely knew crashing for days.

We were all running from something, or towards something but none of us knew what.

At night, you could hear the sounds of Gillott Road outside, cars slowing, deals being made, voices calling out.

I lived with my mate from school, Dan Crookes, the kind of lad who could sniff out a good time before anyone else even knew it was happening. On campus, if something was kicking off, chances were Dan was already in the middle of it, usually pulling the strings with a grin. While our housemates were mostly white and English students, from Yorkshire, London, Bristol and Kent, the crowds at the Gillott Road parties told a different story.

Local lads and lasses of Jamaican, Indian and Brummie heritage mingled with other students from all parts of the country. The music was the only common language, a pulse that cut across accents and skin tones, drawing everyone into the same beat.

And then there was Woody.

A local Brummie with the spirit of a carnival and the stamina of a sherpa.

We met through one of my housemates in my first year at Uni, drawn together by music, humour and good vibes. Woody's energy was contagious, the kind of bloke who could turn up to a party, take over the decks and have the whole room moving in ten minutes flat. He didn't just love music, he lived it. Hip-hop, house, jungle, garage, soul, disco, his playlists were like underground history lessons.

Among all the grime and madness, people like Dan and Woody were sparks of light, Dan with his scheming grin, Woody with his carnival energy. They made the chaos feel less like darkness and more like living.

And while the beat kept us moving, the shadows crept in at the edges.

Beyond the basslines and the dancing, past the blur of nights that bled into dawn, another world hovered, darker, sharper, and far less forgiving.

It was edgy. Lawless. And we were living right in the thick of it.

This was also when I came into contact with the darker edge of Birmingham, through party circles, university acquaintances and a web of chance connections.

Some of my mates knew people who ran in the city's notorious football firms, the Zulus from Birmingham City FC as well as Aston Villa's hardcore. One of their top lads even ended up living with us for a month, kicked out of his own place and needing a crash pad.

Our home turned into something out of a film. Wild parties. BBQ smoke curling out into the night. Blokes with reputations. Whispers of violence and loyalty.

There was something intoxicating about it. Fearless men with presence and stories, living by their own rules.

And the names? Straight out of a Guy Ritchie script. Porsche Paul. Si the Brief. Gary the Hairdresser. Rumour. Villa Sam. Gangster and comedy genius in equal measure. Half the time, you didn't know whether to laugh or lock the door.

It looked like power. It looked like escape.

But beneath the bravado was something else. A weight. A cost.

I stood at the edge of that world, tempted more than I liked to admit.

There was a glamour to it, fast money, fearlessness, the sense that you didn't have to answer to anyone. I could feel it pulling at me, offering a shortcut to the respect I hadn't yet earned.

But I also felt something else.

The echo of my father.

I didn't know him yet. Not properly. But I knew enough to sense that he had walked a version of this road. And something in me, some buried instinct, screamed that if I stepped across that line, I might not come back.

So I stayed close but never crossed.

I danced at the edge of darkness. Flirted with the fire. But in the end, I turned away and saved myself from a path I might never have returned from.

Walking away didn't mean the struggle was over. It just meant the fight would take a different shape.

The Grind Years – Five Jobs, No Map

When you drop out of university, there's no ceremony. No crowd. No applause.

Just silence and the thud of real life knocking at your door.

After leaving uni, I found myself in a strange no-man's-land. No degree. No plan. Just a sharp need to survive and an even sharper sense that I couldn't go back.

I was still living in Birmingham but the city looked different now. Less exciting. More demanding.

No more student discounts. No more lectures to skip. Just bills.

And so began the grind.

Each one a hustle. Each one a lesson, even if I couldn't see it at the time.

Telesales. Sitting in a grim office, dialling strangers who wanted nothing to do with me. The phone slammed down so many times I started hearing it in my sleep.

Door-to-door sales. Trudging through estates in the rain, trying to sell things no one needed to people who didn't want to be disturbed. Some were kind. Most weren't. One day was enough to know this wasn't me.

Advertising sales. Stretch targets. Non-stop cold calls. Constant pressure. I remember one job where I didn't make a single sale for a couple of months. My confidence took a beating. I started wondering if I was just pretending, if all the talent people once saw in me had been smoke and mirrors.

Then came a small start-up venture with two older blokes, smart, driven, full of promise. For a while, it felt like it might be the thing. Long hours. Small wins. But in the end, it fizzled out like the rest. A dream that couldn't pay the rent.

I was spinning plates. None of them would stay up.

Each time something ended, I started over. CV updated. Shirt ironed. Hope clinging by a thread.

There were nights I sat alone wondering if I was destined for mediocrity.

If this, scraping by, chasing jobs, being broke, was all there was.

Enter Cedric

One of the people who shaped me most during this time was Cedric.

Cedric wasn't a boss or a mentor in any official sense. He was one of those men you don't forget. I met him at my second telesales job, The Telecom Bureau. An older Black man from Birmingham, around ten years my senior. Second-generation Jamaican, born in Birmingham in the late '60s, shaped by basslines, hustle and Brummie swagger.

He wasn't tall but he didn't need height to carry a room. He had presence. Magnetic. Effortless. A wide-toothed smile that could light up a dull Tuesday at the office and a glint in his eye like he knew something you didn't. His laugh was high-pitched, almost mischievous, the kind that cut through the noise and made people grin before they even knew why. When he dropped his voice, though, people listened. Charisma in stereo.

He had lived fast in his younger days but had rebuilt himself from the inside out.

He spoke about purpose. About discipline. About keeping your word, even when no one's watching. He introduced me to self-help tapes (Zig Ziglar, his personal favourite), goal-setting, early morning routines.

He didn't preach. He showed up with earned dignity, hard work and grounded strength, never needing applause. In Cedric, I saw an image of strength that was real, not the bravado of the streets, not the polish of the elite but something steady. Earned. Rooted.

He also gave me something else, something I wouldn't fully understand until much later. A steady stream of wisdom. Short, sharp quotes and mantras he'd picked up from years of learning and unlearning:

"He who has conquered doubt and fear has conquered failure."

"You can get everything in life you want if you will just help enough other people get what they want."

"Attitude determines your altitude."

But the one that echoed loudest, the one that changed how I saw the world, was this:

"You are a product of your environment."

I wrote those quotes down in my diary, almost religiously. At the time, they felt like small sparks of hope.

Looking back, I realise they were blueprints. Cedric wasn't just teaching me how to hustle.

He was teaching me how to build an environment I could thrive in.

That lesson became the spine of every chapter that followed.

And yet... something else was happening underneath. I was learning. Toughening. Watching. Listening. Picking up cues from people who had made it work and just as importantly, from those who hadn't.

The grind jobs exposed me to a cross-section of Britain I'd never encountered at QEGS or even on the rugby field.

My colleagues came from everywhere:

At the Telecom Bureau, there was Sean, a sharp-tongued older Irishman whose humour masked a losing battle with drink.

Kofi, the quiet genius from Handsworth, who crushed sales targets between additional studies.

Nadia, a British-Pakistani single mum who had in effect two jobs and still managed to run rings around the management team.

The office wasn't glamorous but it was a living, breathing portrait of graft and survival. For the first time, I was working alongside people from so many different races, religions and backgrounds, not as competitors but as equals trying to make it through.

Maria – A Quiet Anchor

At the same time, something beautiful was unfolding back home.

In 2000, my mum gave birth to my baby sister, Maria.

I was twenty. Still stumbling through jobs. Still unsure who I was meant to be. But the moment I held her, something shifted. A quiet recalibration.

I'd travel back to Leeds just to push her pram through Leeds City Centre and the streets I grew up on, chest out, beaming with pride. Her laugh was pure. Her eyes, wide, unjudging, saw none of the failure I felt at the time. Just her big brother.

In a world spinning fast, her presence was still. Gentle. Certain. She didn't speak but she spoke to something in me. A reminder of who I was before the noise, before the late nights, before the doubts started whispering louder than my dreams.

Sometimes I'd look at her and think: maybe I haven't ruined it all. Maybe there's still something good in me, something worth protecting.

Maria gave me a why, even before I had the how.

She anchored me. Not with advice or wisdom but with innocence. With wonder. With the subtle, silent gravity of love that doesn't need to say a word to be felt.

Back in Birmingham, the grind continued. I was still broke. Still uncertain. But something had shifted. Between Cedric's quiet strength and Maria's quiet joy, I began to gather the raw materials for the man I would one day become, even if I couldn't name it yet.

They didn't offer a map. But together, they offered something more enduring: orientation. A sense of where true north might lie.

The Breakthrough

And then, in 2003, it happened.

I got a call back from a respected multinational company, a job I had no business landing on paper. I didn't have a degree.

I didn't tick the boxes. But something in me sparked during the interview process. I was hungry. Battle-tested. Resilient.

They made me jump through twelve rounds of interviews, over a couple of months.

Twelve.

Each one tougher than the last. Every time I walked into the room, I felt like an imposter. But I kept adapting. Kept learning. Kept holding my nerve.

I remember one interview in particular, with a Regional Director who oozed confidence and old-school polish. He arrived in a convertible Jaguar XJ12, effortlessly stylish in a tailored suit, cufflinks catching the light. The kind of man who'd clearly been groomed for leadership since prep school.

To say I was intimidated was an understatement.

He grilled me with precision, sharp questions delivered with calm authority. And I held my own. Until he asked a question I hadn't prepared for. A simple one, really. One I'd heard a hundred times before.

"So… what do your parents do?"

I froze.

In that moment, the air changed. I could feel the heat rise through my chest, that familiar flicker of shame and calculation. What do I say? What can I say?

I told him my mum had worked in sales, which was true. But then came the dilemma. My father?

I paused... Then lied.

"A dentist," I said.

It was the most respectable job I could think of in the moment. Something that would protect me. Something that might close the gap between the man in the Jaguar and the boy from Morley trying to cross a chasm.

It wasn't pride. It was survival.

Because in that world, I wasn't just being assessed for competence, I was being measured for class, for polish, for pedigree. And I knew that saying "I've never met my father" would slot me straight into a stereotype I had spent my whole life trying to outrun.

I walked out of that interview with my heart thudding. Not because I'd stumbled but because I'd said what I thought they needed to hear. Even then, I knew: it wasn't who I was. It was what I needed to say to keep the door open.

I waited, unsure whether I'd crossed a line or navigated one. When the call came, it was a yes.

And though the win came with a whisper of compromise, it still felt like progress. I'd made it through the door, on my terms, as much as theirs.

It wasn't just a job. It was a lifeline. A launchpad. A sign that maybe all the setbacks had been building me for something greater.

When the call came, I didn't call my mates. I called my mum. I wanted her to know the fight hadn't been in vain.

I wasn't just surviving anymore. I was beginning to rise.

Turning Point – From Grind to Growth

Getting the job didn't feel like winning the lottery.

It felt like breathing again.

After four years of drifting, doubting and grinding, I finally had structure. A salary. A reason to wake up early. And maybe most importantly, a place where I could start rebuilding my confidence.

This wasn't just about money. It was about momentum.

For the first time in years, I felt like I was moving forward.

Every new postcode, every upgrade in pay, it all felt like proof I was moving my mum and I both forward, even if she never asked me to.

The company was sharp. Global. Professional. Everyone seemed polished, well-educated, buttoned-up.

And there I was, no degree, rougher edges, zero corporate experience.

I didn't belong on paper.

They sent me to the Coventry office, far from glamorous, especially compared to the energy and prestige of Birmingham. But I didn't care. This was my shot. I would've taken a broom cupboard in Scunthorpe if it meant getting a foot in the door.

I knew how to read people. I knew how to adapt. I knew how to work hard without complaint.

The grind had trained me in ways no lecture ever could.

I was fortunate, too. Josh Edmunds, a young manager from London, had been sent up to Coventry to steady the ship. He brought energy, polish and a clear sense of standards. He saw something in me early and helped shape it. From Josh, I learned the fundamentals: preparation, presence and how to listen between the lines of what clients and candidates were really saying.

I watched. I learned. I mirrored. I sharpened.

I said yes to everything, projects, travel, pressure. And I delivered. Every time. Not because I was trying to impress them.

But because I was trying to prove to myself that I could do this. That I did belong.

I wasn't going back.

I wasn't just climbing a career ladder, I was climbing out of the story that said lads like me didn't belong in these rooms.

What surprised me most was how quickly things started to change.

Within months, I was earning more than I'd ever imagined possible. Not a fortune but enough. Enough to upgrade from frozen pizzas to dinner out. Enough to afford suits that fit.

And around that time, something else changed too, my circle.

It was then I became close with Alistair Norman and Paul Ricciardi. Along with our mutual friend Brian, who I lived with (and could share a thousand hilarious stories about...), we spent countless nights out in Birmingham's coolest clubs, shared meals, holidays, unforgettable stag dos, always surrounded by a wider crew, Rich, Rob, Kev, Chloe, Faye, Christina, Moz & Donna, as well as Matt Colton. It was the first time I felt surrounded not just by mates but by examples.

Alistair and Paul were a handful of years older, already successful in their own right. They didn't preach. They simply lived with purpose and integrity. They showed me, without saying it, what it looked like to build a good life, professional success, true friendship, real joy.

And in Paul's case, I later saw what brilliant fatherhood could look like. The way he and Chloe raised their daughters stayed with me. Still does.

Though we're only in touch occasionally these days, those friendships left an imprint. They helped shape my aspirations, not just for career but for character. Looking back, I realise I saw them as older brothers. Guides I didn't know I needed, showing me another way to be a man.

But even as I entered this new chapter, part of me carried the old one.

I never forgot the rejection. The empty bank account. The nights staring at the ceiling wondering if I'd blown it.

And that memory became fuel.

I worked hard, relentlessly some days, restlessly on others. I wasn't perfect. I still doubted myself. Some days I smashed targets, other days I fumbled meetings or stared at the screen unsure if I belonged there at all.

But I kept showing up. Kept learning. Kept leaning into the responsibility I felt, not just to succeed but to honour everyone who had seen something in me.

My mum. My grandparents. Cedric. James. The Shortes. Even my Headmaster.

Each of them, in their own way, had held up a mirror, reminding me not just who I was but who I could become.

Their belief was my ballast.

And while I didn't have it all figured out, something was shifting.

I was no longer surviving. I was beginning to move forward, with questions still in my pocket but a deeper hunger in my bones that felt more like direction than desperation.

And yet, something inside me still felt unsettled.

Because even as I was climbing, I was still carrying questions. About identity. About where I came from. About the father I didn't know and the roots I hadn't explored.

Professionally, I was rising. But inside, I still felt like a shadow of the man I was trying to become, shaping the outer life faster than I could catch up within.

But that job was the turning point.

It took me out of survival mode and gave me real momentum.

It gave me a taste of what was possible.

And once I'd had that taste, I couldn't go back to just existing.

I wanted to build. I wanted to lead. I wanted to see how far this could go.

Soon, my journey would take me beyond Birmingham, beyond the UK entirely. Into new cities. New countries. New cultures.

But before I left, I took one last long look at the place that had shaped me.

Twelve apartments in six years.

Rats in the oven. Wild parties. Women and whisky.

Football firms and job rejections.

Nights out that tested your liver. Music that made your soul two-step.

Laughter that came from survival. Tears that dried before they dropped.

Birmingham had broken me down but it had also built me back up.

It gave me the fight. The fire. The foundation.

And perhaps most importantly, it showed me how powerful it is when someone believes in you.

And how powerful it is when you don't.

I knew, deep down, that wherever I went next, I'd carry a piece of it with me.

Always.

The Blueprint – Chapter 4: Hustling Without a Net

Key Truth

"No safety net. Just instincts, grit and the will to rise."

Quote

"You never know how strong you are until being strong is your only choice." - Bob Marley

---

Theme: Grit and Growth in the Wilderness Years

Leaving home without a guide, no father, no mentor, no map, can feel like being dropped into a storm with nothing but your instincts. For anyone who's ever juggled jobs to survive, hustled through self-doubt, or felt the sting of early failure, this is your blueprint in motion.

And if you've ever done it while also navigating the challenges of race, mixed identity or working-class roots, the hustle hits even harder but so does the growth.

This is for the ones who had no fallback plan, who spun the chaos into courage and who are still turning survival into strength.

Unlike the emotional anchors of childhood, this chapter focuses on self-construction during your wilderness years, when you became your own architect.

---

1. Freedom without discipline is a trap

When you've craved freedom your whole life, the absence of limits can feel like success. But freedom without intention is just motion without meaning. Discipline isn't a restriction, it's a steering wheel. Without it, freedom becomes noise. With it, freedom becomes direction.

Why This Matters:
Freedom feels like success when you've escaped control, but too much of it, too soon, becomes quicksand. Without rhythm or structure, ambition drifts. These moments teach us the leadership trait of self-regulation, how to anchor freedom with clarity. Disciplined freedom becomes the seedbed of responsible autonomy and decision-making.

My Reality:
Birmingham gave me everything I thought I wanted, space, nightlife, the buzz of attention, the thrill of romance and no one checking in. But I had no rhythm, no scaffolding. Days turned into nights. Nights into stories I didn't recognise myself in. I wasn't building a life, I was dodging myself.

Lived Experience:
After dropping out, I told people I was "figuring things out." In truth, I was floating. Parties masked the anxiety. The hours slipped. And eventually, I realised: freedom without purpose is

just an open cage. Learning to self-govern became a muscle I had to build, one decision at a time.

Make it Real:
Write down where you currently feel the most "free." Then ask: is that freedom moving me forward, or numbing something I'm not facing?

Reflection Prompts:

- What part of me is calling this freedom when it's actually drift?
- What boundary could turn this chaos into clarity?
- Where do I need to lead myself more clearly, not just escape?

---

2. The hustle is the classroom no one talks about

The jobs no one celebrates often teach the skills no one else learns. In the grind, behind the bar, on the sales floor, in the chaos, you're collecting lessons in leadership, resilience and emotional intelligence.

Why This Matters:
Society doesn't reward hustle years, but they sharpen real-world leadership. Working multiple roles builds adaptability, grit, and people skills especially under pressure. These roles

teach active listening, emotional regulation, and the ability to navigate ambiguity. You don't just work those jobs. If you're present, they work on you.

My Reality:
I cycled through telesales, door-to-door sales, cocktail bars, start-ups. None of it was glamorous. But it taught me how to sell, how to bounce back, how to work a room, how to read people. I didn't know it then but I was earning my stripes.

Lived Lesson:
Working the cloakroom in different clubs, I'd listen, really listen, to every conversation. Who got the best tables? Who tipped? Who demanded respect and who commanded it silently? That cloakroom became my business school. I didn't just learn sales. I learned presence.

Make it Real:
List three undervalued jobs you've had. Now map one leadership or life skill you learned from each. Own that knowledge. That's your hidden MBA.

Reflection Prompts:

- What street-level lessons shaped my leadership today?
- How can I honour those years as preparation, not failure?

- Where does my emotional intelligence reflect lived, not taught, experience?

---

3. Failure builds the muscle of reinvention

When you've got no safety net, failure doesn't just sting, it scars. But scars aren't the end of the story. They mark the moment you started building something stronger. When you're forced to pivot, you learn to become both the author and the architect of your next chapter.

Why This Matters:
Too often, we treat failure like a full stop, when it's actually a drafting table. If you've ever had to sketch a new plan with shaky hands and no guidance, you know how solid those new foundations can become. Reinvention isn't a luxury. It's architectural. And it might just be the strongest structure you'll ever build.

My Reality:
Dropping out wasn't just academic. It was emotional. A blow to everything I thought I was building. But rebuilding forced me to learn how to rewrite my story in real time.

Lived Lesson:
Three job rejections in one week. I sat on my bed with a rejected CV in one hand and a blank one in the other. I

rewrote it, not just the CV but the story I told about myself. That act of reinvention unlocked the next chapter.

Make it Real:
Think of a failure you've been hiding. Reframe it: What did it build in you that success couldn't?

Reflection Prompts:

- What strength came from a loss I thought would break me?
- What would owning that chapter out loud make space for now?
- Where has failure become my foundation?

---

4. Quiet seeds that grew anyway

Not all mentors arrive with speeches. Some come with cassette tapes. Others arrive wrapped in giggles and baby blankets. Whether it's a quiet word, a steady presence, or the simple act of being seen, some seeds don't announce themselves. They take root quietly and bloom when you're finally ready to receive them.

Why This Matters:
Great leadership often stems from observation, not instruction. Quiet mentors and anchoring relationships model

consistency, integrity, and care, traits we later carry into the way we lead. These presences shape our values and worldview long before we give them credit. Not every leader speaks loudly. Some just live powerfully.

My Reality:

Cedric didn't coach me with speeches, he modelled resilience. And Maria, my baby sister, didn't need words to change me. Her laughter reminded me what softness felt like. Her presence anchored me to who I was, before the chaos. She didn't know it but she was a mirror. A why. A silent seed of responsibility and love that took root just when I needed it.

Lived Lesson:

One night after work, Cedric handed me a Zig Ziglar cassette and said nothing. Just nodded. That opened the door to growth. But just as powerful were the visits home, where I'd take Maria out in her pram, just the two of us, rolling through the same streets that once raised me. I wasn't around all the time. But in those moments, I was *there*. Her laughter didn't ask for perfection. Just presence. And each time, something inside me softened and strengthened. Those seeds would one day shape how I lead, too.

Make it Real:

Identify one "silent sower" in your life, someone whose presence shifted your direction without fanfare. Honour them today, through gratitude, memory, or a gesture that keeps their legacy alive.

Reflection Prompts:

- Who shaped me without saying much?
- Whose quiet example still echoes in how I show up?
- Where can I model consistency without performance?

---

5. Build your environment, build your future

Your surroundings shape your standards. When you're growing without a guide, your environment becomes your blueprint. If you want to shift your future, upgrade the air you breathe.

Why This Matters:
You can't rise in a room that expects you to stay small. But one shift, a new peer, a different rhythm, a mentor in proximity, can alter your arc. Environments shape belief systems. Exposure to someone operating at a higher level activates ambition and possibility. Your network, routines, and daily inputs influence how you show up, as a leader, parent or partner. This is how vision gets seeded: proximity becomes possibility.

My Reality:

Cedric's desk was across from mine. That one detail changed my trajectory. Just by being near someone who believed in growth, I started to believe I could grow too. That's when the shift began.

Lived Lesson:

I used to jot down Cedric's quotes quietly, never thinking much of it at the time. He never saw me do it and I never told him. But two decades later, I found my old diary from that time, filled with his mantras and realised how deeply they had taken root. I hadn't forced them in. They'd simply woven themselves into my thinking, like quiet seeds that grew without asking.

Make it Real:

Audit your inputs: who you're around, what you consume, where you spend your time. Choose one upgrade, a new room, a new habit, or one person you'll move closer to who lifts your standards.

Reflection Prompts:

- Who quietly expects me to rise?
- What part of my environment needs to change so I can breathe bigger?

- What vision am I quietly absorbing and is it the one I want?

What the Hustle Taught Me:

Birmingham didn't just leave me with bruises, it laid the foundations for my endurance. Those hustle years taught me how to turn rejection into rocket fuel, how to say yes when I didn't feel ready and how to build a future from fragments. Whether navigating poverty, cultural complexity, or both, remember: today's grind is tomorrow's foundation.

Still, as much as the grind shaped me, I was restless. I wasn't just moving cities, I was moving mindsets.

Birmingham had been my crucible. It taught me that even in chaos, you can craft resilience. That even without a roadmap, you can navigate forward. That mentors and environments are more than support, they are strategy.

And that sometimes, your greatest anchor comes not from those with wisdom but from those with wonder.

So, when the call came from London, the so-called city of ambition, I didn't just pack my bags. I packed the lessons, the scars and the quiet wisdom that Birmingham had etched into my blueprint.

The next chapter wouldn't just be about geography.

It would be about becoming intentional.

And as I'd soon learn, the streets of London weren't paved with gold.

They were paved with lessons.

5

LONDON – THE STREETS WEREN'T PAVED WITH GOLD

Belonging, Brotherhood and the Fight to Rise in London

After Birmingham, I thought London would be the answer. The place where ambition and achievement finally aligned. The city of suits, skyscrapers and second chances.

But the streets weren't paved with gold. They were paved with overdrafts, Oyster cards and hard lessons in class and belonging.

I moved to Fulham, where my old friend Dan Whiting had been living for a while. After a couple of months, we found a top-floor flat on the Fulham Road, just down from Chelsea Football Club's Stamford Bridge stadium, tucked inside a red-brick Victorian building with a turret that became our living room. From the outside, it had charm. Inside, it felt like the start of something grown-up. But the reality landed fast. The single-pane windows let in every shout, every siren, every late-night pub spill-out. Peace was rare. Sleep, rarer – especially on match days!

Dan had landed a role as a currency broker in the City, with punishing 6 a.m. starts and the fast-paced grind of City life. By the time I got home at 8 p.m., he was out cold on the sofa. Most weekends he was off with his girlfriend. We saw less of each other than we thought we would. The friendship was still there, solid, warm but we were living on parallel tracks, each of us chasing something in our own way.

Those first six months were hard. Really hard.

But they weren't all heavy.

Despite the grind of settling in, Dan and I still had some cracking moments, usually fuelled by food, Guinness or nostalgia. Dan took on the role of tour guide with great pride, dragging me from one Gourmet Burger Kitchen to another, convinced he was leading me through a Michelin-level tasting menu of West London's finest buns. We explored Borough Market like it held all the answers, usually with some good wine in our hands by midday and no plans of stopping. Those afternoons drifted into all-day drinking sessions, just the two of us laughing about everything and nothing and for a few hours, it really felt like we were fifteen again.

We were relearning how to be friends in a new phase of life, no longer boys from primary school, not yet the men we'd eventually become. And though things between us would become strained for a while, those early months still held a kind of warmth. A reminder that even when life feels uncertain, there's something sacred in shared history, the kind that doesn't need explaining.

London wasn't just the UK's capital then, it was the beating heart of a global era.

From 2004 to 2006, the city was riding a wave of prosperity and cultural swagger. The Square Mile and Canary Wharf pulsed with finance, drawing talent from every corner of the world. The 2012 Olympics had been secured, injecting a sense of ambition. British music, fashion and media were thriving, Coldplay, Amy Winehouse and Dizzee Rascal topped charts, while designers like Alexander McQueen and Stella McCartney redefined global style. Tony Blair's New Labour promised upward mobility and for many, London seemed like a living symbol of what was possible.

But behind the skyline and the champagne gleam, the city also sharpened divisions, between those who belonged to that success story and those who were simply trying to survive within it.

I arrived full of hope. But hope doesn't pay rent.

I didn't have much money. I didn't have many friends.

During the week, there was a kind of rhythm. Two, sometimes three nights a week, certainly Thursdays and Fridays, I'd be out with colleagues near the office in Holborn, leaning into the after-work drinks culture like my life depended on it. Pub rounds turned into late nights, tipsy laughter under streetlights and conversations that felt deep at the time but rarely lasted past last orders. It was a temporary escape. The alcohol dulled the pressure. For a few hours, I wasn't worrying about money or identity or where I was heading. I was just another young guy in London, laughing too loudly and drinking more than I should.

But when the laughter faded and the night wore off, reality returned. Money was so tight, I'd sometimes borrow Dan's expensive Clinique skincare when I couldn't afford my own. One day, I found a handwritten note tucked in his washbag: "Stop nicking my stuff!"

The shame I felt in that moment… it's stayed with me, even now. Not because Dan meant anything harsh by it but because it was a mirror. A reminder of how close to the edge I was living.

Work, thankfully, was a lifeline, if not a glamorous one. To make the move to London happen, I'd taken a step down. From the senior team I'd earned my way into in Coventry, I was now in a smaller, less-respected business unit. A quiet demotion, even if no one called it that out loud. My pride stung but I swallowed it. I was in London. That was what mattered.

I told myself I'd claw my way back up. And I would.

Every morning, as I buttoned my shirt in the half-lit bathroom mirror, I had to fight the creeping sense that I was an imposter. That sooner or later, someone would notice. Quietly, under my breath, I'd repeat the same line:

"You belong here. You've earned this."

Some days I believed it. Some days I didn't. But I said it anyway. And in time, the belief caught up with the words.

But even as I tried to climb, life was pulling me in another direction.

My mum, now raising Maria, my baby sister, had finally found the strength to leave a relationship that had turned harmful. The man, Maria's father, had hurt her, both emotionally and physically. She needed a fresh start. A steadier environment. A space where she could breathe again. I couldn't stand by and do nothing.

So when she asked me to help her buy a house, there was only ever one answer. I agreed to take on part of her mortgage, me, flat broke, barely managing my own rent, now signing up for a second set of financial commitments. Some weeks, I started with less than a tenner in my pocket. Bus fare was a calculation. Getting caught without a valid pass was a constant risk. I lived in the grey zone between survival and collapse.

But I never crumbled. I wouldn't let myself. Not when falling felt like confirming every fear I'd carried since Birmingham, that I didn't belong in this version of the world I was trying to claim.

There were small bright spots.

Old friends like Michael Walker were in London too and seeing him kept me tethered to something real. We'd watch sport, have a few beers and laugh until our stomachs hurt, the kind of laughter that time-travelled, back to Morley, to schooldays, to a version of ourselves untouched by ambition or pressure. With Phil Thomas, who I'd met during the Birmingham grind years, it was the odd post-work pint that had a habit of turning into six before you even noticed. To this day, I've never seen anyone sink a pint faster than Phil. An evening with Phil was like lighting a fuse, you never quite knew what would follow, only that it wouldn't be dull.

On rare weekends, Dan and I would head out to his work events, high-speed, high-volume parties with a mix of Essex lads in sharp suits and old-money Southerners whose ease and entitlement were of a type I'd never seen up North. At first, I tried to blend in. Laugh at the right jokes, nod at the right moments. But it was obvious. I wasn't one of them. The class divide wasn't subtle. It was steep.

In London, class wasn't abstract, it was a daily negotiation. Every word, every gesture, every outfit carried weight. It wasn't just tiring. Some nights, it left me questioning who I was becoming.

In the North, working-class grit and sharp wit could still carry you into a room. London operated on different codes. Conversations felt like tests. Accents revealed your upbringing. A university degree wasn't just a qualification, it was a passport. Family names opened doors I didn't even know existed. I felt the class divide more sharply here than anywhere else. I didn't quite belong to any one group. Not racially, not socially, not economically. And maybe that's why I began to notice others who stood slightly outside the lines too.

That's probably why watching Dan in those same rooms was so fascinating. He moved through it all effortlessly. The ultimate chameleon, able to blend in without ever blending out. He kept his Yorkshire accent, his dry wit and a sense of self that never seemed to waver, no matter how manicured the crowd or messy the night.

My God, the man could drink but somehow, he always kept his line. In a world where most blurred boundaries chasing highs beyond alcohol, Dan held his own with clarity and control. Come Monday, like clockwork, he'd be up and on the trading floor by 6 a.m., calm, sharp, unshaken. Looking back, it was remarkable. Almost everyone I knew from that world eventually burned out. But Dan never did.

He was the exception. Most of us were still working out where we fit. I found my footing not through conformity but connection, especially with the internationals. Aussies, Kiwis, Americans, Spaniards, Poles, Italians, Asians. People who didn't ask, "Where did you go to school?" as a measure of worth.

Their accents, like mine, stood out.

But where theirs were met with curiosity, mine often came with assumptions. I was proud of my Yorkshire roots but in London I started to notice the way certain vowels could tighten a room. Over time, without meaning to, my edges softened. The North never left me but somewhere along the way, it started to lose its hold on my tongue.

Even as my voice adapted, I kept gravitating toward those reshaping their identity in real time, like I was. Their ambition often came from the same place, proving themselves far from home.

Over shared pints and late-night conversations, we didn't talk about not fitting in, not directly. We swapped stories about our countries, our upbringings, the blandness of British food (with me playing its unlikely defender) and the madness of London rent. We laughed at each other's slang, compared hangover cures, talked about dreams that felt just out of reach. It wasn't vulnerability, not exactly. But it was connection. And for the first time, I realised that my difference, which had always felt like a barrier, was starting to become a bridge.

That said, I didn't only connect with people from far-flung places. Some of my closest friendships from that time were with English guys I met through the office, people like Damien, Tom, Paddy and Charlie Cole. With them, the bond was rooted in familiarity, shared ambition and the kind of banter that made the long days bearable. At one point, we took on a legendary all-day Circle Line pub crawl, eight of us started, only a few of us finished and the stories from that day could fill a book (though no one remembers them clearly enough to write it).

We're not in regular touch these days, just the odd email or LinkedIn exchange but a few years later, they flew out for a weekend none of us will ever forget. Long nights, big laughs, and the kind of memories that outlast even the best job titles.

Looking back now, it doesn't surprise me that all of them went on to live and work abroad. Maybe we all shared a restlessness, a quiet hunger to see what lay beyond the postcode we started in.

Back at the office though, things were clearer, it was still my comfort zone and in that space, I stood out. I was regularly a top performer, earning sales incentives, trips abroad and those long, boozy Friday lunches that spilled into unpredictable evenings with the MDs, where deals were forgotten and stories flowed.

Yet even with the friendships, the fun, the flirtations with success, I couldn't shake a deeper drift setting in. The highs were real, but they didn't last and they didn't fill what was quietly hollowing out inside.

Still, before things got better, they got harder.

For nearly a year in London, I drifted. Without sport, without structure, I lost my edge. I performed well enough at work but emotionally, I was flat. Numb. No spark. I was becoming someone I didn't quite recognise.

Some evenings, I'd light up, just to dull the silence. Weed mostly. A quiet haze to blur the edges of another day that felt exactly like the one before.

Some nights, I'd sit alone in that Fulham flat, staring up at the cracked ceiling, wondering if all the striving meant anything when there was no one to share it with. I'd made it to the capital but the capital hadn't made space for me. Behind the after-work drinks and forced smiles, the city could feel as cold and lonely as the night itself.

Until rugby returned.

Seven or eight months into my time in London, I joined Hammersmith & Fulham RFC. And something shifted.

The moment I stepped onto the training pitch, muscle memory kicked in. Sweat, bruises, shouts, it all came flooding back. The rugby lads didn't care about accents or education. They cared if you showed up, took hits, made tackles.

And I did.

I trained hard. Played harder. Slowly, I found rhythm again. Discipline. Brotherhood. My confidence started to return, not just at rugby but everywhere.

At Hammersmith, the team was a mix of Londoners and internationals, Australians, Kiwis, South Africans, Irish lads, even the odd Canadian or Frenchman. Many, like me, were carving out lives far from where they'd grown up. On the pitch, none of that mattered. You earned respect through hits, tackles and trust. Off the pitch, the stories flowed. I learned about New Zealand's small-town pride, South Africa's battles with identity, Australia's love of underdogs. In a city that often felt cold and coded, the rugby field gave me a brotherhood that crossed continents. It was the first time I realised that shared struggle, far from home, could build family just as much as blood or birthplace.

The more I played, the more I found myself again. I was selected to represent Middlesex at county level, a quiet but meaningful win. Years after playing cricket for Yorkshire, here I was, carrying that same fire onto a rugby pitch in London. It wasn't about trophies. It was about feeling like I belonged again, on my own terms.

Beyond the matches, I felt more grounded. Stronger. The rhythm of training, camaraderie, even bruises gave me something London hadn't yet offered, a sense of place that didn't require performance.

And then one night in Fulham, of all places, that bridge led me to her, an Argentinian woman who would quietly change the rhythm of my life.

Beautiful, sharp, fiercely independent. There was an instant connection but more than that, a recognition. She understood what it meant to be a stranger in a city that didn't slow down for anyone. Her world moved fast, a young executive at Accenture, confident, talented and yet, in each other's company, time seemed to pause.

Looking back now, I realise something I hadn't seen at the time. After moving to London, I never dated an English woman again. Not once.

Why was that?

Was it the cultural distance? The unspoken rules and expectations I hadn't grown up with? Or something deeper, an instinctive shift away from spaces where I'd felt most judged, most unseen?

Maybe I was searching for connection without performance. Love without translation.

And in London, I found something close. A relationship that began as a spark and slowly settled into something steadier. She was warm, ambitious and came from a world that intrigued me, different but not distant.

In the midst of navigating identity and survival in London, this new connection gave me room to breathe. To feel seen without explaining.

It was the beginning of a bond that would follow me into the next chapter, both emotionally and geographically.

Then came the annual company rugby match: England vs. France. That year, it was held to coincide with the real Six Nations fixture in Paris. A corporate tradition nonetheless, high-stakes, where our UK and French offices squared off for pride and bragging rights.

And for me, a moment that would change everything.

I played like a man possessed, quick, aggressive, focused. I *wanted* it.

I don't think I'd realised how much I'd needed that release until I felt it, tackle by tackle, sprint by sprint. All the weight I'd carried, the doubt, the loneliness, the quiet ache for direction, poured out onto that pitch.

I walked off the pitch as Player of the Match.

Afterwards, I was invited to watch the real England vs. France match at the Stade de France, with the French senior executives. Later that evening, we gathered in an elegant Parisian bar bathed in golden light, the Arc de Triomphe glowing behind us. Crystal glasses clinked. Laughter moved easily between languages.

And then, almost casually, I found myself seated beside the French Managing Director. He leaned in, drink in hand, eyes steady and said:

"You ever think about working in Paris?"

At first, I thought he was joking.

But he wasn't.

He'd seen something in me, not just the physical performance but the presence, the grit, the calm under pressure. Within a couple of months, the offer was on the table: a transfer to Paris. A return to a senior business unit. A reset.

And just like that, a door opened.

But the decision wasn't easy.

I'd just started to feel stable in London. I'd fought tooth and nail to build a life there. I had friends. A flat. A girlfriend. Rugby. And now I was being asked to begin again, in a different country, speaking a different language, learning a whole new code of belonging.

On returning to London a few days later, I remember getting off the tube at Stamford Bridge and walking home that night, the city humming around me, the air thick with possibility and doubt. I thought of Birmingham. Of failing. Of starting over again and again.

And I asked myself:

What if this is the last time someone opens the door for you?

And in that moment, I knew.

The next chapter wasn't in London.

It was waiting for me, across the Channel, beneath the boulevards, inside a city I barely knew, waiting for the man I was finally becoming.

The streets weren't paved with gold.

But they had led me here.

The Blueprint – Chapter 5 - Finding Your Edge in Ruthless Environments

Key Truth

"Class may divide but purpose connects."

Quote

"Your new life is going to cost you your old one."

- Stephen Bartlett

London wasn't just a city for me, it was a baptism by fire. It exposed me to harsh realities: financial scarcity, pride-swallowing setbacks and the tension of stepping down just to keep climbing. Whether you've walked the streets of a city like London or simply faced seasons where you felt like you were clawing to survive, this blueprint's for you.

When you grow up without a guide, navigating complex intersections of race, class and ambition, success can feel like a battle fought in isolation. But every hardship becomes a hidden lesson, shaping you for the rooms you'll later walk into with quiet authority.

---

1. Humility without defeat

Your ego will whisper that stepping back is failure. But growth often hides in reverse, when you pause, realign and surrender pride to play the long game.

Why This Matters:

In fast-paced cities and ambitious circles, status can feel like currency. Job titles, pay brackets and LinkedIn headlines become identity. But if you measure your worth by external metrics alone, you'll forget who you were before the race began. Sometimes, it's the quieter moves, the ones that bruise your pride, that create your biggest breakthroughs. These moments don't just shape humility, they build self-direction, emotional maturity and the ability to lead from within rather than from image.

Early experiences of swallowing pride without losing purpose often become the blueprint for grounded leadership: the kind that doesn't flinch when ego isn't fed.

My Reality:

When I took that junior role in London, I'd just left behind years of grinding in Birmingham. I was earning the same salary, not adjusted for London - and it stung. I'd downshifted on paper, even as I was climbing internally. But that move planted me in the company, a network and a city that would change my life. From the outside, it looked like a step back. But from within, it was a slingshot.

Lived Lesson:

I remember getting on the Tube some mornings with a knot in my stomach, watching peers talk about bonuses, titles, promotions, while I was quietly starting over. But that season taught me something deeper than ambition: resilience without recognition. Years later, when I had to guide teams through layoffs, delayed promotions, or strategic pivots, that same humility became a hidden strength. I knew how to lead without applause. I'd done it before.

Make it Real:

Identify one area in your life where your pride is resisting a pivot. Is there a strategic retreat you've avoided out of fear it might look like failure? Write down what this pause could make room for, a relationship, a redirection, a new rhythm. Then ask yourself: How might modelling this humility help someone around you take their own brave next step?

Reflection Prompts:

- Where am I clinging to titles instead of growth?
- What step back today could become a setup for tomorrow?
- How can I lead with steadiness, not just status?

---

2. The hidden curriculum of scarcity

Scarcity doesn't just limit your choices, it sharpens your instincts. When you've had to make something out of nothing, you carry a quiet intelligence that no textbook can teach.

Why This Matters:

Abundance can breed comfort but scarcity breeds strategy. It forces you to see angles others miss, to plan deeper, stretch further, listen harder. Leadership isn't just built in boardrooms; it's built in bus rides, unpaid bills and quiet decisions made under pressure. That's where resourcefulness becomes a reflex and foresight becomes survival. Scarcity, while painful, can gift you the discipline to prepare, the agility to respond, and the courage to persist without validation.

My Reality:

There were weeks in London when I had less than ten pounds in my account but you'd never have known it. I still turned up sharp, still backed others when I could, still carried myself with pride. Because when you grow up without a net, you learn early how to walk the tightrope.

Lived Lesson:

Scarcity taught me patience when the world was rushing. It taught me generosity without surplus and how to keep showing up even when nothing was certain. That season didn't just test me, it trained me. Today, when stakes are high and pressure mounts, I draw from that same muscle memory. I don't panic. I adapt.

And now, when I see someone hesitating or hiding behind pride, I understand why. I've been there.

Make it Real:
Write down five lessons scarcity taught you, not just about money but about people, self-worth, trust and timing. Now trace them forward: how do those insights shape how you lead, love, plan or perform today?

Reflection Prompts:

- Where did scarcity sharpen my edge?
- What did I learn in lack that I still carry in abundance?
- How can I support others who are also building without a blueprint?

---

3. Brotherhood / Sisterhood and community are emotional infrastructure

Resilience isn't a solo sport. Even the strongest will bend without ballast. Real strength is sustained by those who see you not for what you do but for who you are underneath the armour.

Why This Matters:
In high-performance environments, it's easy to confuse achievement with affirmation. But hustle without human connection eventually hollows you out.

For me, it often came in the form of brotherhood - men who stood beside me when I wasn't performing, winning, or proving. But for others, it might be sisterhood, chosen family, elders, mentors. Whatever form it takes, connection isn't a luxury. It's a stabiliser.

The people who see you behind the performance , who reflect back your worth when you forget it yourself, those are the ones who keep you standing when the rest of the world only sees the surface.

My Reality:
Dan Whiting wasn't just a flatmate. In that tiny London apartment, with barely enough room to breathe, he gave me a sense of home. The kind of quiet presence that says, *I see you. Even when you're not winning.* At H&F RFC, the rugby pitch wasn't just a game. It was the one place where the noise fell away. Where camaraderie, bruises and trust filled a space that performance couldn't reach.

Lived Lesson:
I used to think strength meant doing it alone. But those years taught me that real strength is reinforced. Brotherhood doesn't

always arrive with fanfare. It's built in the quiet moments, the showing up, the shared silence after a hard day.

And later, in leadership, I learned this: when someone feels seen beyond their output, they don't just perform. They thrive. Community isn't soft. It's strategic.

Make it Real:

Identify your three closest sources of emotional support. Reach out to each one this week, not with a performance update but with a moment of truth, appreciation or just presence. Then reflect: how does being truly seen change how you carry the weight?

Reflection Prompts:

- Who knows me behind the scenes, not just in the spotlight?
- What spaces allow me to show up unfiltered?
- How can I model leadership that's built on connection, not just control?

---

4. Performance is a door opener, even in the shadows

When you don't walk into rooms with the right surname, old school tie, or unspoken connections, your work becomes your weapon. Your performance, your proof.

Why This Matters:

When you're *building from absence, not advantage,* there are no shortcuts, just moments. And in environments where pedigree holds power, performance becomes your passport. This isn't about overachieving for approval. It's about showing up with consistency and integrity until the room adjusts to your presence.

That quiet consistency becomes a leadership strength, especially when others are watching how you show up under pressure, not just what you say when the spotlights on.

My Reality:

One corporate rugby match. That's all it took. A crunching tackle here, a burst of leadership there and suddenly the spotlight turned my way. I hadn't said a word in a business context but I'd let my boots do the talking on the pitch. That evening an invitation arrived. Paris. A door I hadn't knocked on was now open, not because of connections but because I showed up when it counted.

Lived Lesson:

I realised that even when the system feels closed, you can still find a side entrance. But it takes relentless consistency. The kind of performance that's so clear, it can't be ignored. That doesn't mean hustling for approval. It means standing so firmly in your craft that the room must adjust its lens. Years later, that same principle shaped how I led, through delivery, not bravado. In unfamiliar spaces, performance became my translator. It built trust before titles ever could.

Make it Real:
What's your "rugby pitch"? Identify one space in your life where your excellence could shift perception. Then double down. Not to impress but to express your full capacity, without dilution. How can your consistency, not just charisma, build quiet trust in those you lead, support or serve?

Reflection Prompts:

- Where am I silently waiting for validation instead of showing what I can do?
- What is one high-integrity action I can take this week that speaks louder than words?
- How might I lead through consistency when connection isn't guaranteed?

---

5. Watch for the quiet handshake

Not all opportunities arrive with a drumroll. Sometimes they come disguised, as a question, a glance, a nod from across the room. In life's most pivotal moments, the real invitations are rarely announced.

Why This Matters:

We're conditioned to chase the spotlight but often, it's in the shadows that your future is watching. Decision-makers don't always signal their presence. They observe.

This lesson teaches the power of consistent presence. Showing up with integrity even when no one seems to be watching builds long-term trust, a trait that quietly defines leaders. These moments create reputational equity, earned not through visibility but through reliability.

My Reality:

There was no job posting, no formal pitch. Just a match on a muddy field, a few moments of grit and someone paying quiet attention. The Paris invitation came not because I asked for it but because I was already prepared when it arrived. It reminded me that showing up fully, even when it seems no one is watching, is a lifelong investment.

Lived Lesson:

Some of life's biggest doors don't swing open from pressure. They slide open from presence. If you treat every room like it matters, eventually the right one will remember how you made them feel and offer you more than you expected.

As a leader, this became a cornerstone: influence is built in how you show up when there's nothing to gain.

Make it Real:

Choose one recurring space you inhabit, be it the office, the gym, a digital platform, or your local café. Now commit to showing up this week with 5% more energy, precision or kindness. You never know who's clocking your consistency.

Reflection Prompts:

- Who might be watching me grow without me even knowing it?
- What does it mean to show up with quiet excellence, regardless of recognition?
- How do I treat low-stakes spaces, as rehearsals for leadership?

What London Taught Me:

London sharpened my grit and showed me that setbacks aren't derailments, they're recalibrations. I also learned that success without connection is a fragile climb. Belonging, community and emotional resilience were not just luxuries, they became the infrastructure that sustained me through the isolation and mental load of trying to assimilate while still growing.

Whether you're navigating race, class, fatherlessness or just climbing without a safety net, the ability to hold your ground in unforgiving environments is priceless. Because when the door opens, to your next opportunity, your next chapter, you'll walk through it prepared, resilient and unstoppable.

That's how I felt when Paris called. London had tested me in every way, mentally, financially, emotionally and yet, I emerged hungrier than ever. The chance to cross the Channel felt like more than a promotion. It felt like a portal into a world I'd only glimpsed from afar. But Paris wasn't just a change of scenery, it was a deeper test, one that would challenge every part of me in ways the streets of London never could.

And so, I stepped forward, into the City of Light, into unfamiliar codes of elegance and power and into a new layer of self-discovery.

6

PARISIAN MIRRORS – ELEGANCE, ECCENTRICITY AND THE EDGES OF BELONGING

From London to Paris, A Departure Without a Map

I still remember standing on the platform at St Pancras, suitcase in one hand, four bags looped awkwardly around my shoulders and arms and a rucksack so heavy it dug into my back. It wasn't pretty but after years of hustling through Birmingham and scraping by in London, the weight felt familiar. Just another step forward. Everything I owned, my entire adult life up to that point, was crammed into those bags. No removal company. No help. Just me, crossing the Channel with nothing but grit and belief.

I'd said my goodbyes to Lucia the night before, my girlfriend of just a few months. It was early days but something between us already felt different. There was a softness, an ease, a chemistry that hinted at more. We didn't speak of the future, not properly but I think we both felt it flickering there, just beyond the edge of what we could name. That goodbye wasn't dramatic. No major tears or promises. Just a long embrace, eyes lingering a little longer, hearts quietly wondering if this was just the start of something bigger.

As the Eurostar pulled away from the platform, a hush came over me. Under the Channel. Into something new. It was September 2006 and Paris was calling.

La Rochelle, Tricolore and a Dash of Humiliation

My French was basic at best. I'd scraped by in school with those dusty *Tricolore* textbooks set in La Rochelle, the ones with cartoon families eating baguettes and riding bikes by the sea. But the reality in Paris was a far cry from that.

My French teachers, Mr. Rylance and Mr. Haigh, would've laughed. Or more likely, kicked me out. Mr. Rylance never had much time for me. He'd send me out of class at least once a week, usually with a disappointed shake of the head. Mr. Haigh would start every lesson with his trademark bark: *"Taisez-vous, asseyez-vous... Mills OUT!"* before I'd even said a word. I was cheeky, easily distracted. French, back then, felt like a punishment.

And now it was my lifeline.

For the first month, I had one-to-one private lessons from 9 to 5 on Avenue de la Grande Armée in the heart of Paris. The company paid for it, which felt surreal, being sponsored to learn a language I'd once been kicked out of class for. Then, after five,

I'd make my way to the office in Neuilly-sur-Seine, one of the most *bourgeois* corners of Paris. The buildings were pristine. People walked slowly, dressed impeccably. Former President Nicolas Sarkozy had once been mayor here. Our office sat opposite Brasserie Pic, where President Sarkozy – at that time - was still occasionally spotted sipping espresso on the terrace, flanked by his bodyguards, like a man running the world.

It was culture shock layered on culture shock. And it wasn't just me feeling it.

Paris, 2006 to 2008, wasn't just a city. It was a mood.

The global financial crisis hadn't hit yet. Luxury felt limitless. The *Grand Boulevards* shimmered with boutiques and café terraces filled with Parisians who made style look effortless. The smell of fresh baguettes mixed with the sharp tang of cigarette smoke drifting from brasseries.

Paris Was a Paradox

Glamour and grime side by side. Grand monuments stood proudly while immigrant neighbourhoods like Seine-Saint-Denis and Clichy-Sous-Bois pulsed with hidden stories. Haute couture shows dazzled the elite while strikes, student protests and simmering debates on immigration and identity filled the streets.

At night, the Eiffel Tower sparkled against a skyline of stone and slate rooftops. By day, the city moved to the rhythm of refinement and quiet tension. Sarkozy's presidency had just begun, promising modernisation but for many, it only sharpened the divides.

Paris was intoxicating. But beneath the beauty raged silent battles, for belonging, for recognition, for a foothold in a society that prized polish but resisted change.

Work, Wine and the Art of Restraint

By the second week, I discovered something that stopped me in my tracks: the brasserie across from our office offered free drinks for employees every Friday evening. I turned to a colleague and asked, "How long does it last?"

He looked puzzled. "Until the last person leaves."

My London instincts kicked in. I pictured a buzzing after-work crowd, the kind of Friday where rounds flowed fast, laughter got louder and things escalated just enough to blur the lines between fun and foolish. Free drinks in London usually meant a sprint to the bar, a race to get tipsy before the tab ran dry. But no. Here, drinks flowed from 5:30 to 9 p.m. and people sipped slowly. They talked politics, travel, their upcoming weekend escapes to Provence and Bretagne. Most of them left tipsy at best. I, on the other hand, had been more than "tipsy" after my first two Fridays. It took me a while to adjust.

This wasn't binge culture. It was culture, full stop. Measured. Elegant. Effortless.

The Mentor and the Maestro

If elegance had a spokesperson, it might have been Yves Renaud. My first true French idol and the person who, more than anyone else in that chapter, helped me glimpse what it meant to move through the world with elegance, confidence and just the right amount of irreverence.

Yves led our executive search division. Early forties, from Cannes, with sun-kissed skin all year round, the kind of tan that made even winter feel like summer when he walked into a room. He was magnetic, charming in that effortless, French way that didn't try too hard because it didn't have to. Yves didn't enter rooms; he glided through them. And yet, it never felt rehearsed. It just felt... *him.*

Impeccably tailored, he wore navy blazers with the kind of effortless finesse that made you second-guess your own outfit, polished JM Weston shoes and a classic Jaeger-LeCoultre Reverso on his wrist. I clocked it straight away, there was something quietly iconic about it, the kind of watch that said everything without needing to speak.

Yves was the embodiment of the bon vivant. He smoked cigars with a wink, drank his red wine slowly and with conviction and somehow managed to carry both gravity and humour in the same breath. Women adored him. Men admired him. He had the good looks of Alain Delon and the charisma of Jean Dujardin but none of it felt performative. It just was.

And yet, despite his polish, Yves was generous. He looked out for me in those early months when I was still figuring out how to walk the tightrope of Parisian business culture. He didn't offer long lectures or formal mentorship sessions. He offered proximity. Access. Invitations. The kind that said: *Watch closely. You'll learn everything I'm not saying out loud.*

We'd often go to Stade de France together to watch the France national rugby team. He always brought an extra cigar just for me, knowing I'd never ask for one. It was his way of saying: *You're in now.* Subtle but meaningful. That was how Yves operated.

There was a grace to the way he moved through his world, never rushed, never flustered. He could close deals, calm egos and hold court at a dinner table with a charisma that did the heavy lifting. I took mental notes constantly: how he responded to pressure, how he made decisions, how he knew *exactly* when to speak and when to stay silent. If Paris was the masterclass, Yves was the head instructor.

But when it came to the day-to-day, it was Eglantine who held the reins. She was my first manager and she had the unenviable task of guiding a relatively uncultured Brit through the mechanics of a Parisian search firm. She could be demanding, even relentless at times, especially when it came to detail. But beneath that was a sharp intelligence and a deep understanding of what people *really* wanted. When the business was over, we could share a laugh, even some wine. But during the day, she taught me the fundamentals: precision, preparation and the psychology of needs. Looking back, she was one of the best managers I've had.

And yet, even with all the structure, all the polish, something quieter began to stir beneath the surface, a feeling I couldn't quite name at the time but would soon have to face. Because beneath the elegance and polish of the Paris office, not everyone was cut from the same cloth and some seams were beginning to show. Beneath the surface of aristocratic names and family legacies, there were a few of us who carried different stories. I connected with everyone in my own way but there was a quiet, unspoken affinity with some colleagues of North African descent and the one other person of Black heritage, whose father had once served as the Congolese Ambassador to France. We didn't speak about it openly. We didn't need to. There was a shared recognition in the way we moved through that world. Each of us understood what it meant to navigate an elite space where the price of belonging wasn't just performance, it was constant self-editing. Our differences, though rarely acknowledged out loud, became a silent bridge.

The Aristocrat with Two Faces

If Yves was the embodiment of considered elegance, then Gilles Fessart de Louvain, was something else entirely.

They were similar in age, early forties, well-groomed, beautifully spoken. On the surface, Gilles could have been plucked from the same mould. He came from an old aristocratic family, the kind whose lineage was spoken about in hushed tones, as though titles and estates were just beneath the surface. He wore it all lightly, too lightly, perhaps. There was no denying his charm. But there was also something… performative. Flashy, even.

The first thing I noticed were the shoes.

Berluti Oxfords in deep oxblood red. Not just polished, glowing. I'd never seen anything like them in England. Not in Leeds, not in London. They looked more like art than footwear, crafted, burnished, sculptural. His suit followed the same rules: crisp lines, perfect proportions, subtle but expensive. He moved like a man who'd never had to chase anything. The world simply arrived at his feet and usually stayed there.

He was handsome, urbane, effortlessly social. His humour could be razor-sharp, sometimes hilarious, often cruel. There were moments when I genuinely laughed with him, admired the ease with which he commanded a room. And then there were moments that made me pause. Jokes that cut too deep. Comments that revealed more than they should. Power games played out in full view of the office, dressed up as banter but leaving bruises all the same.

I'll never forget that first Friday I spent in the Paris office. The clock ticked to 5pm. Without warning, Gilles, seated at the head of our large open-plan room, stood up, walked to the tall window beside his desk and threw it open. A warm autumn breeze drifted in. He took off his jacket, placed his stunning Berluti shoes on the desk like trophies, lit a fat cigar and leaned back with all the confidence in the world.

He exhaled, long and slow.

"Bienvenue à Paris, Ashley."

The whole office erupted in laughter.

Coming from London, I couldn't believe what I was seeing. In any UK office, this would've been a sackable offence. But here? It was theatre. And Gilles was centre stage.

He existed at the intersection of comedy and control. One moment he was the life of the party, champagne, stories, the glint of mischief in his eye. The next, he could turn icy, critical, cutting, especially with the women in the office. We had many and many were beautiful. Gilles's interactions with them were always flirtatious, often inappropriate, occasionally brilliant but tinged with entitlement.

It was a strange experience, watching someone so magnetic operate with such impunity. He could be outrageously funny and then instantly mean. A master of the double entendre, the whispered joke, the wink that left you unsure whether to laugh or recoil. For a while, I just observed. Took it all in. I was new. Foreign. Still learning the terrain.

But over time, I began to see it for what it was.

Where Yves modelled sophistication, Gilles wielded privilege. One led with generosity. The other with dominance.

They were two sides of the same coin, both powerful, both influential but their leadership could not have been more different. And in that contrast, I started to refine not just my approach to work but my vision of the man I wanted to become.

But even as I studied the men around me, quietly absorbing their strategies and their style, deeper questions began to surface, about not just who I was becoming but how I was being seen.

The city was sharpening me, my presence, my language, my understanding of unspoken codes.

I was becoming sophisticated.

But at what cost?

Each new layer of refinement carried a cost, the risk of forgetting who I had been before crossing the Channel. Was I adapting... or was I quietly erasing the rawer, grittier parts of myself that had once been my armour?

At first, I silenced the doubt. Adaptation was survival. But over time, the question refused to stay quiet.

As I studied the rules and rhythms of this new world, there was another layer I rarely spoke of.

My British passport opened doors. My suit, my sales results, my quiet charm, they all smoothed my entry into spaces I once thought unreachable.

But my skin, my roots, my difference, they drew eyes. Not hostile but curious. Assessing. Measuring.

In the British corporate world, race was often a visible divide. In France, it was subtler. Quieter. *Rarely named but always present.*

At first, I told myself I was imagining it. But over time, I recognised the small tells, the double-takes in meetings, the extra questions about my background, the careful curiosity that colleagues from privileged families never seemed to face.

I wasn't just navigating wealth. I was navigating whiteness, Frenchness and the unspoken codes of a society that prized quiet conformity beneath its veneer of sophistication.

I connected easily with international colleagues. But when it came to certain circles, the old families, the closed-door networks, there was a ceiling I couldn't quite see but I could always feel.

And that silent negotiation became part of my daily armour, at times conscious, at times instinctive.

Weekends, Wandering and Finding My Place in France

Weekends became a patchwork of discovery. Some were social, dinners with colleagues, impromptu soirées in candlelit apartments, the clink of glasses beneath Haussmann ceilings, conversations that danced between politics, film and where to find the best local fromagerie. I was still learning the rhythm, still translating more than just words. Most nights, I probably understood 80% of what was being said. But I nodded, I smiled, I stayed in the language. My pride wouldn't let me switch to

English. I forced myself through the discomfort, out of respect, out of grit, out of something deeper I couldn't yet name.

I would pause, close my eyes briefly and *visualise myself speaking French with calm and clarity.* I whispered a quiet mantra, almost like a pre-game chant:

"Mistakes aren't weakness. They're evidence of courage."

It became my armour. The errors would come of course they would. But each one was proof I was daring to grow, not proof I didn't belong.

And while I sometimes left those nights with a headache from the mental gymnastics, I also left with a sense of belonging earned, not given. They were sophisticated evenings, yes but also full of laughter, wine and the unmistakable joy of being young and determined in the heart of Paris. Alongside that, I struck up friendships that have stood the test of time, with colleagues like Stanislas, Mathieu, and Thomas, as well as Steve Berry, often built around sport, whether watching a match or getting out to play whenever a free weekend allowed.

Other weekends, when my friends were not around, I wandered alone. Headphones in, hands in my coat pockets, I'd walk for hours, across the Pont Alexandre III at golden hour, past the street artists in the Latin Quarter, into the winding calm of Saint-Germain-des-Prés. I'd lose track of time in the quieter corners of the Marais or tucked beneath the trees of the Jardin du Luxembourg.

It looked peaceful from the outside. And in some ways, it was. But beneath the surface, there was always a tension, a low hum of sadness that I wasn't out socialising, mingling, living the full Parisian dream the way I imagined others were. I wasn't yet fully at ease in my own company, not quite comfortable with the quieter parts of myself.

So I walked, not because I always wanted to be alone but because it was the only space where I didn't have to perform. I could just be. No French to stumble through. No social codes to decode. Just my I-Pod, music in my ears and the city unfolding before me, one uncertain step at a time.

Montmartre, where I lived, became my home in more ways than one. Its winding cobbled streets, little cafés tucked beneath ivy-covered balconies, the soft strum of a busker's guitar echoing from the steps of Sacré-Cœur, it all felt like a dream rendered in stone. There was something beautifully human about that hill. Raw. Artistic. Slightly worn at the edges but proud.

And then there were the weekends I shared with someone I loved.

She visited every other month and when she did, the city lit up. We wandered through nearly every corner of Paris, late-night cafés in Le Marais, boutique-lined streets near Place Victor Hugo, art galleries tucked behind ivy-covered courtyards, even centre court at Roland Garros.

On long weekends, we slipped out of the city. Alsace, with its fairy-tale villages and crisp white wines. The Loire Valley, where grand châteaux rose like paintings come to life. And Bretagne, wild, wind-blown and oddly familiar. It reminded me of Yorkshire in some unspoken way, only with crêpes and cider instead of chip butties and ale.

Those weren't just travels. They were memories in motion, small moments that gave shape to something deeper. I didn't know it then but those weekends were laying the emotional groundwork for a love that would stretch across countries and years.

France began to reveal itself as more than just Paris. It was a continent disguised as a country, each region its own world. Different food, different dialects, different histories. I found something oddly comforting in that. The idea that a place could be many things at once and still belong to itself.

Over time, I wasn't just understanding the French, I was beginning to understand France. Its proud complexity. Its contradictions. Its rituals of refinement and its flashes of rebellion. Its deep, almost romantic belief in beauty for its own sake.

And somehow, without even realising it, I was falling in love, not just with a woman, or a city, or a job but with the act of becoming someone new.

But becoming someone new didn't mean leaving everything behind. Especially not family.

Each summer, I made sure my mum and my younger sister could visit me, sharing with them the world I was discovering, even as I was still learning how to navigate it myself.

Those summers in Paris remain vivid. My sister, wide-eyed at the Eiffel Tower, my mum sipping coffee in little cafés while I tried to explain the menu in half-broken French. I played tour guide and provider. But more than that, I became something else.

With my sister, the role of brother blurred into something heavier. I was her protector. In many ways the father figure I felt she needed. Even then, in my twenties, I felt the quiet weight of that duty. Making sure she was safe. That she saw the beauty the world could offer. That she knew someone would always look out for her, no matter what.

And with my mum, the dynamic was shifting too. I wasn't just her son anymore. I was becoming her anchor. The one who could offer stability when life still felt uncertain for her. The son she had once raised, now becoming her protector in ways neither of us had fully expected.

Those visits were a reminder: no matter how far I travelled, family wasn't something I could, or wanted to, leave behind.

And yet, even with their presence in those bright summer weeks, my day-to-day life in Paris remained a solo climb. The duality of provider and aspirant. Family man and cultural chameleon. Brother. Son. Emerging leader.

It was a delicate balance and looking back, perhaps the first glimpse of the man I was still learning to become.

The Art of Elegance and the Education of a Lifetime

I didn't speak the language fluently, not yet. But I made it my mission to learn as much as possible. I practised every day, studied every nuance, listened intently to how my colleagues greeted one another, how they ordered their coffee, how they used silence like punctuation. In France, silence wasn't awkward. It was presence. A moment to think. A moment to be.

What I lacked in pedigree, I made up for in delivery. Quietly, consistently, I performed. Quarter after quarter, my name appeared among the company's top European performers. The reward? Access. Invitations. Exposure to a world I'd never imagined, much less felt worthy of entering.

It wasn't about money. It was about code.

The firm's high performers were recognised not just with bonuses but with experience. I was flown to ski resorts like Verbier and Courchevel, places where the air itself felt expensive. I sat at tables in Michelin-starred restaurants, learning the unspoken choreography of fine dining: which fork to use, how to hold your glass, when to speak and when to simply nod with understated approval.

The first time I was served pigeon, I didn't flinch. Not outwardly. Internally, I was on high alert, trying to work out how to navigate the meal without revealing I was out of my depth. Part of me couldn't stop thinking about the carrier pigeons back in Yorkshire or the pub I used to cycle past called *The Carriers*, where the only thing flying was bar banter and pork scratchings. A few weeks later, I found myself at a champagne reception and casually asked for "Veev Click-kot." The man beside me, effortlessly elegant in his navy suit, smiled kindly and said, "Ah, you mean *Veuve Clicquot*," correcting me with a grace that was almost more disarming than a blunt put-down.

That was Paris. It didn't scold you. It let you sit beside excellence until you either absorbed it or exposed yourself.

And so I absorbed.

I learned how to speak less and mean more. How to wear clothes that whispered confidence instead of shouting status. I found my rhythm in conversation, in presence, in knowing when to lean in and when to let the moment breathe. Even the smallest gestures had weight, like the right cologne that lingered subtly after a handshake, or the quiet confidence of a watch that peeked out just enough to be noticed but never announced.

It wasn't about becoming someone else. It was about refining who I already was.

Because for all the suits, cigars and fine wines, I never stopped feeling the fire I brought with me, from Morley, from Birmingham, from the grit of those years when I had nothing but ambition and instinct. Paris didn't soften me. It sharpened me. It taught me how to wield presence like armour own a room without raising my voice.

But even as I refined the outer edges, something inside was stirring.

There were nights I'd come home to my 4th floor Montmartre apartment, its slanted ceilings, wooden beams and a view of Paris rooftops that felt plucked from a film and I'd sit at the window, glass of red in hand and ask myself: *Am I becoming the man I wanted to be, or the man this world wants me to become?*

I'd come so far. But sometimes, it still felt like I was playing a role in someone else's play.

The Ceiling You Can't Always See

Despite the results, the fluency I'd fought for, not just in French but in tone, in presence, in the unspoken language of influence, I began to feel it.

The limit.

Not of ability but of belonging.

In meeting rooms, decisions often seemed pre-determined, closed circles speaking in shorthand, making space only for those cut from the same cloth. The cadence of a Parisian accent could carry more authority than my metrics ever could. I wasn't resented. I was respected. But also... managed. Admired but not truly embraced.

France applauded performance. But it promoted familiarity. Excellence earned you a seat. Heritage handed you the room.

I'd studied the rules, mastered the code but there was a ceiling I couldn't quite name, only feel.

Not glass. Legacy.

Not spoken. Understood.

And quietly, life outside the office had shifted, too.

Love in Motion

Her name was Lucia.

We met in London but it was France that taught us how to love in motion. Two ambitious people, chasing futures in different cities but still choosing each other.

Those weekends in Paris, the cafés, the escapes to Alsace, the long drives through the Loire and the windswept calm of Bretagne, they weren't just trips. They were our thread. Moments of togetherness that stitched time and distance into something that felt like home.

For nearly two years, we lived between worlds. Long weekends, late-night calls, a spark that distance somehow fed rather than starved.

And when she finally moved to Paris, it felt like a new beginning.

Candlelit dinners, laughter echoing through side streets, long walks under lamplight that felt like promises.

But three months later, my path led to Geneva. She followed. And the rhythm of reunion gave way to the routine of reality.

I loved her. No question.

Through her, I travelled to Buenos Aires, met her family and discovered a world of warmth, tradition and connection. A culture that stretched me, softened me.

But she missed home. After five years in Europe, she longed to find herself outside of us. And in the midst of the financial crisis, Geneva offered few answers.

She had once thrived in London and Paris. In Geneva, she felt stuck.

It wore on her. It wore on us.

The truth is, love built across borders can survive distance but not always the weight of stillness.

It wasn't failure. It was life.

And when the decision came to end it, it hurt - for both of us. There was love. Real love.

But sometimes, the kindest thing you can do is let go before love turns into something it was never meant to be.

Still, it taught me something.

That love isn't just chemistry. It's timing, context, shared momentum.

We didn't fail each other.

We simply outgrew the season we once shared.

And in that letting go, I learned that endings can carry dignity too.

Lucia was a mirror during one of the biggest transitions of my life.

Proof that love can grow, even in motion.

She didn't just walk beside my journey.

She helped shape it.

And part of the reason I walked into Paris with my heart open, ready for reinvention.

As the financial crisis began to rumble across Europe, I knew, it was time to move again.

Not because Paris had closed the door.

But because I'd outgrown the version of myself that walked through it.

A City That Changed Me Without Claiming Me

When I boarded the train to Geneva, I didn't feel rejection. I felt release.

Paris hadn't failed me. It had refined me.

Not into someone else but into someone more precise.

It taught me how to read a room without losing myself in it.

How to stay sharp while appearing smooth.

How to move through spaces that weren't built for me and still leave a mark.

I had arrived with broken French and everything I owned in five bags.

I left with confidence, cultural fluency and the beginnings of something deeper: clarity.

But the question still lingered.

Was I building a life of success or still chasing a sense of worth?

Paris didn't answer that.

But it gave me the courage to ask it, out loud.

Geneva wouldn't bring resolution.

But it would bring movement.

And sometimes, that's the only way truth reveals itself.

The Blueprint – Chapter 6: Thriving in Elite Rooms Without Dimming Your Light

Key Truth

"Learn their rules but never lose your rhythm."

Quote

"I have learned that as long as I hold fast to my beliefs and values and follow my own moral compass, then the only expectations I need to live up to are my own." - Barack Obama

---

Theme: Navigating Privilege Without Losing Your Identity

Paris was a masterclass in codes, spoken and unspoken. It invited me into rooms I once thought were sealed shut. But it also revealed the subtle costs of access: the silences, the scrutiny, the invisible pressure to soften your story so it fits the setting. When you've come from working-class roots, when your name or accent or skin isn't the default in elite rooms, presence alone becomes a kind of rebellion.

This Blueprint is for those navigating spaces they weren't born into, those decoding boardrooms, fine dining rituals, or aristocratic workplaces while quietly wondering if they still belong. It's for the culturally displaced, the socially ascending, the ones carrying silent burdens while performing excellence. These are the lessons that allowed me to expand the blueprint, without erasing the original sketch.

---

1. Adaptation is a skillset, not self-betrayal

Adapting to elite environments isn't weakness, it's wisdom. When you enter a world where the rules weren't written for you, learning how to move within them is survival. But there's a difference between adapting and erasing. One expands you. The other hollows you.

Why This Matters:

When you come from a different background, be it race, class, gender, or geography, elite rooms often demand adjustment. But adaptation doesn't have to mean assimilation. Done intentionally, it becomes a form of power: the ability to shift fluently while staying anchored in who you are. Whether you're the first in your family to enter corporate life or the only one in the room with your story, your ability to adapt is not a betrayal of where you're from, it's a testament to your range. It's strategic navigation. The very trait that once felt like camouflage becomes cultural fluency: a vital strength in today's diverse teams and global contexts.

My Reality:

To survive in Paris, I had to learn new codes, how to move, speak, listen. At client dinners where I didn't understand half the wine list or in meetings where silence carried more weight than speech, I learned to observe and adjust. But I never let go of my own voice. I wasn't French. I was becoming fluent, not forgetful.

Lived Lesson:

In my early days, I found myself hesitating at lunch when everyone ordered confidently in rapid French. I'd stumble, ask for translations or just smile and nod, unsure. But rather than shy away, I kept showing up. With each awkward exchange, I slowly found my rhythm and the fluency that followed became a quiet act of ownership.

Over time, that small persistence became presence. Years later, it's the same resilience I draw on when stepping into unfamiliar boardrooms. I don't need to belong to lead, I just need to listen, learn, and stay anchored.

Make it Real:

Identify one environment where you feel out of place. Then list three behaviours or communication styles used in that space, not to mimic but to decode. Learn the language. Keep your accent.

Reflection Prompts:

- Where in my life have I confused adaptation with betrayal of my background?
- What part of myself do I still hesitate to bring into high-status environments and why?
- What leadership edge might be hiding in my ability to shift while staying centred?

2. The room isn't always the reward

Power doesn't always shout. Sometimes it whispers in tone, posture or silence. When you enter rooms shaped by legacy, where inclusion isn't always earned but inherited, learning the rhythm becomes essential. But mimicry is not mastery. You're there to learn, not to disappear.

Why This Matters:

Navigating elite or unfamiliar spaces means understanding not just what is said but how things are said and what goes unspoken. These unspoken rules often reflect deeper norms around class, race, or gender. But learning them doesn't mean accepting them as truth. It means you're equipping yourself to move with intentionality and edge.

Leaders who emerge from the margins learn to see what others miss. That insight becomes strategic composure, an ability to hold presence without posturing.

My Reality:

Some of the most powerful people in Paris rarely raised their voices. Their authority was quiet but so was their prejudice. I had to learn the rhythm without copying the song. I watched how presence was crafted, how approval was coded but I never let the performance become my identity.

Lived Lesson:

I began to notice how influence moved through glances,

pauses and gestures in the Paris office, especially in meetings run by men like Gilles. The real decisions weren't made at the table; they were made in eye contact before the meeting ever began.

That sharpened my ability to read nuance, and later, to lead teams where power wasn't just positional, it was relational.

Make it Real:
Next time you're in a room that feels "above your level," spend 10 minutes only observing. What's not being said? How are power and inclusion communicated?

Reflection Prompts:

- What silent expectations shaped how I saw myself in childhood and how do they still show up now?
- How can I remain present without performing?
- What signals of power or exclusion do I now notice, and how might I use that awareness to lead more inclusively?

---

3. Exposure shatters mental ceilings

Sometimes the limits we feel aren't real, they're inherited. When you're the first to enter a space of privilege or prestige, your very presence starts to expand what's possible, not just for you but for everyone watching.

Why This Matters:

We don't just inherit bloodlines, we inherit ceilings. Many of us internalise an invisible boundary around what's possible "for people like us." Exposure to new rooms, new rituals and new reference points helps rewire those old beliefs. This isn't about becoming someone else, it's about expanding the range of who you've always been.

In leadership, this becomes visionary thinking: the courage to imagine new futures, not just for yourself but for the people watching your climb.

My Reality:

At first, the idea of living in an apartment in Paris or speaking in a boardroom full of aristocrats seemed wild. But by year two, it felt normal. And outside the office, hosting my mother and sister in the city once felt like an unimaginable privilege but it became part of my new normal too.

Lived Lesson:

When I walked my little sister through the streets of Paris, guiding her up Montmartre or through the Jardins du Luxembourg, it struck me: we weren't visitors anymore. We belonged here too. Her wide-eyed wonder reminded me how far I'd come not just for myself but for her future too. That moment helped shift something deeper in me, what I believed was possible for our family and one day, for my own child. Now, I lead with that lens: creating space where others can expand their vision too.

Make it Real:
Intentionally expose yourself to something aspirational, an event, a conversation, a setting, once a month. Journal what feels uncomfortable and what becomes natural over time.

Reflection Prompts:

- What ceilings did I internalise as a child and how do they still shape what I believe I'm allowed to want?
- Where do I still shrink to avoid discomfort instead of stepping forward into growth?
- Who's watching me quietly expand what's possible?

---

4. Build bridges between worlds

You weren't made to live in just one world. You were built to move between them. When your story spans cultures, classes or codes, your strength is in your fluency, not in fitting in but in linking what others keep separate.

Why This Matters:
Bridge-builders are rare and powerful. If you grew up mixed-

race, between classes, or navigating multiple social realities, you carry a unique gift: you can see the world from more than one vantage point. In a divided world, that's not just useful. It's transformative. In leadership, this becomes an edge: being able to speak multiple cultural "languages," empathise across difference and create belonging where none existed.

My Reality:
I wasn't the most refined but I was the most versatile. I could talk rugby with the doorman and geopolitics with a CEO. I could walk the streets of Montmartre in the morning and close a deal in Neuilly by evening. That duality became my edge.

Lived Lesson:
In the office, I could navigate complex boardroom dynamics. But at night, I'd walk the streets of Paris with headphones on, letting the city talk back to me. That space between performance and peace, between the sharp suit and the scuffed trainers, became my real power.

Later, it allowed me to lead teams that didn't look, sound, or think the same and still find unity.

Make it Real:
Identify three "worlds" you move between (e.g., working-class family, elite workplace, international friendship group). Write down one strength you gain from each.

Reflection Prompts:

- Where have I downplayed my ability to connect worlds, out of fear of seeming "too different" for each?
- How can I use my cross-cultural, cross-class, or cross-identity experience as leadership capital, not liability?
- What unique lens do I offer in rooms where sameness is the norm?

---

5. Luxury without purpose is hollow

Elegance can polish your presence but it won't fill your soul. There's a difference between enjoying refinement and being defined by it. When your roots come from lack, success can sometimes trick you into performing fullness instead of building it.

Why This Matters:
Material success, nice watches, fine wines, Michelin stars, can offer a sense of validation, especially if you grew up with less. But meaning isn't in what you wear. It's in what you stand for. If you don't define wealth on your terms, the world will sell you a version that shines but doesn't satisfy.

My Reality:

At one point, I was regularly dining in five-star hotels but still felt emotionally empty. That's when I realised: the outer life looked complete but the inner life still needed tending. Prestige without purpose is a lonely performance.

Lived Lesson:

I remember sitting at a mountain resort in Courchevel, surrounded by opulence I never imagined growing up. On the outside, I was all smiles, laughing, enjoying the moment, playing the part with ease. And sure, I had a good time. But instead of feeling proud, I felt distant, from myself, from home, from purpose. It wasn't an epiphany, but a quiet awakening. That moment taught me to ask deeper questions and those questions now guide how I lead, build and parent, with substance, not just surface.

Make it Real:

Define your version of "enough." What values matter more than your next promotion or purchase?

Reflection Prompts:

- What early hunger for validation still drives my definition of success today?
- Where am I pursuing appearances over alignment and how might I come back to meaning?

- How do I help others measure worth by impact, not just image?

What Paris Taught Me:

Paris taught me how to hold my own in rooms where the rules were written long before I arrived. It taught me how to move with grace, speak with precision and carry presence without apology. But it also reminded me: sophistication is not superiority. Elegance doesn't erase struggle. And you don't need to trade your fire for finesse.

The truth is: you can be both.
You can know your wines *and* remember what it's like to split a bag of chips five ways.
You can wear the luxury timepiece *and* carry the hustle that taught you why time matters.
You can master the codes *without letting them master you.*

And you can learn how to lead in public rooms while still protecting what matters most behind closed doors.

As the Paris chapter closed, Geneva called. Another step deeper into the elite world, structured, discreet, quietly powerful. A world of sharp suits and heavy wooden doors.

But beneath the success, something else stirred.

I was approaching 30.

And with it came the ache that no accolade could ease.

The quiet question no salary could answer:

Who am I, *really* and where is the part of me that's still missing?

7

THE SEARCH FOR THE MISSING HALF - FINDING MY FATHER, RECLAIMING MYSELF

I had never met my father. I knew he was from the Caribbean but not his name, his face, or his voice. He was a ghost, a missing piece in a story I could never quite complete. His absence had become so constant, it nearly felt normal. Nearly. No matter what I accomplished or how far I travelled, there was always that space, that unanswered question. By the time I turned 30, I knew it was time to find the answer.

By the Time I Turned 30

By 30, I had built a life that once would have felt unimaginable back in Morley. I'd crossed borders, geographic, cultural, emotional, navigating worlds I was never meant to enter, worlds where nobody looked like me. From Birmingham's backstreets to London's glass towers, from Paris's old-world refinement to Geneva's discreet wealth, I moved through cultures and languages like a chameleon, mastering skills on the fly, learning to survive, then thrive, in rooms built for others.

I was earning well, respected in my field, building a future I could be proud of. And yet, one part of me remained untouched, unanswered, unseen.

Who was my father?

That question had lived quietly in the background for years, present but parked, now it demanded attention.

A Name Without a Face

Growing up, my father was more myth than man, an outline, a shadow. My mum never spoke of him, not in anger, not in sadness, not even in passing. His existence sat somewhere between taboo and denial, like a missing page in a family photo album, carefully removed, yet the space he left behind shaped me silently, profoundly.

Every year, the first Sunday after my birthday arrived with a heaviness I never spoke of, Father's Day. While my friends wrapped homemade cards in pride and laughter, I gradually withdrew. At school, when we were asked to draw a picture of our dads or write a few lines about them, I'd sit with my pencil hovering over the page, heart pounding. Sometimes I sketched a made-up man, a smiling figure in a suit, with strong shoulders and kind eyes. Other times, I'd pretend I needed the toilet, just to buy myself time or avoid the task altogether.

I never cried, never complained but the pain was there, internal, constant, a ritual of absence repeated every single year. I never let it show, not to my teachers, not to my mates, not even to myself most of the time. I buried it deep, convinced that silence was strength but inside a quiet ache throbbed.

Then one day, I found my birth certificate. I was about eleven, snooping through one of my mum's drawers, half-curious and half-bored, when among old papers and keepsakes I pulled out a thin, official document bearing my name. I stared at it for a while, my thumb tracing the bold black letters that spelled out my full name, until I saw the line for "Father's Name."

Instead of a name, it read: Unknown.

That word hit harder than I expected. Unknown, not absent, not unnamed, not even "not provided," just unknown. There was something brutal about the coldness of that word on such a personal document, like a stamp of rejection I had never agreed to. My existence was officially acknowledged, yet somehow still denied. At the time, that single word felt like the first blow.

What I didn't know then was that an entirely different life had nearly been signed into being. I wasn't just missing a father, I had almost been missing from my own story.

I didn't cry. I just stood there, staring, shame creeping in like a slow, invisible fog. I folded the certificate and put it back where I found it but something shifted in me that day. The idea that my own story had been signed off by the state with a question mark left a mark. From that moment, the ache wasn't just emotional, it was documented, official, real.

Still, life moved on.

In the absence of a blueprint, I built my own definition of manhood: strength, resilience, self-reliance. I pieced it together from fragments, rugby coaches who pushed me harder, older lads who walked with swagger and purpose, teachers who saw a spark I hadn't yet named.

I studied heroes, some who looked like me, the grace and defiance of Jeremy Guscott, England Rugby's first mixed-race centre who played my position, the commanding presence of Viv Richards, the West Indies' legendary cricket captain, the killer instinct of Michael Jordan, the silent authority of greats who didn't just play, they dominated. I clung to those glimpses of greatness, not because I fully understood them but because they showed me what might be possible.

When Barack Obama was elected in 2008, a mixed-race man raised without his father, it hit me deeper than I could admit. There was something in his story, the way he rose with grace despite the absence, that mirrored my own inner search. It made me believe, for the first time, that maybe I wasn't broken, maybe I was just unfinished. But even with that hope, there was still a gap. A name wasn't enough and certainly, "Unknown" wasn't enough. I needed more.

I remember listening to his speech on the night of his election victory, November 4th 2008, sitting in my small apartment in Montmartre, Paris, watching history unfold from my sofa as evening darkness wrapped around the city. I felt a strange mix of astonishment, pride and fear (the threat of his assassination felt so real that day...), as if history might be stolen before it had even begun.

And then something broke.

After holding it together for so long, I found myself in tears, uncontrollably, not just for what the world had witnessed but for everything I hadn't yet faced. It was as if twenty years of silent grief had been waiting for that exact moment to be released.

With hindsight, I think that night cracked something open. Combined with reading Obama's first book - *Dreams from My Father*, it stirred something in me that had long been buried. Within a few months, I would begin the search, not just for him but for the missing half of myself.

Starting the Search

The decision to find him didn't arrive like lightning, it came like a tide, slow, rising, impossible to ignore. At first, it was just a whisper in the back of my mind, then a tightening in my chest whenever I passed a father and son, until eventually it became a truth I could no longer outrun: I had to know.

Whilst in Geneva, where I had moved after that famous election victory, I reached out to a private search company in the UK, polished, reassuring, confident. "We can help," they said, "we've done this before." I paid the fee and gave them every detail I had, which wasn't much. Eventually, my mum had shared what she believed was his name, though she wasn't certain. It was more memory than fact, a fragile lead. And then I waited.

Weeks turned into months. I chased, I called, I emailed. Sometimes they replied with cautious optimism, other times they went silent. The waiting gnawed at me, it wasn't just frustration, it felt like holding my breath for weeks, unsure what would come next. Hope pulled me forward, fear held me back.

What if he didn't want to be found?

What if he had died?

What if he had known about me all along and chosen to avoid me?

There were moments I almost gave up. I'd close the file on my laptop and tell myself: You're fine without him, you've done alright, let it go. But I couldn't, the question wouldn't die quietly.

And then, months later, the phone rang.

The Call That Changed Everything

There were no fireworks, just an unexpected ring, midday, midweek. A man from the agency was on the other end. His voice was warm but measured, like he knew the weight of what he was about to say.

"We've made contact," he said, "but not directly with him."

There was a pause.

"We spoke with a woman, Danielle. She's his daughter."

I froze.

A sister?

It was the first time I'd ever heard her name, Danielle. A complete stranger, yet somehow… not. A sister I never knew existed. The idea landed somewhere between shock and recognition, like finding a photograph you're in but have no memory of taking.

"She confirmed the name you gave us," the man continued. "He's her father and… she's happy to pass his number on to you."

I remember the sensation, my mind spinning, my body frozen. I barely heard the rest of the call. I thanked him, scribbled down the number and stared at the piece of paper like it might catch fire in my hands.

The thoughts came fast and chaotic.

Danielle. Did she know about me before today? What did she think when the agency called? Why had she agreed so willingly?

And then, him.

What would he say when I called? Would he even pick up? What if I heard his voice and felt… nothing?

Or worse, what if I felt everything?

But the biggest fear of all was this, what if this moment, the one I'd imagined and feared for most of my life, left me feeling even more alone?

I sat with those questions for hours.

Then finally, heart pounding, I picked up the phone. My hand trembled slightly as I dialled.

One ring. Two. Three.

Then...

He answered.

The First Conversation

His voice was deeper than I'd imagined, slower, confident. It wasn't awkward at first but it wasn't easy either. There were long pauses, polite questions, tentative words. It was more of a hello than a reckoning, a cautious introduction, like two people circling something too large to name just yet.

Neither of us dove into the past. We weren't ready, not over the phone. The call was a bridge, a necessary one but it didn't carry the weight of answers, just the possibility of them.

We agreed to meet in person.

He was open, calm, not surprised, not overly emotional, just steady. There was something in that steadiness that grounded me, even as my head swam with a thousand thoughts.

We didn't speak long. When I hung up, my hands were trembling. A man I had wondered about for thirty years was no longer an idea. He had a voice now, a location.

And soon, the man I'd imagined for three decades would have a face.

The Meeting in Nottingham

We agreed to meet in person a week later, not in Geneva or London but in Nottingham, a city with grit in its bones. Unpolished, working-class, unpretentious. In its quiet toughness, it felt right. No theatre, just reality. A place that, in some strange way, matched the moment.

We met at a small West Indian restaurant in a part of Nottingham where Caribbean culture ran deep, in the food, in the music, in the rhythm of the street. Honest, authentic, no-frills. The kind of place you wouldn't stumble into unless you knew it was there. The air was thick with spice, ginger, scotch bonnet and something deeper, more rooted.

The walls were painted a dull mustard yellow, the furniture dark wood and worn from years of elbows and stories. It wasn't loud but it buzzed with conversation, reggae humming gently in the background.

The restaurant was split across two levels. We sat at the back of the raised section, half a floor above the rest. From there, you could see it all, the door, the counter, every face that came and went. He had chosen that spot. Later, I understood why.

He arrived just as I was folding my hands, trying to slow my breathing. And when he walked in, everything paused.

He was taller than I expected, much taller. Slim built but he looked hard, really hard, like a man who had been through a lot and lived to tell it, even if he didn't always want to. His head was shaved, smooth like polished stone. Something about him immediately reminded me of Michael Jordan but slightly darker.

It struck me in a way I didn't expect. I'm relatively light-skinned for a mixed-race man, Obama-light, I used to joke and seeing him, this man who shared my blood but looked like he came from a completely different palette, hit me with something I didn't yet have words for. Not shame. Not confusion. Just… difference. A quiet reckoning with who I was and who I wasn't unfolding in real time.

His presence was sharp, alert. I noticed the way his eyes scanned the room, always moving, always clocking exits, angles, reflections in the windows. Every few minutes, he glanced behind and above him, as though checking for something, or someone. It wasn't paranoia. It was muscle memory, the kind you earn when life has taught you to never fully relax.

When he sat down, I noticed the way his shoulders angled, not slouched, not defensive, just ready.

He ordered for both of us without asking. "Two curry goat and rice," he said, his voice low and raspy. "And two Guinness."

There was something familiar in the way he spoke, not to me but to the space itself. Like he had been here before, like this was his terrain. One of the staff nodded and disappeared without a word.

I looked at him. He looked at me. We said nothing, just sat there in the stillness, letting the moment breathe. Then he smiled. Not wide. Not performative. But real. And in that subtle lift of his mouth, something hit me with the force of a mirror shattering.

Myself.

The same cheekbones, the curve of the jaw and then, the eyes. That unmistakable twinkle, a glint of charm laced with mischief. I'd seen it before, staring back at me from the mirror, never knowing where it came from. Now I did.

There he was. My father. No longer a question mark or an idea I carried in pieces. A man. And not just any man, my origin point.

I wanted to speak, something profound, something that could honour the gravity of it all but my mouth was dry, my throat tight. All I could manage was a quiet, "Alright?"

He nodded. "Yeah, man." Then he began to speak.

His voice was deep, unhurried, a Caribbean lilt weathered by years in England. There was rhythm in it and weight. Every sentence felt like it had lived a life before being spoken.

Somewhere between the stories and sips of Guinness, he dropped it casually, "I'm from Jamaica." The words landed like a body blow. My stomach flipped, breath caught in my chest.

Jamaica.

The island I'd imagined but never known. For thirty years, I hadn't even known which island I came from. Jamaica? Barbados? Trinidad? St. Kitts? My mum didn't know either. It had always been a blank space. Until now. And just like that, it had a name.

Something primal rose in me, pride, curiosity, the thrill of discovery. A strange mix of familiarity and distance. Jamaica, the island of resistance and rhythm. Bob Marley, Marcus Garvey, Olympic gold and ancestral fire. I'd admired it from afar, from a space of awe and abstraction. But now, it was personal.

Yet pride wasn't the only thing rising. Alongside it came something more uneasy.

Jamaica wasn't just sunshine and swagger. It was also burdened, by headlines, by history, by violence and pain. One of the highest murder rates in the world. A place of power and struggle, beauty and grief. A country with two faces, the cultural titan that danced across the global stage and the wounded island fighting systemic wounds beneath the surface.

It was bold, defiant, beautiful but it was also fractured, scarred. A place where joy and trauma existed in every breath and now, somehow, I was connected to both.

That duality didn't leave me when I stepped out of the restaurant. It followed me, in my thoughts, in my skin, in every glance in the mirror. I was Jamaican but I hadn't grown up eating ackee and saltfish. I didn't speak Patois. I'd never set foot on the island, couldn't name the parishes, didn't know the national heroes. The music was familiar, yes but the roots? Not yet.

At first, the realisation made me feel like a fraud. Could I claim a culture I'd never lived in? Was it mine to hold, or just a story I now wanted to borrow?

And yet, deep down, something in me recognised it. The rhythm. The pride. The fire in the blood.

It wasn't about geography, it was about belonging. And for the first time in my life, I had something to point to. Not just a race or a region but a country, a people, a lineage.

But with that recognition came responsibility. If I was going to claim Jamaica, I had to learn it, understand it. Not just wear the colours but carry the stories, both beautiful and brutal. Because that's what it meant to inherit something real, to take the gift and the wound, to love a place not for what it could offer me but for what it revealed about who I was.

From that day forward, Jamaica lived inside me. Not fully formed, not yet understood but present. Waiting.

He kept speaking. We didn't linger there long. The story kept moving and I kept listening, not just with my ears but with my whole body, leaning in, scanning every detail, trying to piece together the shape of a life I'd only just begun to meet.

The food arrived. Steam curled between us, the scent of curry goat and rice rising through the low hum of the restaurant. He poured the Guinness, passed one across to me and raised his glass slightly. A quiet toast. No words. Just an acknowledgement.

We ate in silence for a while. Not awkward but weighted. Full.

But just as I began to steady myself, still absorbing the weight of Jamaica, still coming to terms with the mirror across the table, he dropped another truth. No warning. No ceremony. Just a sentence that cracked the ground beneath me.

The Revelation

We kept talking. The conversation didn't unfold in neat lines, it meandered like memory, circling back, drifting forward, tugging at loose threads.

And as I sat there, still piecing together what it meant to carry Jamaica in my DNA, he said it, almost offhand, like it was nothing.

"You've got brothers and sisters, you know."

I looked up, startled. "What?"

"Yeah. You've got five of 'em."

He said it like he was naming a football squad.

An older brother, an older sister, two youngers and a little one. Luke, Danielle, John, Jordan and Laura. Four different mums.

Six of us.

Apart from my younger half-sister, born when I was twenty, these were lives I never knew existed. Stories unfolding parallel to mine, running beside me like train tracks hidden behind a wall of silence.

My body went cold, not with fear but with the quiet shock of something too big to process all at once. The restaurant faded. The clink of cutlery, the chatter around us, it all slipped away. It felt like someone had opened a door inside my chest and let in a wind I hadn't braced for.

I thought of my own life, shaped in solitude, anchored by my mother's strength. I'd been raised as an only child. For years, my half-sister was the only sibling I'd ever known.

And now, there were five more.

Five.

Each one carrying a thread of the same story, the same blood, the same absence.

And not one of them knew me.

"Do they know about me?" I asked, cautious, already suspecting the answer.

He paused, then shook his head. "Not all of them."

Just like that, I became the secret, the one in the shadows, the brother on the other side of silence.

Yet somehow, there was tenderness in the way he said it, as if he understood the weight of it, even if the words still faltered in his mouth.

But the night wasn't done with its revelations.

Meeting Danielle

After the restaurant, there were no tears, no emotional breakdowns. Just a quiet stillness between us. The kind that follows something weighty but unfinished. We both knew there would be time for feelings later. For now, my father simply stood, adjusted his coat and said, "Come on. Let's go meet your sister."

We took a short drive across Nottingham, the streets calm and slick with evening rain. The car pulled up outside a modest, well-kept house, warm light glowing behind the curtains.

"This is Monica's place," he said. "Danielle's waiting."

Monica answered the door, a lovely older Black woman with soft features and a kindness that felt almost too gentle for the rough-edged man standing beside me. She smiled warmly.

"You must be Ashley. He told us you might be coming."

She ushered us in and there, standing just behind her in the hallway, was Danielle.

Her eyes glistened the moment she saw me. Before either of us could speak, she stepped forward and wrapped me in a hug, strong, real, the kind of embrace that carried weight.

As she held me, I caught the faint scent of coconut oil. Familiar. Grounding. Like the hair of aunties and cousins in the Shorte family. A smell I hadn't realised I'd missed. The soft texture of her jumper brushed against my cheek, casual but comforting, like the kind of clothes worn in family living rooms where formality didn't matter.

Tears slid down her face.

"You look just like him," she whispered. "But I see your own light too."

That hug didn't feel like meeting a stranger. It felt like recognising someone you'd somehow always known.

Blood remembers, even when time forgets.

We talked for a while. Light conversation at first, the kind siblings might have if they'd grown up together. She asked about my life, Paris, work, the usual. I asked about hers. We didn't dive into the past, not yet. We let the present settle first.

And as the evening unfolded in Monica's warm, modest front room, with my father seated nearby, watching quietly, I felt something I hadn't expected.

There was something about the connection with my sister, Danielle, that felt unexpectedly deep, natural even, like roots threading through soil I hadn't realised I was still searching for. Her warmth, her tears, the ease between us, it all felt familiar in a way that had nothing to do with time and everything to do with recognition.

Not just connection.

Belonging.

I wasn't just meeting my sister, I was reclaiming a piece of myself that had always been missing.

The Second Night – Rhythm, Danger and Belonging

The next night, my father had something different planned.

"This time," he said, "you'll meet your older brother."

Luke.

Born in London, tall and rangy with gold tooth flashing behind an easy grin, Stone Island long coat buttoned to the top. Same eyes, same defiant smile as my father, a chip off the old block.

And instantly, I recognised something else too. Luke was the man my mum had been protecting me from becoming. The style, the swagger, the streetwise alertness that felt magnetic but dangerous.

Yet when he greeted me, there was no bravado. Just warmth. A brother's handshake that turned into a pull-in hug.

"You're family now, bruv," he said quietly.

That night wasn't about casual conversation. It was about stepping into my father's world, into their world.

We drove to one of Nottingham's most renowned clubs, a legendary Reggae and Dub night, headlined by none other than David Rodigan. The queue wrapped around the block, the air electric, bass already pulsing from inside, the smell of weed hanging in the cold night air.

A sea of faces, dark skin, gold chains, puffer jackets, dreadlocks, high-top fades. My people, Jamaicans, Bajans, Trinidadians, Londoners, Brummies, gathered under one roof. A shared rhythm, a cultural heartbeat, pulsing through the room.

As we approached the front, my father caught the eye of the doorman. A nod. No words. The rope parted like the Red Sea. We moved inside.

We were in the VIP section near the DJ booth, close enough to feel the speakers rumble through the floor. The bassline hit like a heartbeat in the chest.

My father and Luke leaned back, rum and cokes in hand, like kings holding court, at ease, in control, commanding presence without saying a word. Eyes clocked us. Men scanned the room, sizing us up the way people do when respect, pride, or ego might be on the line.

And with them at my side, I felt untouchable. Protected. Elevated. Bulletproof.

So I did something to match that feeling and ordered champagne.

Not because it was asked for but because I wanted them to see me. Not just as the younger one, or the newcomer but as a man.

Looking back, it wasn't necessary. But in that moment, it felt vital. A signal. A symbol. Not just that I belonged but that I could carry weight in this space. I wasn't a guest in this space. I was one of them.

As I leaned in to place the order, I felt my father's eyes on me. Not overt, just a glance. A discreet, measured look across the table. Approval, maybe. Or assessment. As if he was seeing me step into a world he had once ruled and perhaps wondering if I would stay in it, or one day move beyond it.

The music took over.

Rodigan's voice cut through the air, commanding the crowd, pulling us into a shared rhythm older than any of us. Reggae. Dancehall. Dub.

Resistance music. Survival music. Celebration music.

It didn't just fill the room. It filled something inside me.

And yet, as the night unfolded, between the champagne toasts, the pull of the bassline, the laughter and knowing looks, I felt something else simmering beneath the surface.

Danger.

This wasn't just a family reunion, it felt more like an initiation. There was an undercurrent running through the night, quiet but unmistakeable. Nottingham's gang culture was never far away, you could see it in the sharp glances, the unspoken calculations playing out in the corners. And I could feel it too, the sense that even though I was protected, this was still a space where things could flip in an instant.

But I didn't fear it, I leaned into it.

For a few hours, I felt like a hundred men, invincible, claimed.

When we finally stepped out into the early morning air, the cold bit at our skin, bringing a different clarity. The rush still coursed through me but so did something else, a quieter knowing.

I had loved the power of that night, the tribe, the respect, the charisma of men who moved through the world with danger in their eyes and rhythm in their blood. It was intoxicating, familiar even. I had known nights like this in Birmingham, back when bravado masked ache and energy kept the questions at bay.

But I also knew this, that path had an ending and it wasn't one I could afford.

I embraced my brother. I embraced my father. I thanked them. Because I understood the language of that night. The men in that room didn't survive by talking. They survived by being seen, by holding their ground, by reading the temperature of a room without ever saying a word.

That rhythm wasn't new to me. It wasn't something I found in that club, it was already inside me, carried in the way I entered rooms, scanned faces, sensed danger before it arrived. My father and Luke didn't need to say it, I already knew.

That night, I had been tested. And I had passed.

But the truth is, I have felt that rhythm pulse through me many times since. Sometimes I have leaned into it. Sometimes I have had to fight it. Either way, it is always there. A question mark I still carry.

And when I walked away, I carried more than the warmth of belonging. I carried the weight of choice.

I could love my roots without being ruled by them. I could honour the fire without letting it burn through me.

And for the first time, I understood that manhood wasn't just about proving strength or taking up space. It was knowing when to rise and when to stay rooted, when to speak and when to trust the quiet voice inside, the one I had spent years doubting but was finally learning to hear.

Sunday – The Final Gathering

The next day, the last before my flight back to Geneva, Danielle and Luke took me to meet my youngest brother, Jordan.

He lived in a small flat not far from the city centre, tall and slim like our father but with softer edges. Jordan was mixed-race, unlike Danielle and Luke, who carried more of our father's darker hue. His eyes were sharp but uncertain, the kind of uncertainty I recognised. A soul still searching, somehow. The kind that came from straddling two worlds, never fully belonging to either. His gaze kept darting toward the door, as though he were ready to leave, or waiting for something to arrive.

There was warmth in his handshake. Politeness, yes but also a hint of something else, that familiar mix of pride and hesitation. The look of a young man still trying to find his footing.

We sat in his living room for a while, making small talk. Football, music, family. Surface things, on the face of it but with deeper meaning when spoken between people only just becoming family. Jordan listened more than he spoke but when he did speak, there was an openness to his voice, like he wanted to claim this connection but wasn't sure if he was allowed to.

In him, I saw a version of myself from years earlier. Warm. Capable. But still trying to figure life out.

Not because of who he was but because of what was missing.

That need for belonging. That ache for a clear identity. One that didn't require explanation. We didn't try to cover thirty years of distance in an afternoon. We just shared time. And sometimes, that's the bravest start there is.

After an hour or so, Danielle and Luke hugged me goodbye. Jordan did too. Tentative at first but real. This wasn't the end of our connection. Then they left me to spend the final hours with our father.

The Last Conversation

I returned to Monica's. Just my father and me this time. No crowd, no music, no champagne. Just the calm of a Sunday afternoon, steady and still, like we had earned the quiet.

We sat in the living room, the same space where Monica had welcomed me two nights earlier. The television murmured in the background, the sound of a football match filling the pauses between us. But beneath the swirl of casual chat, something deeper stirred, not just a connection through DNA but through the quiet gravity of who he was.

He was a man who had lived at full tilt, a force of nature. Music, football, charisma, power. But also rage. And absence. His life was marked by hard choices and long silences, edges sharpened by survival.

He had moved through the world outside the rules, sometimes by defiance, sometimes because the rules were never made for him. There were gaps in his story, places where time had passed but words hadn't followed. The silence said enough.

I didn't need every detail. The specifics didn't matter as much as the weight behind those pauses. I knew that language, the unspoken kind. I knew what it meant to carry pain in silence, to walk through life in survival mode.

He had lived on the margins and he had paid the price. Maybe I saw it clearly because I had grown up with my own kind of struggle. Different streets, same fire.

I looked at him again. Really looked.

He wasn't the villain I had conjured in my loneliest moments. And he wasn't the hero I had hoped might one day turn up and make everything make sense. He was a man. Flawed. Magnetic. Real.

And in that moment, I felt something I never expected, love. Not the kind built over years of birthdays and football matches and late-night chats in the kitchen. This was something deeper, something older, something primal. The kind of love that says, I see you. And in seeing you, I see myself.

With that recognition, something inside me finally exhaled.

But love didn't cancel the questions.

Where had he been? Did he ever think of me? Did he ever wonder what I looked like, what kind of man I had become? Did he regret not being there?

I wanted to ask them all. I wanted to know everything. But the moment wasn't built for interrogation. It was built for something else.

Connection. Not closure. Not blame.

It was about reclaiming the parts of me that had lived in uncertainty.

The elegant man in Geneva. The cheeky boy in Morley. The young man drifting through Birmingham nights. The polished professional holding his own in Parisian boardrooms. The child who sat in class every June, quietly colouring in an imaginary dad on Father's Day.

All of them were me.

But now, there was more.

Now, there was this man. This story. This ancestry.

Jamaica, no longer just a word but a truth I now carried.

When we finally stood to leave, my father embraced me. It wasn't long. It wasn't awkward. But it was firm. Solid. Felt.

I stepped outside into the Nottingham afternoon, the air cool against my skin. Everything looked the same.

But I wasn't.

I had entered the weekend with a question. I left with a mirror.

Something had shifted and there was no going back.

And somewhere deep down, I knew, I would have to go there. To Jamaica. Not just to visit.

To complete the journey.

The Blueprint – Chapter 7: The Courage to Search for What's Missing

Key Truth

"You're not searching for him, you're searching for yourself."

Quote

"I was born a crime. But I was never a mistake." - Trevor Noah

---

Some of us grow up with a question that shadows everything we do:
Where is the person who was supposed to guide me?

For me, that question lived in silence. It echoed on Father's Days, in school assemblies, in the blank space on my birth certificate where a name should have been. My father wasn't just absent, he was unknown. Thirty years of wondering, of building a life without a blueprint, until one day I chose to look.

But searching for him wasn't just about finding a man, it was about finding me. You are not missing. You are gathering. Piece by piece. Silence by silence. The truth isn't what completes you, it's what sets you free to continue.

For anyone who has ever carried a missing piece, be it a parent, a mentor, a culture, or a truth, this is your Blueprint. The search itself can be your teacher.

---

1. The absence shapes you, but it doesn't define you

Absence can echo louder than presence. It shapes how we view strength, safety, even love. But you are more than what you lacked. The space left behind can become a source of power, not just pain.

Why This Matters:
It's easy to believe that a missing parent, especially a father, means you're incomplete or destined to fail. But absence doesn't equate to brokenness. It often forces self-reliance, sharpens awareness and accelerates maturity. These become quiet leadership foundations: emotional discipline, independent thinking and the ability to navigate life without constant reassurance. The shape of the wound may never fully disappear, but it can become the outline of strength.

My Reality:
Growing up without a father left me with a void, but also a drive. I had no template, no guiding voice, so I became my own compass. Every decision, mistake and breakthrough was made by feeling my way forward. The absence didn't destroy me, it refined me.
And while I built my own definition of manhood, I also came to understand my mother's silence not as absence but as protection. She wasn't just keeping out pain. She was carrying it alone.

Lived Lesson:

Each year, Father's Day arrived like a silent alarm. I'd sit in class with a pencil hovering above blank paper while others drew pictures of their dads. Sometimes I'd make someone up. Sometimes I'd pretend I needed the toilet. That quiet ritual, year after year, taught me to protect myself from public pain. But it also taught me emotional discipline. The absence shaped me. But it didn't own me. That quiet strength became the bedrock of how I now hold space for others.

Make it Real:

Write down three traits or values you've developed as a result of growing up without a consistent parental guide. How have they helped you navigate challenges or become a role model in your own right?

Reflection Prompts:

- What strengths has my "missing piece" quietly given me and am I ready to own them, not just survive them?
- In what ways have I overcompensated to hide the impact of absence? What would it look like to release that pressure?
- How does this early void shape how I protect, lead or support others today?

2. The search takes more courage than the result

To search is to risk disappointment. But not searching at all keeps you locked in a story you didn't choose. The courage to look, despite the fear, changes everything.

Why This Matters:

It's not the answer that defines your growth, it's the willingness to ask the question in the first place. Searching, especially for someone who abandoned or disappeared, is an act of vulnerability. It calls forward self-inquiry, bravery and emotional risk tolerance, key traits in those who lead and live with integrity. You confront not just the possibility of rejection but the truths about yourself that you might not be ready to face.

My Reality:

Picking up the phone to call my father, after decades of silence, was the hardest thing I've ever done. I wasn't just searching for my father. I was searching for the part of myself that wanted to stop apologising for wondering. The part that believed silence was safer than truth.

Lived Lesson:

Dialling his number, I stared at the digits for hours. My hand trembled, not just with nerves but with everything those numbers represented, thirty years of silence, shame, and imagining. The moment he answered, I realised something: the act of calling was already a victory. That kind of courage didn't transform me overnight. It took time, time to process, to reflect, to better understand myself. But slowly, that moment became a turning point. It planted the seed for how I would eventually hold space for difficult conversations and show up with greater transparency. Not perfectly. But more honestly.

Make it Real:

What question are you afraid to ask? Who or what are you avoiding seeking out? Write it down. Sit with it. Then take one brave step - however small - towards asking it.

Reflection Prompts:

- What am I avoiding because I fear the answer and what might shift in me if I simply had the courage to ask?
- What has my fear of rejection stopped me from exploring and is the cost of not knowing greater than the risk of finding out?
- How can the act of seeking become part of how I lead or relate?

---

3. Answers don't heal everything but they start the process

Truth doesn't always arrive wrapped in comfort. But even painful truths can break the grip of imagination, allowing real healing to begin. Knowing something, finally, can be the first form of freedom.

Why This Matters:

The truth can be jagged. It doesn't always arrive with resolution or a tidy bow. But hearing it can shift your inner dialogue. It gives you something to push against, something real. And in that realness, healing can begin. Over time, this ability to face uncomfortable truths develops into a quiet leadership strength: emotional maturity, a tolerance for ambiguity, and the capacity to hold difficult realities without rushing to fix or flee. It doesn't happen in one moment but piece by piece, you build the muscles for deeper connection and braver leadership.

My Reality:

When he said, "I'm from Jamaica," it was like someone had turned on a light in a room I didn't know I was sitting in. That one sentence didn't fix everything but it opened a door to identity that had been sealed shut for too long.

Lived Lesson:

For three decades, I didn't know which island in the Caribbean I came from. No country, no flag, no roots. When I heard the word "Jamaica" from my father's mouth, it unlocked something deeper than pride, it gave structure to a part of me that had always floated unanchored.

That moment didn't erase the ache but it gave it context. And context was enough to begin healing. Over the years, that moment became a reference point for how I navigate identity, culture and difference not with certainty but with openness. That willingness to look beneath the surface would eventually shape how I connect, how I listen and how I build trust across lines of difference.

Make it Real:
Identify a truth in your life you've been avoiding, about your family, your history, your identity. Consider journaling or speaking it aloud. Truth opens the way for transformation.

Reflection Prompts:

- What truth have I been afraid to face and what freedom might it offer if I gave it a voice?
- What stories have I created in the absence of facts and how have those stories shaped my identity or relationships?
- What inner story do I now have the power to rewrite with new clarity?

---

4. Identity is an inheritance – and a choice

Your story begins with what you inherit - but it doesn't end there. Identity isn't just given. It's also chosen. And you have the right to shape what you carry forward.

Why This Matters:

You may inherit bloodlines, culture, even trauma, but your identity is ultimately yours to shape. Accept what is true but never forget your power to evolve beyond it.

Over time, this becomes one of the deepest leadership competencies: self-definition. Those who lead well aren't stuck imitating what came before they build something new with what they've inherited. They choose what to carry, what to change and what to build from scratch.

My Reality:

Discovering siblings I'd never met and a father with his own jagged past, was overwhelming. But I realised I didn't have to carry all of his story. I could honour it, learn from it and then choose the kind of man I wanted to become.

Lived Lesson:

In the club with my father and brother, surrounded by bass, bravado and invisible threat, I felt the pull of identity, the allure of being part of a tribe. But even as I leaned in, I knew I could walk out. That moment taught me that inheritance doesn't demand imitation.

You can step into your history, carry its weight with pride and still move forward on your own terms. That realisation didn't happen all at once. It came slowly, through decisions made in silence, through building a life that honoured where I came from, without being limited by it. That same discernment would later help me lead with integrity, choosing what aligned, and letting go of what didn't.

Make it Real:

Draw two columns. On one side, list the parts of your identity you've inherited. On the other, write what you choose to keep, change, or evolve. This is how you reclaim authorship of your story.

Reflection Prompts:

- What parts of my inheritance serve me and which ones am I ready to respectfully release or reshape?
- If I gave myself permission to shape my identity on my own terms, what would I keep, what would I change and what would I begin to build?
- Where have I been living someone else's story and what would it feel like to start writing my own?

---

5. Healing the father wound allows you to parent yourself

The deepest healing doesn't come from getting what you missed. It comes from becoming what you needed. At some point, the search turns inward and that's where power lives.

Why This Matters:

Until we heal the wounds of absence, we may spend a lifetime outsourcing our worth, seeking validation, leadership and protection externally. True healing is learning to reparent yourself. To become the guide, protector and presence you always needed.

That work is never instant but it builds emotional resilience, internal security, and leadership grounded in authenticity rather than approval. It's how we shift from performing to truly guiding.

My Reality:

I'd spent years searching for a father to guide me. But it turns out, I'd been building that guide within myself all along. Meeting him didn't end the journey. It gave it new meaning.

Lived Lesson:

As I sat across from him on that final day in Monica's living room, TV murmuring in the background, silence thick between us, I didn't yet have all the answers. I saw a man full of contradictions and I felt the ache of everything unsaid. At the time, I thought I understood what his absence had shaped in me.

But I was still piecing it together. Only later through fatherhood, therapy, love and leadership. I realised: I hadn't just survived fatherlessness. I had been fathering myself quietly, all along. And when I started trusting that inner guide, not just seeking external validation, I became a better father, partner and leader not perfect, but present.

Make it Real:

Write a letter from the future version of you, the parent, mentor, or guide you needed when you were younger. What would they tell you today? Then, start acting on that advice.

Reflection Prompts:

- If I became the guide I've been waiting for, what would I stop chasing and what would I start trusting in myself?
- What version of me, past or present, most needs parenting right now and how can I show up for that part of myself?
- How do I show up differently, for myself and others, when I stop performing for approval and start leading from self-trust?

What Finding Him Showed Me:

Some absences leave an echo but searching for my father - and finding him - taught me that the search itself was the rite of passage. It wasn't about getting the perfect answer, it was about making peace with the complexity. You may never fully fill the gap but you learn that you've carried enough within you all along.

Meeting him didn't erase the story behind me but it gave me a new lens through which to see it. And while that meeting shifted my understanding, life kept moving. The future was already unfolding, even as I looked back.

Not long after, a new path emerged, a job, a city, a world that would feel different from anything that came before. Zurich was calling and with it came the invitation to move forward, carrying the answers I had found, the questions still unanswered and the man I was becoming.

PART III:

BUILDING AND BREAKING

8

A NEW LIFE IN ZURICH

Meeting my father changed something in me. Not in the way I had imagined, not as some grand emotional reckoning, not as a moment of closure. But as a shift in perspective. A quiet, internal realisation.

For years, I had believed a part of me was missing. That his absence had left a hole in my soul, a wound that never fully healed.

But after that meeting in Nottingham, I began to realise: the void I had carried wasn't empty, it was filled with the life I had built despite it.

And that life kept moving. Fast.

By the end of that same year, 2010, I left Geneva and moved to Zurich.

A new city. A new rhythm. A new test.

I didn't know it then but I was about to enter a world that would stretch me in ways I hadn't yet imagined.

Geneva to Zurich: The Transition Before the Transformation

I was still working for the same company I'd joined in 2003. It had taken me across cities and countries, from Birmingham to London, Paris to Geneva and now, to Zurich. Eight years in, I had become one of their most consistent performers.

But Zurich wasn't just another stop. It was a reset.

I arrived with the weight of recent revelations still settling in my chest. I'd met the man whose name had once been "Unknown" on my birth certificate. That meeting was still echoing, his presence, his truths, the mirror he held up to me. But life, as always, kept moving. No pause. No breath. No time to process.

Within two months of settling in, I changed rugby clubs, moving from my Geneva side to Grasshopper Club Zurich. It wasn't just a sports decision. It was familiarity. Continuity. In a world that demanded constant adaptation, rugby was the one place I didn't have to perform. It was the place where everything made sense.

In Geneva, rugby had grounded me. We'd won the Swiss First Division Championship two years in a row. It was a rare kind of joy, earned through bruises, sweat and the brotherhood that forms when strangers chase the same cause. Those seasons gave me something money and status never could: a deep sense of belonging and memories so vivid they're etched into my bones. They remain some of the purest joy I've ever known, hard to replicate and impossible to forget.

In Zurich, that spirit continued.

Grasshoppers weren't the best team when I arrived but we had hunger. Grit. A few of us joined around the same time, along with a new coach from Australia; Cam and together, we quietly changed the culture. There was a shift. A new belief. A new fight.

The following season, we won the Swiss National Cup.

It was more than silverware. It was a statement. That belief matters. That effort still counts. That something raw and real can rise even in a city of silent capital and closed circles.

Soon after, I received a call-up to play for Switzerland's national sevens team at the European Championships, this time, not just as a player but as captain.

Me.

A working-class kid from Morley. The boy quietly colouring in imaginary dads at school.

Now wearing the armband. Now leading a nation on the field.

Alright....it wasn't a Six Nations call-up for England, and Switzerland's hardly a rugby powerhouse. But still.

It was humbling. Surreal. A moment that made everything, the failures, the fights, the doubts, feel like part of a bigger story.

But as much as rugby rooted me, Zurich tested me.

Because this wasn't just a city that admired excellence. It expected legacy. It didn't ask where you were going, it assumed you already belonged.

And that... was a very different kind of game.

A City of Quiet Power

Zurich was pristine. Structured. Discreet.

It wasn't showy like Dubai or aggressive like London. It didn't shout. It whispered.

But make no mistake, it was powerful.

And power, here, came with pedigree. Not the Parisian aristocracy kind, with double-barrelled surnames and summer châteaus but something more reserved and more intimidating. Zurich was wealth that had never known scarcity. Confidence that didn't need to be earned. Influence that didn't announce itself.

This was a city where you could stand beside a man in faded jeans and discover he owned half the Bahnhofstrasse. Where a woman in a wool coat and flats might have inherited five apartment buildings and a stake in a private bank. Old families. Quiet capital. Influence tucked behind modest façades.

I had arrived with eight years of hustle in my hands, a diluted Yorkshire accent and an instinct for adaptation shaped by years of navigating circles where I was always the exception, not the expectation.

Even before I'd found my professional footing in Zurich, I could feel the shift.

Business conversations were slower. More measured. Relationships unfolded over time, not over coffee. Deals weren't made in boardrooms, they were crafted over alpine hikes, sealed with subtle nods at lakeside lunches, or woven quietly into family connections that stretched back decades.

There was an unspoken cadence to it all. A kind of coded elegance that favoured discretion over charisma, longevity over ambition.

I knew how to hustle. I'd spent years doing it, pushing doors open, proving myself, learning how to speak the language of ambition in every city I landed in.

But Zurich didn't respond to hustle.

It responded to heritage.

And that changed everything.

I wasn't the only one finding my way through the invisible codes of Swiss society. Most of us did, instinctively, without ever naming it. My international circle was full of well-educated professionals: Swedish, Indian, Italian, British, Dutch, French and American. We came from different countries but shared the same quiet truth, none of us had truly integrated. Despite our careers in consulting, finance, law and tech, polished on paper, fluent in every expected code, we were still outsiders to the old Swiss families and the deep, reserved social networks they kept to themselves. Even among those who had lived here for years, "real" Swiss friends were rare.

At the time, most of us were too young, or too busy building careers, to fully articulate what we were feeling. But looking back, I see it clearly now. We weren't just adjusting to a new city. We were learning how to exist beside a culture that was polite, professional but ultimately closed.

A Seat at Her Table

It was around this time that I met her, the woman who would later become my wife.

She was, without question, the most beautiful woman I had ever encountered, stunning, intelligent, quick-witted, passionate and effortlessly magnetic. But it wasn't just her looks that drew me in. It was her energy. The kind of presence that turned heads when she entered a room. Her laugh carried, her charisma filled space. People noticed. And from the very first moment, something clicked.

The conversation didn't feel like discovery, it felt like remembering. Like we'd known each other long before we met. There was no performance, no trying. We were simply taken, both of us. What I didn't yet know was just how different our worlds were.

She came from a family well known in Swiss circles, one of those names that opened doors without ever needing to knock. Her father had built his reputation over decades, stewarding a family with a long history in Swiss business.

This wasn't new money. It wasn't loud.

It was old. Inherited. Institutional.

Woven into the very fabric of the country.

Summers were spent at the lake house. Winters in their properties in St. Moritz. And her father, he was one of the most impeccably dressed men I'd ever laid eyes on. Flawless tan, his grooming immaculate, his skin almost ageless. He looked a decade younger than his years and moved with an air of supreme confidence. Everything about him, his cars, his presence, the boat on the lake, spoke of a life lived at scale.

The world I was entering felt both surreal and strangely real. Because now, somehow, I wasn't just glimpsing it.

I was finding a place inside it.

That first Christmas, we travelled to one of the most beautiful villages in Engadin. Her family's chalet wasn't just a home. It was a statement. A vast property complete with stables. Fresh snow blanketed the rooftops like a postcard scene come to life.

And that evening, I found myself seated at a huge table, her mother, her father, her… and me.

The setting was cinematic.

Hand-crafted pinewood walls. Candlelight. The low hum of jazz somewhere in the background. Crystal glasses. Silver cutlery that had weight to it, the kind that made even silence feel curated. Conversation drifted across topics I'd never grown up around, ski routes, architecture, investments, generational strategy.

I nodded. I laughed. I added a few comments of my own. Thankfully, my partner's parents were warm, outgoing and genuinely welcoming.

There was laughter, curiosity and a natural ease to the way they hosted.
It softened the edges of the setting, what could've felt like a performance became something else: an invitation.

And yet, even as I was welcomed, the contrast lingered. It was a world I'd never known, whose language I was learning, still unsure if fluency would ever mean belonging.

But inside, something in me tightened.
I realised: I was the only one at the table who hadn't grown up with this world as my backdrop. For me, arrival had required motion. Everyone else had started the journey much closer. A quiet voice rose inside:

You're visiting their world. Will you ever truly live in it?

The feelings were layered.
Pride, for crossing a thousand invisible borders to sit at that table. Doubt, for wondering if arrival meant acceptance or just admiration. And beneath it all, a quieter fear: that no matter how much I achieved... I might always feel like I was borrowing someone else's chair. Because belonging isn't something you can buy.

It has to be given. Or built.

It was the awareness that some rooms are furnished with comfort you can't fake.

Legacy is hard to mimic. It's a posture. A rhythm. A casual entitlement that only time and inheritance, can produce.

I smiled. I listened. I mirrored the ease and confidence around me, while silently rehearsing polite conversation in my head. Adaptation was my shield. But later that night, standing alone in the guest room, the mask slipped.

I looked in the mirror. Crisp shirt untucked. Smile faded. And the question came.

Was I adapting… or disappearing?

Korn Ferry and the Quiet Ascent

A few months prior, I made another move, professionally this time, and joined Korn Ferry, the Goldman Sachs of our industry, the number one executive search and leadership advisory firm in the world. This wasn't just another job, this was the top of the mountain.

I was now working alongside former Chairmen, CEOs and leaders from multi-generational family enterprises across Switzerland and Europe. I would go on to work on mandates that shaped companies and influenced industries.

From the outside, I had arrived, but on the inside, I was wondering if my voice fit or if I was just performing. And deeper still, would they hear the working-class kid beneath the polished sentences, would they sense the fear I carried into every new room?

The doubts weren't constant, but they surfaced before every new client pitch, every lunch where the conversation drifted to boarding schools, sailing regattas and art auctions I could barely fake knowledge of.

To survive those moments, I created quiet rituals. Before meetings, I'd straighten my tie, not just for appearance but for grounding, a small act of order when everything inside felt uncertain.

"You are a product of your environment," Cedric used to say that back in Birmingham, usually when I was fronting or doubting myself. He meant it as a warning but also an invitation. You become what surrounds you, yes, but you also get to choose what surrounds you.

And in Zurich, I chose carefully. Morley, Birmingham, London, Paris, Geneva, each city had left its mark and each chapter had shaped the man.

Before social events, my inner script wasn't about being authentic, not yet. It was simpler. When the doubts grew louder than the room, I'd whisper back: you've done this before. London, Paris, Geneva. You've navigated harder rooms. You will again.

I kept an Anchor File, just a folder in Outlook filled with client praise, candidate feedback and the rare, heartfelt note from a Senior Partner thanking me for the quality of my work, not for show, for the moments when doubt came creeping.

Proof that I wasn't just passing through. I was contributing.

I thought of the Paris pitch where a CEO once gripped my hand after we finalised a placement and said, *"You were the only one who really understood what we needed."*

Moments like that weren't just memories. They were evidence. Markers that the boy from Morley wasn't just visiting these spaces, he was shaping them.

It didn't erase imposter syndrome, but it gave me something sturdier than fear: proof.

Still, the mental weight never fully lifted. The constant measuring, the silent questions before each new room, they sharpened my instincts, yes, but some days, they stole my peace.

What I didn't yet understand was that this kind of weight doesn't always show up like struggle. Sometimes, it wears achievement like armour. Sometimes, it passes as pride. The full shape of it and the cost would reveal itself in time.

The Cost of Access

Zurich gave me many things, a six-figure income, a home in one of the safest, cleanest cities in the world, a love that lit me up, and a window into a life I never thought I'd touch. But it also gave me a question: am I thriving, or performing?

Because in those rooms, in the company of generational wealth and effortless privilege, my story wasn't just different, it was incomprehensible. I had grown up in a terraced house in Morley, chased by skinheads, stretching a tenner into next week, hustling through telesales, cocktail bars and broken dreams.

Now, I was advising leading business figures, trusted by people who'd never known my world, navigating a life that looked nothing like the one I came from. I could play the role, but I missed the boy who didn't have to, the one who didn't need to code-switch, who didn't measure his words, who didn't feel like he had to edit the truth to be palatable.

That tension followed me everywhere, not just in boardrooms or at family dinners, but in the everyday spaces where identity wasn't discussed, it was observed, measured and too often, misunderstood.

Brother, Beats and Belonging

But Zurich wasn't all silent codes and boardrooms, there was lightness too, adventure, and a brotherhood I didn't expect to find. His name was Kyuta, Swiss-Japanese, father from Canton Schwyz, mother from Yokohama. Fluent in English, French, and Japanese. Fluent too in style and swagger.

We had met years earlier in Geneva, working at the same company. He was the Marketing lead. Even then, he had a quiet gravity, the kind of guy who could walk into any room, from a board meeting to a basement club and instantly belong.

If I was the hustler, Kyuta was the vibe. An eclectic mix of punk, rock, hip-hop and house. Beastie Boys meets Ice-T meets Daft Punk, with a dash of Pharrell, refined but always a little rebellious. All wrapped up in a Swiss-Japanese blend that nobody could quite copy.

After my break-up with Lucia, we became inseparable. Two single guys in their early thirties, crisscrossing Europe, Stockholm, Berlin, Milan. VIP parties, secret mansion raves, underground clubs. Kyuta knew everyone, knew everywhere. And when we arrived, we didn't just attend, we belonged. Or at least, it felt that way for a night.

By day, we were professionals. By night, explorers, testing the edges of culture, music and freedom. There was laughter, brotherhood, moments when the weight of Zurich's closed doors disappeared and all that remained was movement and sound.

And yet, even Kyuta - Q - for all his magnetism, mostly socialised with internationals, the ex-pat crowd. The coolest Swiss guy in every room, but with few real Swiss friends. We never spoke about it, but I suspect he felt it too. That subtle, steady weight. The sense that no matter how fluent, how stylish, how successful, we were still dancing on the edge of belonging.

And when you linger at the edge long enough, people notice. Even if they don't mean to. Even if they don't say a word. Their eyes say it for them.

The Looks

In the city's boardrooms and restaurants, on Bahnhofstrasse and Bellevue, even in Coop and Migros, I was almost always the only person of colour – particularly when I first arrived in Zürich in 2010.

People looked. Not with malice. Surprise, more than suspicion.

At first, I thought I was imagining it, that maybe my paranoia had followed me up the mountain. Until one winter morning, at a quiet ski resort just outside Zurich, the truth caught up with me, somewhere between the car park and the gondola.

Ski pass zipped into my jacket, boots awkward and unbroken, I took my place in the queue. Families chatted in Swiss German. Children weaved through the snow with practiced ease, already fluent in the mountain's language.

Then came the glances. One. Then two. Then a ripple of glances, subtle but unmistakable. Older couples. Teenagers. The lift attendant with a moustache that deserved its own passport. Each look carried the same unspoken question: How did you get here?

Not you as in rude. But you as in unexpected. Like seeing Idris Elba at an Aldi.

And that's when I realised, I wasn't just carrying skis, I was carrying history.

Switzerland, for all its precision and prosperity, hadn't had much practice with visible difference. Unlike Britain or France, it bore no colonial scars in Africa or the Caribbean. Its reckoning with multiculturalism had only truly begun in the '90s, when the Balkan wars brought new names to old doorbells.

This wasn't hostility. Just unfamiliarity.

And while I smiled, nodded and got on with it, part of me knew, Switzerland hadn't prepared for people like me.

But I was here now, pass, poles and all.

Looking Forward, Looking Inward

Zurich was the peak, a world of Prime Towers, quiet power and curated grace. On the surface, it shimmered. Career ascending, relationship strong, life enviable. But peaks come with altitude, and altitude can thin the air.

We were building something, together. Love, laughter, routines that felt like rhythm. Weekends in the mountains, wild nights with friends and whispered dreams as the music faded into Sunday.

She believed in me, in us, and I was proud of the life we were carving out. But I was also shape-shifting, adapting so often, so completely, I sometimes lost the sound of my own voice.

I could belong in almost any room but I wasn't always sure I belonged to myself. Success felt earned but also performed.

A quiet question began to hum beneath it all: What have I softened, silenced or shaved down to stay welcome in these spaces?

I pushed forward, building, leading, believing, not just for the life we were living but for the one I'd always dreamed of.

Maybe part of that dream was born years ago, on the living room floor, flipping through my mum's old *Vogue* and *Tatler* magazines. A world of elegance and arrival. A life that looked nothing like ours, but still pulled at something in me. I didn't realise it then, but some part of me had been chasing that feeling ever since.

Yet, even as Zurich embraced me, some part of me remained on mute. I wasn't lost but I wasn't quite found either.

The Blueprint – Chapter 8: Holding Your Ground in a World That Moves Quietly

Key Truth

"Adapt without disappearing."

Quote

"Culture does not make people. People make culture." - Chimamanda Ngozi Adichie

---

Theme: Balancing Assimilation with Authenticity

Zurich introduced me to yet another world, the hushed corridors of old money, the subtle codes of quiet influence. I wasn't new to adaptation. But here, adaptation had to be silent, invisible, precise. It wasn't about hustle or bravado. It was about understanding legacies, discretion and how wealth operated beneath the surface.

In rooms like these, there are no rulebooks. Only expectations. Only eyes.

And if you've never seen someone like you in those rooms before, the questions don't stop at the door. But neither does your power.

For anyone stepping into elite or unfamiliar environments, whether it's a boardroom, a generational family home, or a place where no one shares your background, this is your *Blueprint*.

Here's what I learned about holding your ground in spaces not built for you.

---

1. Adapt without disappearing

Adaptation is a survival instinct. But there's a fine line between blending in and erasing yourself. Especially in elite or unfamiliar environments, where so much of the language is unspoken, coded in gestures, glances and silences. This lesson is about mastering that fluency without losing your frequency.

Why This Matters:
In elite spaces, the instinct is often to conform. To shrink to fit. But true adaptation honours your values while learning the rules of the room. Power often hides in subtlety, those who thrive learn to read the unsaid. Still, fluency is not the same as forgetting your voice. Survival means knowing the code. Authenticity means not becoming it. And in leadership, this becomes a quiet superpower: the ability to read complex dynamics while staying anchored in who you are. This kind of cultural fluency builds both trust and strategic influence, especially when stakes are high and norms are unspoken.

My Reality:

Zürich demanded precision. In the early years, I was still learning the rhythm, how to speak fluent professional, decode subtle status signals and move without disturbing the calm surface. At first, I second-guessed myself constantly, unsure if I belonged or was simply being tolerated. But over time, I found my rhythm. I stopped trying to vanish and started showing up fully. I learned to stand straight without stiffening, to shift without erasing. I brought both street-smarts and corporate savvy into rooms of inherited wealth, where my presence was an exception but never an accident.

Lived Lesson:

I remember one private client dinner. A colleague, not used to the unspoken codes, interrupted, over-explained and cracked jokes that fell flat. The client smiled politely but never called back. That night taught me something simple but crucial: in some rooms, *how* you speak matters more than *what* you say. I learned to listen first. To note the cadence and cues. And when I did speak, I brought my story. That's not code-switching. That's cultural fluency. It's knowing how to navigate the room, without ever leaving yourself at the door. Years later, this ability to move with awareness while staying rooted became essential in boardrooms, negotiations, and even parenting, where listening before reacting often revealed the real issue beneath the noise.

Make it Real:

List three core values that define you. Now write one sentence on how you protect them, even in rooms where they feel out of place. Then, observe a "closed" environment this week (a meeting, a dinner, a family gathering). What unspoken signals are being sent? How can you show up with both awareness and authenticity?

Reflection Prompts:

- What parts of myself do I tend to mute when I enter unfamiliar or elite spaces? Why?
- What's my edge and how do I keep it sharp without cutting myself off?
- How does my ability to read the room shape how I lead, guide, or advocate for others?

---

2. Love doesn't require losing yourself

When love crosses lines, of culture, class or identity, it can be beautiful. Expansive. But it can also bring invisible compromises. The cost of connection shouldn't be self-erasure. Love rooted in truth leaves room for all of you.

Why This Matters:

Romantic relationships often ask us to soften edges, stretch perspectives and bridge difference. That can be growth. But if you find yourself filtering who you are just to keep the peace, it's not growth, it's erosion. You don't have to disappear to be loved. In leadership too, especially relational leadership, this lesson matters. Authentic influence begins where self-suppression ends. When we lead from truth, we model psychological safety, not performance.

My Reality:
Falling in love with someone from a world of privilege opened doors and dilemmas. Her upbringing was steeped in structure, certainty and old wealth. Mine was built on hustle, instinct and learning how to read every room. At first, I found pride in navigating her world with grace. But over time, I noticed the subtle edits I was making. Laughs held back. Stories trimmed. My own past softened, like a book rewritten for polite company. I was present. But not always fully.

Lived Lesson:
There was a moment at a family gathering in Sardinia, wine flowing, laughter circling around old stories and fun times all together, when I caught myself mid-sentence, pausing before mentioning my mum's struggles or our first house with damp walls and second-hand furniture. It wasn't shame. It was reflex. A quiet calculation of what "fit." I eventually realised: if love costs your truth, the price is too high. It took me years to stop softening my past for comfort. But that unlearning helped me

show up with more integrity not just at home, but as a leader. Because if I couldn't bring all of me into my most intimate relationship, how could I ask others to do the same in the teams I led?

Make it Real:
In your closest relationship, ask yourself: Where do I feel most seen? Where do I hold something back? Write down one way you can bring more of your truth into that space this week.

Reflection Prompts:

- In what moments have I muted my background or culture to keep someone else comfortable?
- What does it look like to be loved *without translation*?
- How does my relationship with truth in love influence the way I lead or support others?

---

3. Difference is a lens, not a limitation

Your difference isn't something to hide or apologise for it's the very thing that sharpens your view. It allows you to see what others miss, ask questions others won't and carry empathy others haven't earned. In rooms where everyone shares the same background, it's often the outsider who holds the clearest mirror.

Why This Matters:

In elite environments, difference can feel like a disadvantage, something to minimise, polish or explain. But the truth is, your difference doesn't disqualify you. It equips you. It gives you perspective, agility and courage. The discomfort it creates in others isn't a flaw, it's often a sign you're bringing something new. In leadership, this ability to see what others can't - and say what others won't -isn't just value-add. It's visionary.

My Reality:

There were countless times in Zürich when I was the only person of colour in the room. The only one with a Northern accent, albeit quite diluted. The only one without a lineage traced through private banks or family businesses. At first, that reality made me question whether I belonged. But over time, I realised it gave me something others didn't have: a dual lens. I could understand the code but also question it. I could bring empathy for the outsider, insight into unseen markets and a hunger that couldn't be inherited. My difference didn't make me less, it made me more complete.

Lived Lesson:

I once sat in a meeting with a global FMCG Chief HR Officer who had spent his entire life in the same elite circles. He asked a question about how to attract "diverse talent" and everyone nodded along politely. I paused. Then I told him that diverse talent doesn't just need an invitation, it needs evidence. That landed differently. Not because it was brave but because it was true. I didn't read it in a whitepaper. I *lived* it. That was the power of seeing through a different lens.

Make it Real:

List three perspectives or instincts you hold that come from your background, your culture, your story, your struggle. Ask yourself: how can I bring these into the rooms I'm in now, not as disclaimers but as insights?

Reflection Prompts:

- Where have I been told, directly or indirectly, that my difference is a disadvantage? - How has that belief shaped my confidence?
- How might my story give me a strategic edge that others overlook?

---

4. Build bridges. Don't wear masks

It's natural to want to belong. To ease the tension in the room. But when you trade too much of yourself for acceptance, what's left isn't connection, it's performance. The goal isn't to camouflage who you are. It's to build bridges that honour both worlds.

Why This Matters:

There's a difference between adjusting and acting. Between presence and performance. Real influence doesn't come from fitting in, it comes from showing up fully. When you bring your truth into elite or unfamiliar spaces, you don't just change the room, you expand it. Leaders who integrate their full identity signal to others that it's safe to do the same and that kind of culture builds resilience and trust.

My Reality:

In Zurich, it took time to understand the power of subtlety, how influence moved quietly through tradition, tone and restraint. At first, I played the part, sanding down my edges to blend in. But over time, I realised the moments that truly connected weren't about polish. They came when I let both sides of me speak, the suited executive and the lad from Morley who still loved hip-hop, rugby and a bit of cheek. The real magic was in the merge.

Lived Lesson:

The first time I shared an important milestone on LinkedIn, I nearly followed the usual script: *"I feel honoured and privileged..."* But something stopped me. Instead of polishing it to perfection, I wrote about why the moment mattered, about coming from a single-parent, working-class background and what it meant to reach that point without a blueprint. The response blew me away: over 100,000 views, thousands of comments and private messages from people who saw their own journey in mine. That post didn't just connect. It cracked something open. In many ways, it gave me the encouragement to eventually pursue my long-held goal of writing this book. And the deeper lesson? When you tell the truth of your story, you create a mirror for others. That's not self-promotion, it's leadership through lived narrative.

Make it Real:

Think of a space, online or offline, where you usually filter your story. It could be LinkedIn, a team meeting or even a group chat. This week, share something a little more honest. Not for attention but for connection. See what shifts.

Reflection Prompts:

- Where am I still curating my story to be impressive, rather than real?
- What's one truth from my journey I've rarely shared and why might now be the right time?
- How might my honesty give others permission to show up more fully too?

---

5. Imposter syndrome grows in silence

When you're the first, the only, or the outsider, the quiet voice of self-doubt can get loud. Not because you're unqualified but because the room wasn't built with you in mind. Imposter syndrome doesn't disappear with success. But it can be confronted with truth.

Why This Matters:
High achievement doesn't silence doubt it often amplifies it. Especially when you've had to build your identity in spaces where no one looked like you. But silence lets insecurity grow. When you bring your wins into the light, you remind yourself and the world, that you didn't get here by luck. You earned it. In leadership, recognising your impact and naming it with humility helps you lead from a place of inner validation, not outer approval.

My Reality:
Zürich was full of unspoken expectations. The more I succeeded, the more I felt the pressure to prove it wasn't a fluke. There were moments I'd walk into meetings feeling like I had to justify my seat at the table before I'd even spoken. I started keeping a quiet folder, just for me. It was filled with client praise, candidate messages, heartfelt notes from colleagues. Not to boast. To survive. To remind myself that I was no imposter, I was making a difference.

Lived Lesson:

After a pitch in Paris, a CEO shook my hand, looked me in the eye and said, "You were the only one who truly understood us." I flew back that night exhausted but changed. That line went straight into the folder. Because when the whisper of doubt came back in Zurich, I needed that voice louder. Not to inflate my ego but to protect my peace. Now, I encourage others to do the same, especially those navigating identity-based doubt in high-pressure spaces. You don't need to shout to lead. But you do need to remember your wins.

Make it Real:

Create your own Anchor File. Digital, handwritten, doesn't matter. Fill it with truth: thank-you notes, wins, kind words, moments you made a difference. Read it when the imposter whisper shows up.

Reflection Prompts:

- What's one success I've downplayed that actually proves I belong?
- When was the last time I reminded myself, not others, of what I've overcome?
- How can I help others name and celebrate their value, especially when they're the only one in the room?

What Zurich Showed Me:

Zurich didn't erase me. But for a while, I lost sight of who I really was.

In that city of quiet power and inherited ease, I learned to move through legacy spaces but sometimes, at the cost of my own reflection. I shaped myself to fit, until one day, I barely recognised the shape.

But slowly, through work, through major life-events, through truth, I found my way back.

I didn't just navigate elite environments, I began to decode them. To see the rules for what they were. To lead without shrinking. To show up without splitting.

And in doing so, I shaped something rare: a self not fractured by worlds but strengthened between them.

If you've ever questioned your place at the table, remember this:

You don't need to round off your edges to belong.

You just need to understand what shaped them.

That's your blueprint.

That's your strength.

That's what makes you unmistakably you.

9

BECOMING THE FATHER I NEVER HAD

By my mid-thirties, I had crossed more borders, real and imagined, than I ever thought possible. My career spanned cities, industries, cultures. I'd earned seats at tables I wasn't born to, met the man whose absence had shaped me and begun to understand my own roots.

And then, at 35 years old, everything shifted again.

It was an unusually hot April day, crystal blue skies stretched endlessly overhead, not a single cloud in sight. There was a clarity to the light, as if the universe itself had paused to mark this day with purpose. Calm. Open. Full of promise.

Because this was the day, the most beautiful day of my life, my daughter was born.

Two Worlds, One Birth

I remember sitting in hospital, one of Zurich's most exclusive private hospitals. Everything around me gleamed with quiet luxury, white-gloved staff, a private suite with plush furnishings, an à la carte menu offering gourmet food and rare red wines. Champagne at your request. Linen curtains. Curated silence.

And all I could think about… was Dewsbury Hospital. That's where I was born. In a rough West Yorkshire mill town, a far cry from this serene, lakefront sanctuary.

My mother had walked into that hospital alone, carrying the weight of a decision she'd already made to give me up for adoption. But three days later, she held me for the first time… and everything changed.

Now here I was, decades later, sitting in a private suite in Zurich, waiting to meet my own daughter. A loving partner beside me. Support all around.

This was legacy, I realised, not just inheritance but interruption. A full-circle moment where one life bent in service of another.

Where generational patterns had the chance to break.

Where silence had the chance to be replaced with presence.

My daughter would enter the world in a completely different way than I had. And I would be there to witness it.

11:40 a.m. to 12:10 p.m. – The Stillness Before Everything

I sat alone in the waiting area outside the delivery suite, dressed in a hospital scrubs, gloves, and mask. Everything around me moved with Swiss precision. A nurse told me they would call me at exactly 12:10 p.m. I stared at the clock, heart pounding beneath the silence.

I checked the time. 11:40 a.m.

Thirty minutes.

At first, the feeling was familiar. The same nerves I'd had before cup finals on the rugby pitch, the tight chest, the quickened breath, the stillness that hides a storm.

But as the minutes ticked by, something else began to rise within me.

Memories of my own childhood flooded my mind, not just the struggles and the breakthroughs but the deep, persistent ache of my father's absence. All at once, the room felt colder, the silence sharper.

A fierce wave of doubt crept in.

Could I genuinely break a pattern so deeply embedded? Would my daughter one day look up and wonder where I was? Would the shadow of absence find its way through generations, despite all my promises?

My chest tightened with a grief I hadn't anticipated. I'd faced down opponents on rugby fields, closed complex business negotiations in leadership rooms, navigated countless moments of uncertainty but nothing had ever felt as daunting as this.

I closed my eyes, breathing slowly, willing myself steady. I reminded myself silently: I am not him. His choices are not mine.

But the echoes lingered, quiet, relentless whispers asking if presence would be enough, if intent could truly overwrite history.

Then, something shifted. Not suddenly, but unmistakably.

The storm quieted. Not because I forced it to but because I had faced it.

Clarity rose from the fear, not as a roar, but as a steadying truth.

My fear wasn't weakness. It was love in disguise, proof that I cared enough to change.

The doubt I'd carried for so long wasn't a sign I'd fail.

It was the signal that I was ready to begin again.

And after that… stillness.

A serenity I hadn't known I was searching for.

Not the calm of avoidance, but the calm of alignment. I felt it settle in my chest, a quiet certainty.

This was the day.

The one that would change everything. Not because I was ready to be perfect.

But because I was finally ready to be present.

At 12:10 p.m. the door opened.

A nurse smiled gently. "Ready?"

I met her gaze, steady now.

"Yes," I said. "I'm really ready."

And I stood up and stepped into the most defining chapter of my life.

The Weight of Fatherhood

The moment I saw her, everything else disappeared. All the struggles, all the striving, all the unspoken questions that had followed me for years, they melted away in an instant.

She was perfect. Half British and Jamaican, half Swiss and Italian. The most extraordinary mix of cultures, continents and bloodlines shaped by struggle and privilege, all wrapped into 3.6 kilograms of pure wonder. She carried the fullness of our stories. And something more, a new beginning.

I remember the weight of her not heavy but anchoring, like something inside me had finally settled. My whole life had been motion, cities, identities, rooms I thought closed to me, but holding her, skin to skin, I stopped completely. I was home.

Her eyes opened briefly, dark, unfocused, searching, and in that flicker of a gaze, something hit me with full force: I am her *father*. And for the first time in my life, that word didn't sting. It didn't ache. It felt whole.

And in that moment, there was nothing else. Nothing else mattered. No past. No proving. Just presence.

This was the most beautiful day of my life.

Not career milestones.

Not the highest highs or wildest wins.

This.

Her.

Nothing has come close to that moment since.

Because in her arrival, something else was born too, a version of me I had never fully known. A man not just surviving the story he came from but beginning a new one entirely.

But right behind the joy came something else, something I wasn't prepared for. A grief. Not for her, for me. For the boy I used to be. The one who never got this moment. The one who had no memory of being held like this. The one who filled out Father's Day cards at school with made-up names. The one who had carried absence like a second shadow.

And now here I was, holding my daughter in the place where I had once been held by no one. It was beautiful. It was devastating. And it was transformative.

Because in that moment, I knew one thing with absolute clarity: I would never leave her. I couldn't. The very idea was impossible, unthinkable.

Looking into her face, I couldn't understand how any father could walk away. And for the first time, I didn't just feel anger at my father's absence, I felt disbelief, a visceral, gut-level rejection of that choice.

Whatever flaws I carried, whatever fears I had, whatever mistakes I might make, abandonment would never be one of them.

Her birth handed me a mirror. And in it, I saw who I needed to become: not perfect, but present. Not performing, but protecting.

I didn't have a blueprint. But I knew how it felt to grow up without one. And I knew, she never would.

Because fatherhood isn't an obligation.

It's a privilege.

One I had waited a lifetime to claim.

Perfection and Protection

But understanding the role didn't mean I understood the rules, especially not in Zurich. In elite Swiss parenting circles, success wasn't just encouraged, it was often engineered.

Children were spoken to like adults, their schedules packed before they could tie their own shoes. Trilingual by six, piano by seven, skiing black diamonds by eight. Birthday parties felt like corporate events.

And before those parties, some children were coached on what to say, how to act, reminders to represent the family well. Tiny diplomats in polished shoes.

Beneath it all was a quiet but constant pressure, raise a prodigy, not just a person.

Coming from Yorkshire, it unsettled me. We weren't prepped for parties, we were told to say thank you and not nick too many sausage rolls. Our childhood wasn't a performance, it was lived in scraped knees and second-hand bikes, not in Swiss polish and parental branding.

I found myself resisting it, the curated smiles, the quiet rehearsals, the sense that a child's joy was being managed like a reputation.

I didn't want that for her. I wanted her to be grounded, not groomed, brave, not perfect.

And that's when I realised, breaking the cycle wasn't just about presence, it was also about protection. Protection from performance, from pressure, from the quiet voice that says you are only as good as your achievements.

So I found myself straddling two instincts, wanting to shield her from the pressure while helping her thrive in the world around her.

I didn't want her to perform, I wanted her to feel free. But I didn't want her to fall behind either, in a culture where toddlers seemed to have LinkedIn-ready lives.

So I walked a line, translating between my past and her present, teaching her to stand tall in both worlds without having to shrink in either.

Because breaking the cycle wasn't just about being there, it was about protecting her from perfection.

But even that wasn't the full weight. There was another layer, one I couldn't always name but I carried it daily. As a Black and mixed-race father in elite European spaces, I felt the silent scrutiny, a quiet, persistent pressure to disprove the story the world had already written about fathers like me.

That we vanish, that we falter, that we fail to show up.

Providing wasn't enough. I wanted to rewrite the script. Too many children like her, especially those with Black heritage, grow up with absence as a central character in their story.

I knew it firsthand, that hollow space, that quiet question. So every lunchbox packed, every tear soothed, every bedtime story told, it was never performative. It was presence. Not ego, just love, measured not in words but in showing up.

For her. For the boys who grew up wondering why no one stayed. For the men trying quietly to do better than what they saw.

Still, even in those beautiful moments, doubt lingered. Could I really end something so deeply embedded? Could love, shown consistently, be enough to rewire what absence had once carved?

I had no blueprint. Just a promise. To rewrite the ending, to live the answer I had once needed, and to do it again tomorrow, and the day after that.

Because fatherhood, for me, was never just a role. It was a resistance. A reclamation. And a quiet revolution.

Breaking the Cycle

The promise I made in that hospital didn't stay in the room. It followed me into airports, boardrooms and sleepless nights. It shaped how I moved, how I worked, how I loved.

Not in the soft, gentle way I had imagined but with fire, focus and drive.

I travelled constantly, two to three days a week, fifty to sixty flights a year. Zurich, London, Paris, Madrid. It was relentless.

But when I was home, I was all in. Nappies, lullabies, imaginary games. Her giggle in the morning was my anchor. She would never grow up with the financial stress I had known, of that I was sure. But I wanted more than provision. I wanted clarity, roots, a living, breathing answer to the question I had carried for so long: where is he?

She would never need to ask. She would know.

Not perfect, but present. Not always nearby, but never out of reach.

That her roots weren't a question mark, they were an anchor. That became the new mission. Not just to parent but to model, to show her what love looks like when it stays.

And just as I was learning to show up fully, life offered a moment to mark it, a winter wedding in St. Moritz.

A Winter Wedding in St. Moritz

Fatherhood had already changed me. It sharpened my focus, deepened my purpose. But life had one more chapter-turning moment waiting, one that carried its own kind of gravity.

Our wedding.

Set in the snow-covered dreamscape of St. Moritz, at the legendary Suvretta House, a grand hotel that had hosted royalty, dignitaries and icons, it was the kind of place I would have once seen only in movies. Now, I was standing beneath its vaulted ceilings, surrounded by people from every chapter of my life.

Friends from Morley and Wakefield mingled with new friends from Zürich and Geneva. Colleagues from Paris and London raised glasses beside members of Zurich's elite. James Shorte and the Shorte family were there, an anchor of love and constancy through every stage of my journey.

Dan Whiting, my best man, stood by my side as he had through so many twists of the journey. My mum and sister, Maria, were radiant, proud, present and finally able to witness fully the life I had built. Mickey Walker, one of my groomsmen, brought his trademark warmth, loyalty and banter, a cornerstone of friendship built over years of weathering life together. And Christian Reichel, another groomsman and a friend I had met through work back in Geneva, stood steady as ever. His wise counsel, sharp mind and ability to challenge me with care had long made him a trusted sounding board through both triumphs and transitions.

Each of them stood not just in support but as symbols of the full span of my life, childhood bonds, professional alliances, chosen brothers. It was a rare convergence of worlds that had shaped me, all gathered in one room, witnessing what I was stepping into.

And then there were the shared friendships, those formed through my partner's devoted inner circle of women. All of them radiant that day, elegance woven into every detail. Over the years, they had become more than her friends. They had become ours. Their grace, loyalty and laughter helped bridge two worlds and their partners had become my friends too, connections built through dinners, travels and the quiet glue of genuine affection.

Among the guests were old friends from QEGS - Jonny, Cal and Ryan O'Neil, who had flown all the way from Australia to be there.

As they raised their glasses with us that day, I felt the strength of those shared bonds. Old roots, deepened. New roots, planted.

It was a strange and beautiful alchemy, the collision of lives that had never been meant to meet. And yet, somehow, they had. Around her. Around us.

The mix of cultures, backgrounds and personalities could have created tension. But instead, it created something electric. Yorkshire laughter met Swiss precision. Parisian charm danced with Caribbean rhythm. And after a few drinks and then a few more, it turned into an almighty party. No awkwardness. Just joy. A release. A shared understanding that we were all there to celebrate something rare. Something real.

There was one moment, just before the meal, where I caught a reflection of myself in a mirror. I was wearing the Jaeger-LeCoultre I had once admired on Yves Renaud's wrist, my French mentor back in Paris. I remembered being 26, sitting across from him, thinking, *I'd love to be in that world.* And yet, here I was. With French friends and former colleagues around me, Stanislas, Jonathan, Jason, Manu and my close friend Mathieu, men who had once welcomed me as an outsider and now stood by me as brothers. Steve Berry, who had looked out for me when I first arrived in Paris and never stopped believing in me, was there too, still steady, still sharp, still soulful and living proof that character leaves a lasting imprint.

They weren't looking down at me. Just… with me.

Woody was there too, bringing that unmistakable Brummie bounce all the way to St. Moritz and especially to the now infamous Table 9, alongside Kyuta, whose grin and mischief matched the mood perfectly. Birmingham was also in the house, through Phil, and through Alastair and Paul too, bound not by birthplace but by the stories we'd lived together in that city. The nights, the laughter, the grit. Those years had shaped us and now they anchored us, even here in the snow.

Still, beneath all the laughter and glamour, there was something else. A quiet weight. The months leading up to the wedding hadn't been easy. I was carrying the weight of some hard truths, ones I needed to own fully. And I knew, deep down, that this day needed to go well. That I needed to rise. Not just for the guests, not just for appearances but for her. For us.

So when the time came to speak, I gave everything I had.

And it landed.

It was the best speech I've ever given in my life. It needed to be.

But as the room rose in applause, one quiet absence echoed louder than the clapping.

I hadn't invited my father. Not out of anger but because, deep down, I still wasn't sure how to place him in this part of my life. I didn't feel ready. But in his place stood a man who had been present through every pivotal turn: Irvine Shorte. During my speech, I made a special point to honour not just him but his entire family. Their presence wasn't symbolic, it was foundational. As I spoke, I caught Irvine's eyes across the room. There was no need for words. The pride on his face, the quiet connection we held in that moment... it was pure. In that room of grandeur, it was that glance that grounded me most. A nod to the man who had never needed a title to be a father figure.

And still, as I stood there taking it all in, another question settled in the back of my mind:

Could I really hold all of this? Could I truly be the father, husband and man they now believed I was?

I watched as tears fell, laughter rippled, heads nodded and even those from the most established circles, the ones you'd expect to stay reserved, leaned in. I spoke not just of love but of journey. Of struggle. Of becoming. And as I looked across the sea of faces, some smiling, some tearful, all of them holding pieces of my story, I felt something shift.

I didn't feel like an outsider trying to fit in.

I felt like a bridge.

Between worlds. Between histories. Between what I'd come from and what I was stepping into.

I remember catching her father's expression during one quiet moment, eyes full of pride as he looked at his daughter. Tears welling but not falling. And for just a second, I thought of my own grandfather, not physically there but etched into everything I was. The man who stirred gravy with one hand and holding his betting slip with the other. Who would have looked around this grand dining hall with narrowed eyes and a smile that said, *Go on, lad.*

And I did.

As I looked around the room, my eyes settled on my mum and sister. Radiant. Proud. Present. After everything we'd come through, here they were, not on the sidelines but right at the heart of it. My mum, who had carried the weight of two roles for so many years. My sister, once the baby who gave my life meaning during its hardest seasons, now stood beside her, graceful, strong and radiant. Watching them both in that moment stirred something deep. It was like glimpsing the full arc of our journey, tough beginnings, quiet resilience and now this: joy, hard-earned and shared.

Because this wasn't just a wedding. It was a reckoning. A quiet declaration that, against all odds, I had walked through the gates, not because I was born into this world but because I built a bridge to it.

And she chose to meet me there.

Our love wasn't built on shared backgrounds. It was built on recognition. On curiosity. On the feeling that we saw each other clearly in a world that often blurred everything else.

That night, I didn't just marry the woman I loved.

I anchored a family.

I claimed a new chapter.

And yet, even in that joy, something within me stirred. I was holding more than love that night. I was carrying years of proving, protecting, performing. I didn't see it then. But the weight was there, quiet, constant. And it was time to name it.

The Weight and Wonder of It All

That winter, everything looked pristine. The mountains glistened, our daughter was thriving, my career was ascending. The world I had fought so hard to enter finally felt like home.

Some weight doesn't look like weight at all.

It wears a suit. Smiles in meetings. Tucks in children at night. It says, "I'm fine," even when the soul aches for rest.

I didn't realise how many kinds of weight I was carrying until I became a father. Until I looked down at her face and felt, all at once, the weight of legacy, the pressure to be perfect, and the ghosts I hadn't yet named.

It would take time, and truth, to name them. But first, I had to feel them.

The Weight of Absence

Growing up without a father wasn't just a gap. It was a silence that shaped everything.

No lap to climb onto, no voice to echo. I taught myself how to tie a tie, how to stand tall, how to mask the ache.

That absence followed me through classrooms, friendships, first loves.

I smiled, achieved, performed, all while wondering if anyone would ever stay.

The Weight of Expectation

Then came success. Boardrooms, luxury, applause.

But with it came the pressure to prove I deserved it. When you grow up without safety, everything feels borrowed. I moved through elite spaces like a guest with a time limit, polished, fluent, watchful. I wore the right watches. Softened my accent. Smoothed the edges of my truth. I worked harder than anyone, not out of ambition but to silence the voice that said, *You don't belong.*

The Weight of Representation

As a Black and mixed-race father in Europe, I carried more than my story.

The world had already written its script about men like me, that we vanish, that we falter.

So I showed up. Every day. Every night. Every milestone. But it wasn't just about nappies and lullabies. It was about proving, quietly and relentlessly, that we are not who they say we are. That weight is noble. But it's still weight.

What I've Learned to Put Down

Some of the weight was never mine. I've started letting go of perfection, of silent apologies, of trying to earn every breath. I no longer carry the need to perform. I just carry the truth.

What I Still Choose to Carry

There's one weight I'll never put down: her. The weight of showing up, of being the man I once searched for. Not flawless, but present. Not finished, but faithful. That's the weight I carry now, not as a burden, but as a vow.

The Blueprint – Chapter 9: Becoming the Father I Needed

Key Truth

"Legacy isn't what you leave, it's what you live."

Quote

"I want to be the father I never had." – LeBron James

Theme: Breaking Generational Patterns

When my daughter was born, everything shifted. The man who grew up fatherless became the father he had once longed for. There was no manual. No inherited blueprint. Just a promise, quiet, determined, to show up in every way I had once wished someone had shown up for me. For anyone stepping into leadership, whether as a parent, mentor, or role model, without having seen it modelled firsthand, this is your blueprint. This is where new legacies are born.

---

1. Presence is the most radical gift

When you've grown up with absence, showing up becomes more than love, it becomes resistance. In a world shaped by neglect or inconsistency, consistency is radical. When you show up, again and again, you're not just parenting. You're rewiring a lineage.

Why This Matters:

Absence creates emotional voids that ripple through generations. Presence, especially when grounded in consistency and care, interrupts those patterns. For leaders, mentors or parents who never had a model to follow, this kind of presence becomes more than support, it becomes repair. The act of showing up, reliably, calmly and without conditions, is one of the most powerful forms of emotional leadership we can offer.

My Reality:

I never had a dad to cheer from the sidelines or guide me through life's messiness. But I made sure my daughter felt me at every step, from her first breath to changing nappies, bedtime and whispered stories. When I was there, I was there fully.

Lived Lesson:

I remember holding her tiny body against my chest, skin to skin, as she breathed her first breaths. The hospital suite was silent but inside me, something roared. For the first time in my life, I wasn't running. I was rooted. That moment wasn't just about birth, it was the beginning of a vow: I will never leave. Years later, that vow still shapes how I lead, not just at home, but in every space where someone is watching to see if I'll show up again.

Make it Real:
Schedule one recurring moment per week to be fully present with your child, mentee, or partner. No screens. No distractions. Just presence.

Reflection Prompts:

- Where in my life am I truly present and where am I simply nearby?
- How do I define presence beyond just physical proximity?
- What impact does my consistency have on those I lead or love?

---

2. Fatherhood is a mirror, not just a role

Parenthood doesn't just reveal the child, it reveals the parent. It dredges up old wounds and invites new questions. And if we're willing, it becomes a mirror through which we heal.

Why This Matters:
When we step into roles of responsibility or care, especially ones we never saw modelled, it can surface unhealed pain. But that mirror isn't just confrontation; it's an invitation. For

leaders and caregivers, this self-awareness becomes the foundation for empathy, emotional regulation and growth. What you refuse to confront, you often unconsciously pass on.

My Reality:

Holding my daughter cracked open the silence around my own father. But instead of retreating, I leaned in. I realised that the man I needed had always been trying to emerge, from inside me.

Lived Lesson:

As I watched her tiny hand curl around my finger, I felt something unexpected: grief. Not for her but for the boy I once was. The one no one held. The one who stared at blank birth certificates. But this time, instead of breaking, I listened. That ache became my compass. And later, that same emotional awareness helped me hold space for others, especially those carrying silent losses of their own.

Make it Real:

Write down three moments when parenting or mentoring triggered old pain. Now, write a new response for each, one that heals forward.

Reflection Prompts:

- What childhood experience still colours how I respond when I feel unacknowledged or afraid?

- How can I turn pain into presence instead of projection?
- Where in my leadership do I need to hold space for others, without repeating old patterns?

---

3. Legacy lives in repetition

Legacy isn't just what you teach, it's what you repeat. People don't remember everything you say or do, but they remember how you made them feel, especially when that feeling is consistent. Repetition builds trust. And trust is the soil where legacy grows. In parenting, leadership and love, what we come back to again and again is what becomes real.

Why This Matters:
We often mistake impact for spectacle. But deep influence is built in routine. The way we lead, parent, or guide others isn't just felt in big moments, it's absorbed in repetition. In leadership, as in parenting, consistency creates psychological safety. That's where trust is born.

My Reality:
From Saturday morning smoothies to the small surprises I brought home after each trip, those rhythms weren't extravagant, but they were dependable.

Lived Lesson:

Whether it was Lego sets, chocolate bars, or just a story from a new city, the gift never mattered. The return did. That truth, repeated, became our foundation not because it dazzled but because it endured. The same holds true in my professional life. I learned that my impact as a leader didn't come from the occasional big speech or grand gesture. It came from the steady hand, the regular check-in, the consistent follow-through. Trust wasn't built through brilliance, it was built through reliability. People remembered that I came back, that I showed up, that I saw them.

Make it Real:

Pick one small gesture and make it sacred. Repeat it. Let the rhythm become the message.

Reflection Prompts:

- What repeated behaviour creates safety for those around me?
- Am I prioritising consistency over showmanship?
- How do I build rituals that outlast me?

---

4. Love without performance

In polished cultures, love can be mistaken for perfection. But children don't need performers. They need protectors, people willing to guard their freedom to be messy, real and enough.

Why This Matters:

In high-achievement spaces, we risk raising performers instead of people. When we model love as conditional on image or polish, we plant the seeds of shame. As parents and leaders, our role is to create psychological permission, to let people be unfinished, unfiltered and still worthy.

My Reality:

In Zurich, I watched childhoods curated like careers. Toddlers prepped to perform. I nearly followed suit until I remembered how stifling that felt. I didn't grow up rehearsed. I grew up real.

Lived Lesson:

Before one of her first birthday parties, I caught myself rehearsing lines with her, what to say, how to smile. I stopped mid-sentence. That wasn't love speaking. That was fear of judgement. I crouched down, held her hands and said: "Just be you and have fun. That's always enough." It took a long time to bring this into my working world but that same belief today shapes how I lead, choosing real over polished.

Make it Real:

Notice when you're managing someone else's image, your child, your team, yourself. Ask: Is this love… or performance?

Reflection Prompts:

- Where am I most tempted to rehearse or edit myself, or others, for approval?
- How do I define worth when no one's clapping?
- What kind of environment do I create for others, safe or curated?

---

5. Carrying the hidden weight

Not all burdens are visible but they shape everything. When you've grown up without a guide, you often carry invisible weight: the pressure to prove, to earn your place, to outrun shame, to repair what was never your fault. These silent loads become part of how you walk through the world. But real leadership begins when we stop performing strength and start understanding what we've been carrying and what we can finally lay down.

Why This Matters:

Those who grow up without blueprints often carry invisible burdens, inherited shame, perfectionism, ancestral pressure, the need to prove. Leadership begins when we confront not just what we project outwardly, but what we bear inwardly. Healing is learning which weights were never ours to carry.

My Reality:
Fatherhood exposed the quiet burdens I hadn't realised I was holding: the fear of repeating patterns, the pressure to disprove stereotypes, the need to perform even when tired.

Lived Lesson:
It took years to realise: not all weight was mine. Some of it belonged to the past. Some to other people's stories. I eventually would begin to put some of it down, perfection, shame, apology and chose instead to carry what matters: presence, love, legacy. In leadership, that shift was transformative. I stopped overcompensating. I no longer needed to be the smartest, the sharpest, or the most polished in the room. I focused instead on clarity, care and steady influence. I discovered that releasing the hidden weight gave me more power, not less and allowed others to do the same.

Make it Real:
Write down three "weights" you feel silently. Now ask: Whose are they? Which ones serve you? Which can you lay down?

Reflection Prompts:

- What invisible load do I carry that no one sees?

- What parts of my drive come from love and which come from fear?
- What would change if I replaced pressure with presence?

What Fatherhood Showed Me:

I carried the absence of my father for 30 years.
But becoming a father showed me this:

You don't need to inherit a legacy to build one.
You just need to begin, again and again.

I once lived with the question: *Where is he?*
Now, my daughter lives with the certainty: *He's here.*

Whether you're raising a child, mentoring someone, or leading a team, you have the power to become the anchor you never had.

Because love, when chosen consistently, especially by those who never received it, is the quiet revolution that rewrites everything.

10

DUBAI – A LIFE BEYOND IMAGINATION

The first time I saw the Dubai skyline, it didn't just rise, it boomed. A city carved out of sand and ambition and I was about to live in its heart.

The offer came unexpectedly, from the President of EMEA, a man I admired not only for his success but for the way he carried it, calm, commanding, principled. The kind of leader I wanted to become. The decision wasn't simple. We had just begun to find our rhythm in Zurich. But when doors like this open, you walk through them.

And so, we did. As a family.

From the moment the plane touched down, the contrast was stark. If Zurich was a whisper of wealth, Dubai was a roar. Everything here shimmered with intention. The skyline towered like ambition itself, steel and glass reaching higher with every floor. The streets buzzed with heat and hunger. And we stepped into a life beyond anything I had ever known.

Our first home was on The Palm, not just the island but within the private residential wing of one of Dubai's most renowned five-star hotels. It was the kind of place where the service was seamless, the views of the Marina skyscrapers were cinematic and every detail felt curated. When we moved out, the next tenant was a Champions League–winning Manchester United striker. My Grandad would've boycotted the place on principle, his loathing for United was legendary. He swore his tea tasted sweeter when they lost.

Despite the shift in setting and the surreal contrast to where we'd come from, we settled in with ease. And somehow, it started to feel like home.

Soon after, we moved to Jumeirah Islands, where we'd spend the rest of our time in Dubai. A gated community of winding lakes and palm-lined streets. A six-bedroom villa with a pool. A gardener. A nanny. A treasured Italian sports car in the drive. A luxury British SUV beside it. It was elegance made effortless, though I still found myself taking the bins out in my slippers on a Sunday morning, which kept things nicely in perspective.

But this time, there was a shift. This villa, this life, it felt like something I had stepped into and shaped. I'd drive through the private gates after long days of work and there was a quiet pride in pulling up to the house.

Not just because of its beauty, or the way it had been so thoughtfully and tastefully furnished by my wife, a soft, elegant blend of Hamptons beach house and desert villa, thoughtfully furnished with care and intention, supported by family generosity and shaped by a clear eye for beauty. But because, in my own way, I had helped build it. Carried it. Not alone. But with a kind of silent determination that had always driven me. Sometimes I'd open the front door, step into the cool stillness of the house and just pause for a second. Take it all in.

Morley to here?

I'd smile to myself, shake my head and exhale a quiet laugh. And yet, beneath the surface of sunlight and sandstone, something else was forming. Not just a life of beauty but a quiet weight. A subtle undertow. One I didn't yet have the words for.

That part would come later.

But for now, there was sunlight pouring through tall windows, the smell of barbecues on warm desert evenings and the laughter of our daughter echoing through the halls.

Desert Joy, Family Light

We weren't just building a life, we were building a community. And in many ways, the friendships we made during those years were just as precious as the place itself.

Tristan and Patricia quickly became anchors, kind, generous, always up for a laugh and equally passionate about discovering great wine and champagne. Rachel and Ahmet lived just a few minutes away, also in Jumeirah Islands, and their three kids were like siblings to our daughter. The bond between them was effortless, the kind that forms when doors stay open and barefoot feet cross thresholds like clockwork. There was a rhythm to our lives in Jumeirah Islands, shared meals, spontaneous drop-ins, laughter that spilled from patios to playrooms. It felt less like a neighbourhood and more like chosen family.

Our home became a revolving door of friendship, barbecues by the pool, children's laughter rising over splashes, adults swapping stories under the desert sun. Music floated from hidden speakers. Glasses clinked. Joy echoed in the stillness long after the music faded.

It wasn't just a house. It was a heartbeat.

A sanctuary of joy and movement.

Most weekends followed a familiar rhythm: Friday afternoons spilling into long, starlit evenings. Halloween parties with carved pumpkins and fancy dress. Birthday celebrations that turned into dance floors beneath fairy lights. Elegant dinners that began with fine wine and ended in stories and belly laughs.

And at the centre of it all, us. A family in full motion.

Our daughter was thriving, still small but already a force of nature: curious, bright, endlessly expressive. She loved the water, the attention, the energy flowing through our home. It was magical to watch her grow surrounded by so much warmth.

My wife created beauty with ease, every table set with care, every corner quietly elegant and full of intention. And I, whenever I could, soaked it in.

On the rare nights when I was home early, I'd pause, glass in hand, tie loosened, watching dusk settle across the pool.

And in that soft desert light, everything felt… full.

I knew I was on the road too much, still catching fifty, sometimes sixty flights a year. But when I was home, I made it count. I didn't just show up, I plugged in, completely. From bedtime stories and car singalongs to lazy Saturday mornings filled with smoothie experiments and perfectly imperfect omelettes, I tried to make every moment stretch, every small ritual feel like something she could hold onto.

It was a chapter of joy. Of life at full tilt.

And yet, even amidst the laughter, there were moments, fleeting but persistent, where I'd step back from it all and ask: *Is this who I am, or who I've become?*

It was a question I hadn't yet found the words for.

But Dubai wasn't just a home. It was a mirror. A city built on vision, speed and unapologetic ambition.

What they had achieved in just a few decades was nothing short of astonishing, transforming a desert outpost into a global hub of innovation, architecture and influence. It was impossible not to be inspired. Living there lifted your gaze. It expanded your sense of what was possible. You moved differently in Dubai, more boldly, more confidently. It made you believe.

And yet… the brilliance of the place also cast sharp shadows. Luxury was everywhere, choreographed, gleaming, relentless. Gold-plated cars. Saturday brunches that rivalled weddings.

Skyscrapers designed to defy gravity. And beneath it all, a tempo that never slowed, where success was measured by the size of your pool, the headcount on your household payroll and whether your early crypto gamble had made you a genius or just late to the next trend.

But in a city of arrivals, departures and curated perfection, something inside me stayed restless.

Dubai magnified everything, success, ambition, image. And in that world, especially for men, there was an unspoken script: confident, unshakable, always in control.

I had come so far and yet, as a man shaped by Yorkshire grit and Jamaican blood, in a hyper-elite expat world, the pressure didn't vanish, it evolved. The weight was still there. Not loud but refined. Polished. The kind that smiles at brunch and strategises its silence. I still felt the need to perform. To prove I belonged. Flawless. Unflappable. Always "on."

There were days I wore the suit and the smile but felt the mask tighten. The pressure was not just professional, it was personal.

What had once felt like strength, stoicism, drive, self-sufficiency, was now starting to feel like armour. Fatherhood was softening me. Loneliness was exposing me.

And the space between the image and the truth was quietly widening.

Friendships could feel fleeting. Plans, provisional.

Conversations often skimmed the surface, pleasant, polished but rarely raw. Everything worked. But not everything landed.

Even professionally, success could feel performative, titles outsized, egos outspeaking experience. It was a place where you could accelerate fast but also lose your footing if you weren't careful.

And as much as I was thriving in this world, deeply grateful for all it had given me, I also felt a quiet tension building.

Because for all its gifts, Dubai had become a place that magnified not only what I had achieved… but what I hadn't yet faced.

It was the pinnacle, yes.

But also a pause.

A glittering horizon that quietly asked: *what now?*

And the answer wouldn't come from the skyline.

It would come, eventually, from a mirror.

But first, there was one more summit to climb.

Boardrooms and Palaces

The world around me kept climbing, even as something within me had started to stir. At work, my role evolved again. My portfolio expanded, my reach deepened. We were advising CEOs, royal court members, ministers and leaders from some of the most prestigious families in the region, working closely with governments from the UAE to Saudi Arabia and all other GCC / Gulf Countries. Often, my role centred on shaping leadership at the very top, helping them build boards, strengthen executive teams and make appointments that would define the future of their organisations.

Sometimes those conversations widened, moving beyond individuals into broader reflections on strategy, structure and transformation. I'd help frame the challenge, offer early counsel and then bring in our expert advisory consultants to take the work forward. I wasn't rewriting government policy. I wasn't leading national reform. But along with my colleagues, I was playing a meaningful role, quietly helping to decide who would.

These were no longer rooms I was trying to enter. These were rooms I now helped shape.

And yet, some of my most important insights didn't come from palaces or ministries. They came in quieter spaces, in corridor chats, project teams and one-on-one check-ins with the women I directly hired and managed. Ambitious professionals from India, Lebanon and the Philippines, each navigating their own version of high performance in a culture that demanded elegance, loyalty and near-constant proof of worth. The Lebanese women, often multilingual and highly educated, carried themselves with poise but even they confided in me about the pressure to always appear impeccable. For the Indian and Filipino women, the hurdles were often steeper, more assumptions to challenge, fewer second chances offered.

Many of them carried the same burdens I did, the need to be twice as good just to be seen as equal. And in those moments, I realised something. This wasn't just my tension. This wasn't just about my imposter syndrome. It was shared. Worn behind bright smiles, immaculate CVs and crisp suits. We were all, in our own ways, carrying the weight of proving we belonged. Maybe that's why our bond ran deeper, because we carried the same weight, even if we wore it differently.

But the more I stepped into these rarefied spaces, the more something began to shift. Not away from the weight but alongside it. A quiet confidence was forming. The tension was still there but I wasn't shrinking from it anymore. I was starting to own the room, slowly but surely.

And then came Riyadh.

The airport hummed with heat and control, all marble floors and muted tones, everything precise and clinical. Then I saw him, a man in a suit, standing tall, holding a white placard.

Mr Ashley Mills.

I paused. Honestly, my first thought was, that can't be for me. I'd never seen my name on a sign like that. Not for a job. Not for an interview. Just… to be greeted.

He stepped forward. "Mr Mills?" He introduced himself as Omar. Immaculate, courteous, professional to the last detail.

"Let me take your bag," he offered, already reaching.

It was just one slim briefcase but something in me, built from years of carrying my own weight, kicked in. "No, thank you," I said, smiling. He blinked, caught slightly off guard, like no one had ever declined before.

We stepped out into the velvet heat of the night, where a blacked-out GMC Yukon XL waited, gleaming like something from a spy film. He opened the door with quiet ceremony. I climbed in.

And for the first time, I didn't feel like I was pretending.

That day, he drove me from meeting to meeting. Billionaire business leaders from the Kingdom's most powerful families. Ministers spearheading national transformation. Even Princes and Princesses, part of the wider Saudi royal family, sat across from me in those rooms. All part of Vision 2030, Saudi Arabia's sweeping plan to modernise its economy, open up to global investment and cautiously expand women's rights in a society long shaped by tradition.

And somehow, I found myself there too, offering what I could. A listening ear, strategic input, helping shape decisions that, in small ways, would ripple into the region's future.

Omar waited patiently outside every meeting. Always ready. Always in place. That evening, as he dropped me at my hotel in the heart of Riyadh's Diplomatic Quarter, where foreign dignitaries and global power players slept behind guarded gates, he reminded me of the next morning's pickup.

"Eight o'clock sharp, Mr Mills."

Sure enough, the next morning at 7:59 a.m., I stepped outside. There he was. Engine running. Door open.

And all I could think was, how did I get here?

From a council house in Morley to this. From side-stepping trouble on the estate to navigating conversations about national vision. From being the kid without a father to being called "Mr Mills" by a driver in a luxury SUV.

It was surreal. Humbling. Electrifying.

And over the next three years, the sky became my second home. Constant take-offs and landings, Dubai to Riyadh, to Jeddah, to Oman, to Kuwait, to Bahrain, cities that once lived only in news reports now etched into memory.

At some point, it began to feel almost normal. But I never let it become forgettable.

Because every time Omar opened that car door, part of me was still that boy from Morley, wide-eyed, alert, and quietly refusing to hand over his one bag.

Behind the Shine – Tears, Truth and a Deeper Reckoning

While life shimmered on the surface, a different current ran beneath.

There were weekends I drank too much, not to celebrate, but to soften something sharp I didn't have words for.

Sometimes, I'd sit outside by the pool as the sun began to dip behind the hills, golden light casting long shadows across the terrace. A glass in hand. Silence all around. The stillness made it harder to hide from myself.

Even with music playing, the silence inside was louder.

I'd play Gregory Porter on repeat, his voice like velvet grief, drawing something out of me I didn't know I'd buried.

The ache wasn't always loud.

It showed up in quiet moments, in stillness, in songs, in the space between meetings.

And sometimes I'd cry.

Quietly.

In the villa.

On planes.

Watching films about underdogs or Black protagonists. stories that didn't just move me, they recognised me. It wasn't about being sad. It was about being seen.

I didn't talk about it then. But I was starting to feel what I hadn't yet admitted:

Success hadn't erased the ache.

And as I moved through Dubai, glittering, ambitious, immaculate, that ache found new reflections. In a city obsessed with perfection, I started noticing who got to be seen, and who stayed invisible.

Dubai's mantra was "Impossible is Nothing."

But that promise came with conditions. If you fit the mould. If you spoke the language. If your skin, passport or salary matched the script.

Labourers, gardeners, "office boys" – *I hated that term then and still do today* - they moved through the city like ghosts. Invisible to many. Essential to all.

And I saw them.

Maybe because I was starting to finally see myself, too. What struck me wasn't just the divide but how easily it was accepted. Racism wasn't limited to old-guard locals. I heard it from polished expats too, the way they spoke about entire nationalities, as if competence was tied to citizenship.

It sat uncomfortably. And for the first time in my career, I pushed back. A hiring decision soaked in coded bias. I named it. Challenged it. Twice. And it changed something in me.

At work, I made it a quiet habit, intentional, never performative, to greet the security guards and office staff by name. To ask about their lives. To see them. So my daughter would see it too. Not as performance. But principle. That's how you treat people. That's who we are.

The moment that stayed with me most came one evening during Ramadan, the sacred month when Muslims fast from sunrise to sunset as an act of faith, discipline and reflection.

As part of an annual company initiative, we were distributing food parcels at a labour camp, just before iftar, the moment the fast is broken at sundown.

Rows of men, tired but dignified waited patiently for the call to eat.

Then I saw Hassan, the security guard from our office building.

He beamed when he saw me.

Pulled me in.

Introduced me to his friends like I was family.

Months later, he told me that moment changed how he saw me.

Truth is, it changed me too.

Because somewhere between the luxury and the load, I finally saw it clearly: Success without compassion is just performance. But success with empathy that's power. That's legacy.

And from the outside, you'd never have known any of it.

The Postcard Life and the Question That Wouldn't Let Go

On paper, it was everything.

The beautiful couple. The villa. The pool. The fast cars. The chocolate Labrador greeting you at the door.

Our daughter running barefoot across marble floors. Laughter spilling from the garden.

A life so polished, it could've passed for a film set, though I often felt like someone who'd wandered onto set without a script.

We had the rare privilege of keeping our penthouse apartment in Zurich, perched above Lake Zurich, with sweeping views and quiet luxuries that always made it feel like home. No matter how far we travelled, it remained our anchor. Every summer, we returned, me for several weeks, the rest of the family for longer stretches. We'd escape the Dubai heat, sip rosé on the terrace and cruise across the lake, sometimes in the little speedboat we somehow ended up buying.

Winters were spent in St. Moritz, at the family chalet, postcard-perfect retreat, quiet and snow-lined.

And in between, it was business class flights on Emirates between Dubai and Zurich, the kind with champagne before take-off, gourmet meals mid-air and a driver waiting on the other side.

It was life at altitude, in every sense, even if I sometimes looked around and thought, is this really me? Our daughter, radiant in her joy, was growing up in a world I could never have imagined as a child, and yet I still wondered if I was giving her the truest version of myself.

Some nights, I'd walk through the door after another whirlwind week, strategy sessions, meetings with senior officials, multiple flights, and feel a strange kind of stillness. Not peace, more like distance. The house was beautiful. My daughter's drawings hung on the fridge. The wine was chilled. But at times, I felt like a guest inside my own life, watching a performance I was still directing.

People saw the surface and assumed the story. He's made it. And in many ways, I had. But beneath it, a question kept pressing against my chest. Have you really earned your place here? Have you truly arrived, or are you still performing?

For all the accolades, I still carried a quiet ache, a chip I had never quite let go of. The academic gap. The unfinished chapter. The missing credentials. I had risen far without them, but something inside whispered that the final ascent, to true partnership, to lasting credibility, might require more.

So, the decision came. Not just for the next promotion, although I told myself that at the time. Not just to prove something to the world, although that mattered too. It was about silencing a voice that had been shouting since I was a boy.

I remember a moment, about 18 months into the firm. I was working on a challenging mandate with a Senior Client Partner from our French office. We'd hit obstacle after obstacle, and despite my best efforts, the strategy wasn't landing. After another pivot, he looked at me across the table and said, with calm, cutting precision, "Ashley, this is just not good enough. I don't want your excuses. I'm more concerned that there's simply not enough intellectual horsepower being applied to this project."

I nodded. Professionally. Calmly. Said something about next steps and tightened focus. But inside, my stomach dropped. The words hit like a slap. Whether he meant it that way or not, it stuck with me for years. Not because it was true, but because a part of me feared it might be. That's the voice I wanted to silence.

It wasn't just about respect from others. It was about respect from myself.

And with that quiet fire in my chest, I took the leap. What I didn't yet realise was that the Executive MBA wouldn't just elevate my résumé. It would break me open, rebuild me, stretch me to the edge of what I thought was possible. It would become the most demanding, disorienting, and ultimately defining experience of my adult life.

And I had no idea how much it would ask of me or reveal.

The Blueprint – Chapter 10: Dubai – Staying Grounded While the World Expands

Key Truth:

"Success without stillness is just another performance."

Quote

"Success is liking yourself, liking what you do, and liking how you do it." - Maya Angelou

---

Theme: Holding Onto Who You Are at the Peak

Dubai was a world beyond anything I had imagined growing up, a life of privilege, beauty and access that defied everything I once thought possible. From Jumeirah Islands to St. Moritz, from poolside barbecues to royal palaces, I had stepped into rooms I once dreamed of and made them part of my daily life.

And yet, in this glittering chapter, the deeper questions began to rise louder than ever.

Because abundance doesn't erase insecurity.
It exposes it.
It asks: Who are you when nothing is missing… but something still feels off?

For anyone navigating success while carrying a complex past, this is your blueprint.

---

1. Success doesn't silence the past - it gives it a microphone

Even in abundance, the past doesn't disappear. It whispers through quiet moments, asking: Have you healed, or just upgraded the scenery? True growth begins when we stop trying to outrun our origins and start integrating them.

Why This Matters:
For anyone who grew up with scarcity, of money, stability, love, success can feel like a cure. But comfort doesn't erase the past. It gives you space to finally feel it. If you've crossed cultural or class thresholds, those early gaps often remain unhealed, waiting beneath the shine.

For leaders who rose from instability, prosperity can become a stage but it also becomes a mirror. True growth requires us not just to ascend but to integrate. To stop decorating the doubt and start addressing it.

My Reality:
I had built a life beyond anything I imagined, villa, driver, business class flights, the works. But in the quiet moments, I could feel the tremor. The boy from Morley, still checking if he was allowed in the room. Sometimes success doesn't silence the doubt, it decorates it. The marble floors, the five-star suites, they can muffle the questions, but they don't answer them.

Lived Lesson:

One night, sipping wine by the pool as my daughter laughed nearby, I should've felt peace. But instead, I felt distance. From myself. From the story I hadn't yet dealt with. The success hadn't erased the ache. It had simply given it space to speak. Years later, I'd realise this was emotional self-awareness knocking, an invitation to lead not just with drive, but with depth.

Make it Real:

Write your personal "success myth." What did you once believe would finally make you feel whole? Now list what actually brings peace or fulfilment and compare.

Reflection Prompts:

- What parts of my story have I tried to outrun?
- What silence am I avoiding by staying busy?
- What truth am I finally ready to acknowledge?

---

2. Designing your life around what matters most

Balance isn't something you find. It's something you build, with clarity, courage and constant course correction. If you don't name what matters, your ambition will choose for you. And it rarely picks love first.

Why This Matters:

For high performers, especially those shaped by scarcity or instability, work becomes identity and proving becomes a habit. Without clear values, work fills every gap. But intentional leadership means defining success across *all* areas of life and building structures that support it. Presence isn't spontaneous. It's scheduled, protected and designed.

My Reality:

In those years, I was trying to be everything to everyone, the executive, the provider, the partner, the father. I rarely said no. I over-prioritised work, convinced that high performance would secure peace for everyone around me. But amidst the overload, I never missed weekends. Saturday mornings became sacred. They weren't perfect but they were consistent. In those moments, I stopped performing and simply showed up. Not everything that grows your CV grows your legacy.

Lived Lesson:

There were weeks I barely touched the ground. But every Saturday morning, we slowed down. I'd teach her how to ride a bike. Cheer her on at Rugbytots. Watch her face light up at Dubai Safari. It wasn't performative balance. It was a quiet rebellion against burnout - a conscious rhythm that kept my values visible. Looking back, that wasn't balance, it was a lifeline. Years later, that rhythm taught me something foundational about leadership: consistency builds trust, and small rituals create psychological safety. Whether leading a team or parenting a child, showing up regularly, even when you're tired, says: *You matter. I'm here.*

Make it Real:

Audit your week like you would a business. Where is your energy going? What gets prioritised, and what gets the leftovers? Choose one recurring moment to protect with the same intentionality you bring to your most important meetings. Not for optics. For presence.

Reflection Prompts:

- What does "success" in my personal life look like and am I honouring it?
- Am I leading at home with the same intentionality I lead with at work?
- What's the cost of being present everywhere but missed at home?

---

3. Belonging must be reclaimed in every room

Even when you've made it, when the car door opens, when your name's on the placard, there's still a part of you that wonders if it's all a mistake. Belonging isn't a place. It's a practice.

Why This Matters:

Imposter syndrome doesn't disappear with titles or wealth. Especially for those who grew up as outsiders, every new room can reignite old questions. But the only way to silence the voice is to speak from your truth. In leadership, reclaiming your story becomes a relational tool. It teaches others to root their presence in purpose, not performance.

My Reality:

The first time I saw a driver hold a sign with my name, Mr. Ashley Mills, I froze. I didn't feel like "Mr." anything. But over time, I realised I didn't need to feel like I belonged in those rooms. I needed to remember the journey that got me there.

Lived Lesson:

There were moments in Riyadh, stepping out of a luxury SUV into marble-lined ministry buildings, where the contrast hit me. I'd catch my reflection in the glass: tailored suit, polished shoes, corporate calm. But in those quiet seconds before a meeting, I'd remember where I'd come from, late buses in Leeds, night shifts in Birmingham, nights in that freezing student flat in Edgbaston. The transformation was real. But so was the past. I didn't carry the same suitcase, but I carried the same story.

Make it Real:

Before your next high-stakes meeting, pause for 60 seconds. Close your eyes and remember three places that shaped you, not credentials but corners of your story. A childhood street. A kitchen table. A moment of survival. Then walk in, not to prove you belong but to *remember* that you already do.

Reflection Prompts:

- What room still makes me feel like I have to prove myself?
- What would change if I walked in knowing I already belong?
- How might my story be the source of my authority, not a footnote to it?

---

4. Legacy outlasts luxury

Luxury turns heads. Legacy turns hearts. You can own the world and still lose what matters. But live with intention and your life becomes a message, even after you're gone.

Why This Matters:
Especially for those who rose from scarcity, it's tempting to equate love with lifestyle. But legacy is not built on aesthetics, accolades, or assets. It's built on relational presence and repeatable values. In both families and organisations, those who prioritise authentic connection over status create cultures that endure.

My Reality:

We had it all, the house, the travel, the life. But my daughter didn't care about any of that. She cared that I was there. That I listened. That she could count on my laugh and my lullabies. The question isn't what they inherit. It's who they remember. And memory isn't shaped by luxury, it's shaped by love.

Lived Lesson:

One evening, after a long week of travel and late-night calls, I was home just in time for bedtime. As I tucked her in, she reached for my hand and asked, "Can you stay a bit longer?" I hesitated, exhausted, emails still waiting, but I lay beside her. We lay there quietly, no words, just breath. After a while, she whispered, "This is my favourite place." Not the holiday villas or island trips. Just that moment. That stillness became a leadership lesson in disguise. What she needed most wasn't provision, it was presence. That realisation has shaped how I show up in every room since: less about controlling outcomes, more about creating spaces of calm, trust, and human connection.

Make it Real:

Ask someone close to you what they admire most about how you show up, not what you have. Then amplify that. Legacy lives in the behaviours they remember, not the things they inherit.

Reflection Prompts:

- What will my children, partner, or closest friends remember most about me?
- Am I living more for admiration or for impact?
- What does legacy mean when no one is watching?

---

5. Compassion is a form of power

In high-performance cultures, compassion is often misread as weakness. But empathy isn't soft. It's strategic. It opens doors others can't even see. It lifts people up. It changes the room.

Why This Matters:
Compassion isn't niceness, it's clarity with heart. It builds trust, bridges divides and elevates voices that are often unheard. For those who've experienced exclusion or invisibility, choosing to see others becomes a form of reclaiming power. Leaders who carry this lens don't just inspire, they *repair*. They model what it looks like to lead with dignity, not dominance.

My Reality:
I saw the hierarchy of Dubai everywhere, from palaces to labour camps. And I chose, quietly but consistently, to acknowledge the unseen. Security guards. Assistants.

Gardeners. Not out of pity, but out of principle. Because success isn't real if you're stepping over people to hold it.

Lived Lesson:

During Eid, I visited a labour camp to help distribute food parcels. When one of the security guards from my office recognised me, beaming with pride, I realised that moment meant more than a thousand client meetings.

That experience reframed power for me. It taught me that leadership doesn't always sit at the head of the table, it moves through every corridor, every handshake, every name remembered. The most transformative influence is often the quietest.

Make it Real:

Start by learning the names of people others ignore. Ask about their family. Shake their hand. Let your presence remind them, and yourself, of what leadership really means.

Reflection Prompts:

- Who in my orbit needs to feel seen right now?
- Where can I show strength through softness this week?
- What version of leadership am I modelling for those with the least power?

What Dubai Showed Me:

Dubai was a high note, a life few could imagine and fewer could sustain. But the real triumph wasn't in what I acquired. It was in what I began to confront.

The quiet ache.
The need for validation.
The chip I still carried.
And the choice to do something about it.

Because growth doesn't happen when the world claps for you, it happens when you start asking better questions.

And for me, that question became louder than ever:
What am I still trying to prove, and to whom?

I didn't know it then, but the answer would take me somewhere I hadn't dared to go:
Back to the mirror.

11

THE MBA AND THE MIRROR

I stared at the screen, finger hovering over the mouse. The final submission portal was open. After two years of late nights, long flights, essays written in hotel lobbies and toddler-filled living rooms, this was it.

Click.

The file uploaded. The page refreshed. And then, nothing. Just silence. Not applause. Not relief. Just a blinking cursor and the hum of the air-conditioning.

I sat back, hands in my lap, and felt emptied.

It should have felt like the summit. And in some ways, it did. A surge of emotion rose as I sat back, tears welling before I even understood why. Relief. Achievement. Something fierce and quiet and overwhelming.

But then came the stillness. And in that stillness, reflection. Because this journey hadn't just tested my intellect. It had touched something deeper, something I'd spent years trying to outrun.

By this point, I was living what most would call a successful life. A career in Dubai, a joyful daughter, summers in Zurich, winters in St. Moritz. I ticked every box success was supposed to. But beneath the surface, a quieter current ran. A voice I'd carried for years. Sometimes a whisper, sometimes a weight. It echoed in boardrooms, even when I was advising prestigious families or sitting beside royalty.

No matter how far I'd come, I still felt like the boy who had dropped out. Still wondering if I truly belonged.

That chip on my shoulder hadn't vanished. It had just learned how to wear cufflinks.

And when you rarely see someone like you at the table, the silence doesn't feel neutral. It begins to echo. Subtly. Quietly. Until the doubt becomes your own.

What the MBA revealed wasn't just academic. It was personal.

I wasn't there to impress others. I was there to meet myself. To reckon with the part of me that had spent years shape-shifting to belong in places where I was never expected.

So, with a demanding job, a young daughter and a life already stretched thin, I said yes. Yes to the challenge.

Yes to the sacrifice.

Yes to the mirror.

What I didn't yet know was how much it would unearth. Or how many truths I'd have to face, starting with my own.

Pushing Beyond the Limits

I enrolled in a top-tier, high-pressure Executive MBA programme at HULT International Business School, while working full-time, travelling across the region weekly and jointly raising a young daughter who still waited for bedtime stories. It wasn't logical. It wasn't easy. But for someone like me, carrying unspoken questions and old ghosts, it was necessary.

Our cohort was a mosaic of the world, fifty professionals from more than thirty nationalities. Emiratis, Saudis, Lebanese, Nigerians, Italians, Argentinians, Chinese. Some ran start-ups. Others led family dynasties. Some had five degrees, others had survived five lives. The diversity was intoxicating. And if I'm honest, at first, intimidating.

Because while the room looked global, not everyone had taken the same road to get there. Yes, there were scrappy, self-made types like me. But many had arrived through quieter privilege, legacy businesses, boarding schools, inherited confidence.

What struck me most wasn't class. It was representation.

I saw plenty of African heritage represented, Nigerians, Ghanaians, Sudanese, often with strong academic foundations and high expectations. But people like me? Mixed-race, Caribbean roots, born in Britain. We were almost never in these rooms. And when I did see someone who looked like me succeeding, more often than not, their background traced back to Africa, not Jamaica.

That stung. Not because I resented their success, they had their own battles to fight, their own barriers to break.

But because I rarely saw my story reflected. It wasn't resentment. It was invisibility.

Even in a room of thirty nationalities, I couldn't help but feel rare. Not just for how I looked. But for the path I'd taken to get here.

There was another truth, too, one I rarely said aloud. Growing up, I hadn't seen many men with my background in corporate leadership. On TV, on sports pitches, on stages yes. But in boardrooms? Almost never. And when you don't see yourself in a space, you start to wonder if you were ever meant to be there.

That's how doubt works. It creeps in quietly. In the half-second pause before speaking. In the instinct to edit yourself. In the need to prove, rather than just be.

That first day felt like school again. I stood in front of the class, heart racing, introducing myself as the kid from Morley who'd landed in Dubai. Some smiled. Some tilted their heads. A voice inside whispered, "Don't mess this up."

But the programme didn't let you stay small. From day one: challenge your limits. Show up fully. Or get left behind.

Lectures began on Friday morning and didn't stop until Monday evening, an intense stretch that consumed the entire weekend. Finishes each night at Midnight were normal. 2 a.m. common. 4 a.m. not unusual.

Group projects with strangers. Cross-cultural debates. Late-night simulations. Boardroom role-plays. Presentations through bloodshot eyes.

And every second weekend: the essay. Not just a few pages, but deep, demanding submissions, often several thousand words long. Some stretched to 15, 30, even 40 pages. Each one a test of clarity, stamina and discipline. Due at 10:00 p.m. sharp, no exceptions.

I submitted most of mine between 9:58 and 10:00 p.m. sweating through the final paragraph, headphones in, at home in my office, writing since 8 a.m., trying to hold both thoughts and family challenges in tension.

Twelve core modules. Six electives. Two years.

Brutal.

But also, quietly beautiful.

Because something started to shift.

Each module I passed, each insight I absorbed, each debate I held my own in, it chipped away at the old story. The one that said I wasn't academic. That I didn't belong in classrooms. That I had missed my chance.

And slowly, that story started to fade. In its place, something stronger began to take root. Not arrogance, not bravado. Just earned pride. A kind of quiet, grounded confidence.

And something else.

I began to notice a gift, an ability to connect, translate, bridge cultures and egos. At first, I called it people skills. But I came to see it for what it was: a superpower.

My dual heritage, once a source of tension, had become my edge. I could speak in boardrooms and back streets. I could relate to the academic, the entrepreneur, the official, the outsider. I could navigate the unspoken.

Yes, the workload was crushing. The travel unrelenting. But in between, I was rebuilding something deeper, not just to earn a degree but to reclaim the part of me I had long underestimated.

And for the first time, I was doing it on my own terms.

The Mirror Cracks

But there was another side to the story, one no grade, however glowing, could hold. Because while I was climbing internally, the ground beneath my home life had begun to shift.

The MBA wasn't just revealing frameworks, it was revealing me. Unpeeling the layers I had worn for decades, ambition, humour, resilience. Not destroying them but demanding I look beneath. Beneath the pride. Beneath the performance. Beneath the survival strategy of always staying one step ahead.

And what I saw in the mirror wasn't always flattering.

The cracks we had once papered over with routine, parenting rhythms, date nights, scheduled togetherness, were no longer holding. There was admiration, yes. Pride, even. But also distance. Love remained. But silence grew.

I was changing, growing sharper, more self-aware, more intentional. But in that growth I felt the gap widen. And that left a mark.

It wasn't one rupture. It was the slow erosion of closeness. The weight of perfectionism, I carried like both a badge and a burden. The impossible task of being everything, father, husband, student, provider, high-performer. Like many men do, I had equated love with provision, presence with performance.

And while I chased that impossible standard, my partner carried so much of the load at home. During those intense MBA weekends, she held our world together, managing our daughter, keeping the rhythm of family life steady while I disappeared into case studies and deadlines. Without her, I would not have made it through.

That support enabled my success, but I came to see how the recognition flowed toward me while the weight of sacrifice often went unseen. That imbalance became part of the quiet strain I felt building between the life I lived outside, and the life we lived within. And in the quiet moments between achievement and exhaustion, I began to feel alone.

I remember returning from an especially brutal module, four days of late nights, high-stakes presentations and soul-sapping peer reviews. I stepped into our villa, bags in hand and felt it: that space between where I had just been and what I'd returned to. The ache of disconnection. The strange sensation of standing inside the life you built, yet no longer feeling at home in it.

Because the programme was transforming me, and with every insight gained, every layer stripped away, the gap widened between who I was becoming and the life I was trying to return to.

That's what no one talks about.

That sometimes, growth doesn't strengthen your roots, it stretches them. That chasing your potential can pull you further from the version of yourself others first loved and from the spaces that once felt safe.

At times, I felt guilt, like I was abandoning the version of me who had once belonged so fully to my family. At times, I felt misunderstood, like I was speaking a new language no one else had learned. But most often, I felt split. Like I was holding two worlds in tension: the world I had grown into and the one I feared I might be growing out of.

That's the quiet tax of transformation. Especially for those of us who have lived in-between.

In-between cultures.

In-between classes.

In-between who we are and who the world expects us to be.

We learn to remould ourselves, not out of inauthenticity, but out of necessity. Belonging was never guaranteed.

Editing ourselves became a survival skill. But the MBA made it harder to edit. It sharpened me but it also exposed what I had buried. And it forced me to realise: the more I grew into myself, the less easily I fit into the life that had once felt like everything.

The MBA had promised clarity. What I hadn't expected was the grief - not the kind born of arguments, but the kind that comes when you finally face what you've spent years burying.

Distinction and the Cost of Becoming

Graduation came quietly.

No cap, no gown, no applause. Just a blinking cursor, a final submission, and the silence that follows two years of relentless motion.

The HULT Business Challenge had nearly broken us.
Six months of high-stakes strategy, pivots and pressure, all aimed at solving a real-world business problem for a corporate giant. Our client? LVMH, the world's largest luxury conglomerate. The brief was ambitious. The expectations higher still. Arguments flared, tensions fractured the group, one teammate was removed, another pulled in midstream. And then, halfway through the challenge, the world changed.

COVID hit. Borders closed. Classrooms emptied. What should have been our final sprint became a scattered scramble of midnight Zoom calls and fragmented messages across time zones. The campus we had come to love vanished into a pixelated grid of faces.

Still, somehow, we finished.

I remember pressing submit on that last deliverable with tears in my eyes, not from exhaustion but from the sheer emptiness that followed. Everything I had, every ounce of belief, energy and fight, I had poured into that moment.

The result? Distinction. A single word. Not about prestige but about redemption.

I had done it.

Twelve core modules. Six electives. Countless essays written on planes, in hotel rooms, in toddler-filled living rooms. Lectures that ran deep into the night. A class of fifty from thirty countries. And me, somehow not just surviving but thriving.

But the real reward wasn't the certificate. It was the people. Because in the pressure and grind of those two years, friendships were shaped that would outlast any module.

Tristan. Fabio. Justin. George. Were friendships that stood out amongst many others.

Different lives. Different worlds. But we clicked.

We challenged each other. Laughed until we cried. Debated until 3 a.m. And in the hardest moments, we held space for one another.

They weren't just classmates.

They were mirrors.

They were anchors.

And for the first time, I felt truly seen by peers who respected the road I'd taken to arrive.

Two years later, long after the pandemic delayed our celebration, we finally stood together again. Not in classrooms but as brothers.

The venue: Dubai Opera.

Date: 18th August 2022.

The Burj Khalifa rising behind us like a monument to the improbable.

I walked across that stage, robe on my shoulders, name called aloud. In the glare of the spotlight, I caught my reflection. It felt surreal, full circle.

But as I stepped offstage, another image rose in my mind. Not the Burj. Not the boardroom.

But the 19-year-old version of me, flat broke, alone in a freezing Birmingham room, wondering if he had already blown his shot at life.

I wanted to tell him:

You make it.

You really do.

And more than that, you are already enough.

There was no dad in the crowd. No shoulder squeeze. No "well done, son."

But two people were etched in my thoughts, my mum, who had carried me through storms and my daughter, who would one day ask what her dad did with the chances she'd never have to fight for.

Maybe that's why the emotion hit harder than expected. Beyond the applause, beyond the robe and the rows of colleagues, something stirred. A quiet storm I didn't yet have language for. A sense that something inside had shifted again.

Just over a year later, at forty, I was promoted to Senior Partner, the highest rank in my industry.

It was the summit I had been climbing toward since the day I walked into the Firm, nearly a decade earlier. In truth, the climb had begun long before: in the telesales rooms where I fought for every sale, on the trains I dodged without tickets just to reach an interview, on the streets of Yorkshire where success was never promised.

It was the product of blood, sweat and tears. Hundreds of flights. Endless sacrifices. Years of silence, of proving, of demons buried but never fully gone. For a quarter of my life, for half my career, I had chased this one rung on the ladder.

And then, suddenly, it was here.

The final step.

The phone call.

A bank holiday afternoon in Dubai.

I was lying on a lounger at a beach resort on the Palm, the sea breeze on my face, the silhouette of the newly built Atlantis Royal shimmering in the distance. When the phone rang, I almost didn't answer. But I did. And in that moment, everything shifted.

My boss's voice was calm, understated, as he shared the news that would become one of the proudest moments of my life.

I thanked him, we spoke briefly, and then I hung up.

And I just sat there.

Not smiling, not celebrating. Just still.

The sun was dipping, the waves moving with a rhythm I hadn't felt in months.

Alone in that moment, I let it land. The boy who once dropped out of university, who carried a thousand questions and just as many doubts, had become a Senior Partner at the top firm in the world.

And no one could take that from me.

There was no champagne. No social post, no crowd – that came later. But I can tell you with certainty, that moment changed something in me. Not because of what I achieved, but because of what I released. The need to prove. The fear of not being enough. The echo of every room I had once entered expecting to be found out.

And as the stillness settled, the voices of the past came rushing back.

I remembered that meeting, that comment, that moment. The French Partner across the table, early in my career: "I'm more concerned there's simply not enough intellectual horsepower being applied to this project."

That wasn't just criticism. It was a seed. A weight I carried silently for years, sharpening, proving, performing. That was the voice I had finally silenced.

That moment didn't come from nowhere.

It was the product of everything I'd walked through, every scar, every sprint and every quiet hand that helped me rise. And in those final years, my wife had carried more than her share of the load at home, making it possible for me to keep moving, for which I will always be grateful.

And everything the MBA had helped me see, about leadership, about presence, about who I truly was beneath the armour.

The MBA didn't just give me a certificate.

It gave me clarity.

It showed me what I was capable of when I stopped hiding behind charm and hustle.

It revealed how much of my striving had been rooted in fear. For years, I had mistaken performance for worth, believing that if I achieved enough, no one would see what I was carrying, that the grind would shield me from the grief.

Like many men, especially those raised without a father, I had learned to translate pain into productivity. To lead with competence when I didn't feel safe showing need.

It looked like ambition but underneath, it was survival.

And it made me confront the true cost of high achievement.

Yes, I had become a Senior Partner.

But I was also a man standing at a precipice, looking back at everything I had built and quietly wondering what it might cost to keep holding it all.

Here's what no one tells you about growth.

It expands you, but it also exposes you.

It sharpens you, but it can slice right through the life you thought was safe.

The MBA gave me tools, it gave me language, it gave me vision.

But the mirror it left behind?

That would take far longer to face.

It didn't just teach me how to lead.

It taught me how to look in the mirror, and keep looking, even when what I saw was uncomfortable.

Because growth doesn't just change what you do. It asks you to choose who you become.

The Blueprint – Chapter 11: The MBA and the Mirror

Key Truth

"You don't need permission to belong."

Quote

"Intelligence plus character, that is the goal of true education."

- Martin Luther King Jr.

Theme: When the Mirror Shows You More Than You Expected

Success stories often celebrate the outcome but rarely explore the cost.
For years, I carried an internal ceiling, the belief that, because I'd dropped out of university, I wasn't cut out for academic or intellectual spaces.

The Executive MBA wasn't just about a certificate.
It was about dismantling old narratives, shaped by class, absence and the subtle exclusions of race.
About confronting the voices, internal and external, that once said:
You don't belong here.

And in doing so, it revealed a deeper truth:
Real growth isn't just about acquiring more.

It's about becoming more and facing everything that comes with that.

This is your blueprint if you've ever told yourself,
"I'm not made for this,"
or if excellence has ever reshaped you in ways you didn't expect.

---

1. Growth isn't just a climb - it's a confrontation

We often treat growth like a straight ascent: higher, better, more. But real growth demands more than progress, it demands reckoning. It digs up the roots you thought were buried. It makes you face the stories you inherited and decide which ones to carry forward and which ones to rewrite.

Why This Matters:
Growth doesn't just add knowledge, it reveals the limits of your self-belief. When you stretch toward your potential, you surface old stories: "You're not smart enough." "People like you don't belong here."

For anyone raised in absence or exclusion, advancement often means confronting inner ceilings not just breaking barriers, but healing what the barriers once protected. For leaders, this confrontation builds emotional depth, humility and the ability to support others through their doubts without judgment.

My Reality:

The MBA wasn't just an academic mountain, it was emotional terrain.

Every essay submitted, every debate survived, every night I stayed up fighting doubt… was a moment of reclaiming. Not just from the system but from the story I'd carried since I dropped out of university.

Lived Lesson:

Some assignments broke me open, not because of the topic but because of what they triggered. I'd sit in hotel rooms or home offices, staring at the screen, not just battling the brief but the inner voice saying: "You're not built for this." But every time I submitted, I silenced that voice. Line by line. Years later, I noticed how this helped me lead others. I could see the fear behind the perfectionism. I recognised the hesitation in someone else's eyes, because I'd lived it and now, I could name it with compassion.

Make it Real:

Write down one old belief about yourself that limits your growth.

Ask: *Who told me this? Is it still true?* Then write three new beliefs rooted in your present strength.

Reflection Prompts:

- What part of your past are you still letting define your future?
- What truth about your current capability are you ready to fully own?
- How does your own growth journey shape the way you mentor or lead others through theirs?

---

2. When growth reveals a quiet grief

Transformation is often painted as triumphant. But growth also comes with loss. As you expand, you shed versions of yourself that once fit. It can be lonely. It can hurt. And sometimes, the hardest part of evolving is realising that not everyone can come with you.

Why This Matters:

We expect growth to bring joy but it can also bring grief. Why? Because when you evolve, you leave something behind: a role you once played, a bond you once needed, a version of you that others recognised.

For those in leadership or mentorship, it's essential to name this. Transformation isn't always triumphant, it's tender. It's the ability to hold loss and expansion at the same time.

My Reality:
The MBA gave me tools but it also gave me distance. I was becoming sharper, more aware… but also more alone. Growth quietly rearranged the closeness I once took for granted.

Lived Lesson:
I remember coming home from a brutal module, exhausted, changed and stepping into a house that no longer felt like home. Not because the people changed but because I had. And that was hard to accept.

But that quiet grief eventually taught me to support others as they grow, without rushing them to celebrate. To recognise when someone on my team, or in my life, needs space not just to succeed, but to let go.

Make it Real:
Name one identity or role you've outgrown. Write a short letter to it, honour it. Then, let it go.

Reflection Prompts:

- What parts of your growth have felt like loss?
- Are you holding on to an old identity just to keep others comfortable?
- How can I support others navigating transformation with empathy, not just strategy?

3. Your background can be your superpower

We're often taught to assimilate, to shrink the parts of ourselves that feel "too different" for elite spaces. But your difference is your power. The roads you've walked give you insight, empathy and adaptability. Your story isn't a liability. It's leverage.

Why This Matters:
In elite spaces, difference is often mistaken for deficiency. But your background isn't a weakness to hide, it's a strength to wield. For those who've navigated class, race, or cultural margins, lived experience sharpens instincts: how to read nuance, connect across gaps and adapt without losing core identity. These are leadership superpowers born not in textbooks, but in real life.

My Reality:
I was one of the only people of Caribbean heritage in my class. At times, it felt isolating. But over time, I realised I had something many didn't: The ability to translate between worlds.

Lived Lesson:
That skill, to relate across cultures, to adapt without losing self, came from being mixed-race, from being "in between." It became my edge.

Not just fitting in but connecting. Not just surviving but bridging.

And in leadership, that's everything. It meant I could understand global clients, speak to different generations, hold space for conflicting views and still be me.

Make it Real:
List three things about your background you once felt insecure about.
Next to each, write one leadership skill it gave you.

Reflection Prompts:

- What part of your story are you still softening for others?
- How would your leadership change if you embraced your full identity?

---

4. Imposter syndrome thrives until you take action

Doubt has a habit of growing in stillness. The longer you wait to feel "ready," the louder it becomes. But confidence isn't a prerequisite, it's a result. And every time you move despite the fear, you chip away at the lie that you don't belong.

Why This Matters:

You can't outthink doubt, you have to out move it. Especially if you've grown up second-guessing your place in the room, waiting to feel "ready" can become a lifelong pause. But in leadership, courage often shows up first. Confidence follows. Taking action becomes the tool that shapes identity and teaches others to do the same.

My Reality:

For years, I carried the shame of dropping out of university. But once I stepped into the MBA, every essay submitted, every idea defended, chipped away at the doubt. Eventually, I wasn't asking if I belonged. I just did.

Lived Lesson:

Submitting my first assignment felt like standing naked in a spotlight. But I didn't wait to feel ready, I acted. And that broke the spell. Years later, I see it in others, brilliant people waiting for permission to begin. I tell them what I now live: start scared. Speak anyway. Lead anyway. That's how courage becomes culture.

Make it Real:

Pick one area in your life where imposter syndrome is loud. Do the thing anyway, apply, pitch, speak, ask. Let action be your answer.

Reflection Prompts:

- Where are you still waiting to feel "ready"?
- What would change if you led with action, not perfection?
- How do you model courage in environments where others may feel unseen or unsure?

---

5. Distinction is a feeling, not a title

There comes a moment when external success stops being the goal. You're no longer chasing applause, you're living alignment. True distinction isn't in the recognition but in the quiet clarity of becoming who you once needed. Not to prove. Just to be.

Why This Matters:
Titles fade. Applause stops. But distinction, the quiet knowing that you've become the person you once needed, that stays. For leaders, this moment of internal alignment becomes your compass. You no longer lead to impress, you lead to serve. You've shifted from performance to presence and that's what people remember.

My Reality:

Yes, I graduated with distinction.

Yes, I became Senior Partner.

But the deepest moment of pride came when I no longer needed to explain myself. I had become the man I once looked for.

Lived Lesson:

I'll never forget that call, beachside, barefoot, hearing the words I'd chased for years: "Senior Partner." But the emotion didn't come from status. It came from release. The quiet laying down of a weight I'd carried for decades.

I no longer needed to prove I belonged. I knew I did.

That clarity changed how I held space for others. I no longer rushed to validate them, I helped them hear their own voice, just as I'd finally heard mine.

Make it Real:

Strip away your job, your achievements, your image.

Ask: *What's left?*

Now invest in that part of you. That's your foundation.

Reflection Prompts:

- Who would you be without the need to prove anything?
- What part of you already feels like "enough" even without recognition?

- How does your presence affirm others who are still finding their own voice or value?

What the MBA Showed Me:

The Executive MBA was more than letters behind my name. It was the moment I stopped carrying the burden of feeling "less than."

If you've ever believed you aren't qualified, educated, or "polished" enough, know this:
Ceilings are often inherited.
But breaking them?
That's always a choice.

And yet, growth alone isn't the goal.
You can build the life you once only dreamed of.
You can climb, lead and excel.
But if you don't stop to ask who you are becoming in the process,
You risk reaching the top and not recognising yourself when you get there.

The mirror doesn't lie.
It reflects not just your success but your essence.

May your next chapter be led not by proving...
But by remembering who you truly are.

12

WHOLE APART: THE BREAKING POINT

For most of my life, I had known how to move forward. When things got hard, I pushed. When doors closed, I found another way in. Every city I lived in, every challenge I faced, I met with motion, upwards, outwards, onwards. Progress was the only language I trusted. And for a long time, it worked.

My marriage had been one of the most meaningful chapters of that journey. We built a life across countries, cultures and seasons, a daughter, a home, a story stitched together by love, intensity and belief in our potential. But even the most beautiful stories can fray at the edges.

We had our highs, laughter, connection, shared adventure and our lows, deep and complicated. Ours was a relationship of sharp contrasts, at times magnetic, at others carrying tensions we both recognised. Like many couples, the rhythm wasn't always easy.

I often retreated into moods I couldn't name, unsure how to articulate what I needed. So I became the fixer, the pleaser, smoothing things over instead of naming what wasn't working. And I can't pretend I didn't make mistakes.

Work consumed me. Sixty flights a year. Conference calls bleeding into holidays. Late nights, constant pressure, the mental spin of performance. I guarded weekends like sacred ground, always coming home, always showing up. But even then, I often arrived depleted, present but thin, there but stretched.

In the pursuit of professional success, I lost sight of what needed to be nourished at home, and I know that created weight for both of us. We came from different worlds, with different models of love, language and life, a contrast that had once sparked curiosity but later revealed harder-to-bridge gaps.

In the beginning, those differences felt rich, full of texture and curiosity. But over time, they revealed deeper divides. And I was changing.

The Executive MBA had cracked something open. Not just intellectually, but emotionally. It surfaced questions I hadn't dared ask before. What do I truly value? What do I respect? Who am I without performance? What kind of man do I want to be, not just in public but in private?

It wasn't just growth, it was awakening. And once your eyes are open, it's hard to pretend they're not.

Our journeys began to take different shapes, and over time, the ways we had once harmonised began to feel more distant.

We both felt it, the weight of unspoken things, the slow erosion of unmet needs, the patterns that quietly wore us down.

Still, we tried. We circled back again and again, hoping to recover the rhythm, the spark, the version of us that once felt unstoppable.

When our daughter reached school age, we made a decision. After a year of primary school in Dubai, she would continue her education in Switzerland. It made sense, for stability, for heritage, for her future.

For a time, we tried to make the distance work, two lives, two cities, bound by one shared hope that space might offer clarity.

But some distances can't be measured in miles.

Even after the MBA, as I asked harder questions and grew in new directions, I still hoped we would find one another again, that somehow we would realign. But deep down, we both knew something had broken long before the goodbye.

When I moved back to Zurich in the summer of 2022, the truth that had been circling for years finally landed. There was a moment, personal, piercing, inescapable, that crystallised everything we hadn't said.

It wasn't about blame. It wasn't about a singular event. Like all relationships, ours had weathered storms on both sides. And I carry regrets, real ones. But something in me shifted that day. The clarity was sudden, though the road there had not been.

The path toward separation was not simple, nor sudden. It came from years of trying, circling back, and realising that what once held us together was no longer enough. And at the centre of it all was our daughter.

Everything I had built over the past decade, every long hour, every promotion, every time I showed up instead of disappearing, was rooted in one unshakable promise, to be the father I never had.

That promise shaped me. It gave me purpose when I had none. It had always carried a desperate hope, that my daughter would never feel what I felt growing up. The ache, the absence, the questions.

So how could we now face the possibility of breaking that vision?

I agonised over it. In my apartment in Dubai, on long-haul flights, alone in Zurich. When is the right time to walk away from a relationship, knowing it could fracture your child's world? Do you stay, for them? Or do you leave, also for them?

I read so many books, watched countless podcasts, searched for a roadmap through the grief. But there is no painless path when a family breaks. Only choices. Only intentions.

And beneath it all, shame clawed at me. Was I just another statistic? Another Black father with a fractured home? Another chapter in the same tired narrative?

For years, I had outrun that fear, dressing it in success, hiding it behind titles, achievements, performance. Telling myself, I'm different. I broke the cycle. But there I was, staring it in the face. And it hurt.

And yet, this wasn't failure. It was a hard, human evolution. Not escape. Not abandonment. But change in form. For her, for our daughter, for myself.

It made me question everything. Was this my legacy? Was this inherited? Was it inevitable?

Those questions didn't go away. In time, they would take me deeper, into history, into healing, into what it means to carry both the scars and the strength of your ancestors. But in that moment, I held to one truth, our daughter deserved parents who were whole, even if that meant they had to stand apart.

So I stayed. Not in the marriage, but in her life. Fully, firmly, fiercely.

Because love doesn't vanish when a relationship ends. If anything, it must grow stronger, strong enough to carry the weight of a different kind of family. A co-created future. A new kind of fatherhood.

And in the end, that was the decision. Not to give up, but to honour the promise in a different form. And though the road ahead was uncertain, I was no longer afraid of standing still.

Because sometimes, real strength isn't about moving forward. Sometimes, it's standing in the wreckage, holding your child's hand and saying, we are still a family, and we will still rise.

But deciding is one thing. Living that decision, especially in the quiet aftermath, is something else entirely.

In the months that followed, I began the slow, sacred work of rebuilding. Not a marriage, but a rhythm we could both contribute to in new ways. Learning how to co-parent in real time, without a manual.

Some days we got it right. Other days, everything felt fragile. There were moments when our daughter's silence said more than words ever could, moments when I questioned whether we had done the right thing. That only deepened the realisation for both of us that moving forward would mean in a new way.

I had to keep reminding myself of something I read once by Robin Sharma - "All change is hard at first, messy in the middle and gorgeous at the end."

This was the messy middle.

I was still in it. Still waking up some mornings with doubt sitting heavy on my chest. Still wondering if I had broken something that could never fully heal.

But underneath it all, I was learning to trust that there was another side. That even if I couldn't see the beauty yet, the decision had been made from love.

And slowly, piece by piece, we began to build something new. Not perfect, but honest. A connection built not from tradition but from intention.

The man I had become was no longer chasing success for its own sake. I was searching for something deeper, something ancestral.

And though I didn't know it yet, the road ahead would carry me back through history, across oceans and into the roots of who I truly was.

It took everything I had to let go. But in that breaking, something new was born. A quieter strength. A deeper truth. And the first real step toward the man and father I was always meant to become.

The Blueprint – Chapter 12: Stillness as Strength

Key Truth

"Sometimes, strength is surrender."

Quote

"The ultimate measure of a man is not where he stands in moments of comfort and convenience but where he stands at times of challenge and controversy." - Martin Luther King Jr.

Theme: Redefining Success Beyond External Markers

For years, I thought strength meant holding everything together, career, image, relationship. I measured success by how well I could maintain the structure around me: no cracks, no doubts, no missing parts.

But sometimes, the bravest thing you can do is take it apart. Not out of anger but out of truth. To look at what you've built and admit: this no longer fits.

Some relationships don't collapse, they shift. Quietly, steadily, out of alignment. And when that happens, the task isn't to force it back, it's to re-evaluate what still stands and what needs to be rebuilt.

This blueprint is for anyone who has stood in the life they built with love, only to realise it's no longer home. For those who grew up without a father and swore they'd write a different story, only to find themselves rewriting again, this time with tenderness and truth.

This is your permission to begin again. Not perfectly. But honestly.

---

1. The hardest question: do you stay for the child?

Absence shaped you. So the thought of creating it for your child can feel unbearable. But presence without peace is its own kind of harm.

Why This Matters:
For those who grew up in fatherless homes, the vow is often silent but fierce: *I'll never leave.* That promise can become a guiding light, or a trap. Because presence in a household filled with tension, resentment, or quiet disconnection can be just as damaging as physical absence. Children are emotionally intuitive. They feel when love is strained, when words go unspoken, when the air gets heavy. Staying "for the child" might soothe our guilt but it doesn't always serve their growth. The real question isn't *Do I stay?* It's *What kind of presence does my child need most?*

My Reality:
I carried that fear like a stone in my chest. The idea of

repeating history was unbearable. I wanted our daughter to have everything I didn't, stability, softness, two loving parents under one roof. But as the years unfolded, I began to ask a harder question: *What are we modelling here?* Love as endurance? Family as performance? I had to confront the possibility that staying might keep the image intact but fracture the soul beneath it. The silence. The strain. The sense that something was quietly unraveling. It was our daughter's emotional safety, not the optics, that needed protecting.

Lived Lesson:
The decision didn't come just from a dramatic explosion. It came from quiet repetition. The same unresolved conversations. The same silences. The same sense that we were both showing up but no longer meeting. I began to understand that staying might preserve structure but not spirit. That real love sometimes means releasing what no longer nurtures. And that leaving doesn't have to mean absence it can mean showing up in a different way, more intentionally than ever.

Make it Real:
Write down three values you want your child to witness in a relationship: not the fantasy but the reality. Ask yourself: Is your current home environment reinforcing or contradicting those values?

Reflection Prompts:

- What message would I want my child to internalise about love, even if our family structure changes?
- If I knew they'd remember how I handled this moment for the rest of their life, what would I want that memory to teach them?
- Where am I maintaining appearances instead of making aligned decisions, for my family or my team?

---

2. Redefining failure

I'd spent years equating success with survival, climbing, earning, enduring. But true success isn't always forward. Sometimes it's inward. Sometimes it's surrender.

When you've worked your whole life to build the opposite of what broke you, the idea of separation can feel like undoing. But true failure isn't when something ends. It's when we keep pretending. Real success isn't about perfection, it's about alignment. In my life I saw how staying misaligned just to preserve the image can feel like collapse.

Why This Matters:
For men from marginalised or underrepresented backgrounds, there's often an added burden: you don't just carry your life, you carry the narrative. The pressure to "break the cycle" can

be so intense that any deviation feels like defeat. But healing doesn't mean replicating what you never had. It means building what's true, even if it looks different.

In leadership too, the fear of failure can become a silent driver, leading to overperformance, burnout and disconnection. But the real collapse doesn't come from ending a structure. It comes from denying the truth of what that structure has become. Whether at home or in leadership, success without alignment is a hollow victory.

My Reality:
I had everything I thought I wanted: a powerful job, a beautiful family, a life that looked polished in every photo. But beneath the surface, I was exhausted. Not just physically, emotionally, spiritually. I had mastered the art of composure but lost touch with honesty. I wasn't lying to others. I was lying to myself. And that realisation didn't come with fireworks. It came in quiet, disorienting waves. But once I saw it, I couldn't unsee it.

Lived Lesson:
In the silence after we separated, I realised I had succeeded in everything but inner peace, the kind that can't be found in status or titles. That reckoning stung. But it also freed me to rebuild on truth.

And yet, I've seen the same in management teams: leaders with perfect resumes but exhausted souls. The lesson? Realignment isn't weakness. It's wisdom. It's knowing when evolution requires ending, not just enduring.

Make it Real:
Write your own definition of success today, without using job titles, income, or relationship status. Circle every element that reflects your true self versus what others expect of you.

Reflection Prompts:

- In what areas of my life have I been performing success rather than experiencing it?
- What part of my identity feels most afraid of "failure," and what would it take to comfort, not silence, that fear?
- How do I define success when no one is watching, at home or in how I lead?

---

3. The power of present fatherhood

Your child doesn't need your perfection. They need your presence, especially when the picture changes.

Why This Matters:
Fatherhood doesn't end with a breakup, it begins again. Separation is not abandonment unless you make it one. Your

presence, emotional, consistent, loving, is the legacy your child remembers.

And the same is true for those in positions of leadership or care, people don't remember your brilliance, they remember your consistency. In parenting or leading, you don't need to have all the answers. But you do need to show up with your whole self, especially when the picture changes.

My Reality:

I promised myself I'd never be the man who disappeared. But I quickly realised that being present in a new family structure isn't instinctive, it takes intention. There were weeks when I was so afraid of doing it wrong that I almost retreated. But I kept returning to a simple truth: she needed to feel safe, not just cared for. That meant sharing small joys, holding space for big feelings and letting her know, consistently, that love hadn't fractured just because the marriage had.

Lived Lesson:

One evening, she asked, "Are we still a family?" I knelt down, looked her in the eyes and said, "Always. Just a different kind." I wanted that to be the truth, not just in words but in the way we lived. Some days, I get closer. Some days, it's still hard. But that moment became a direction. A quiet promise I continue to walk toward.

That moment taught me what relational safety looks like, something every child deserves, and every team needs. The reassurance that "we're still in this," even if the format changes.

Make it Real:
Start a weekly ritual with your child, however simple. A walk, a story, a note in their lunchbox. Make your love visible and regular.

Reflection Prompts:

- What is one memory I want my child to hold when they think of this chapter of our lives?
- Am I giving them what I longed for at their age or simply repeating the model I inherited?
- Am I confusing provision with presence?

---

4. Let the awakening lead you

Sometimes clarity doesn't arrive as vision, it arrives as ache. And if you follow it with honesty, it'll take you somewhere whole. There comes a moment, after the grief, after the rupture, where a new voice emerges. The one that asks: What patterns brought me here? This is the awakening. The place where endings become teachers. Where pain becomes a portal.

Why This Matters:
Too often, we rush to rebuild, another relationship, another

distraction, another success story. But if you don't pause to reflect, you'll replicate. You'll carry the same dynamics into a new shape. Healing starts with slowing down. With listening to your own evolution.

And the same is true in leadership. We promote, restructure, pivot, without examining the deeper dynamics that led us here. Awakening requires stillness. A slowing down. A listening in. Not just for healing but for transformation. The best leaders don't just rebuild, they reimagine, from a place of honest reckoning.

My Reality:
After the separation, I didn't just lose a relationship, I lost a version of myself. The polished one. The provider. The man who had it all together. And when that version fell away, I met someone quieter. Stiller. Not pushing, just listening. I realised how many roles I'd been performing, not from alignment but from fear. My ego took a hit. I was humbled. But in that humility, I found space to be honest. And in that space, I began to rebuild, truthfully this time.

Lived Lesson:
I journaled for weeks without editing. Just letting the rawness surface, grief, confusion, flickers of peace. On the page, I could be unfiltered. There was no audience to impress, no image to uphold. Just me, a pen and the truth. What emerged wasn't failure but fragments of a self I'd buried under duty. Journaling

became the quiet mirror I didn't know I needed. And from those pages, something new began to take shape not perfect but real.

I now see that reflective practices, whether journaling, coaching, or silent walks, are not luxuries, they're leadership tools. They create space for consciousness to emerge before action takes over.

Make it Real:
Begin a "truth audit." List three beliefs about love success, or fatherhood you've never questioned and ask: Do these still serve me?

Reflection Prompts:

- Who did I become to survive my past? And do I still need him?
- What part of me is waiting for permission to emerge?
- How often do I slow down enough to ask: What's truly mine to carry forward and what belongs to an old version of me?

---

5. Don't let grief become bitterness

When you've been hurt, by life, by love, by yourself, grief can harden. It calcifies into resentment, blame, detachment. But if you want to lead love and father differently, you must learn to grieve well. Bitterness keeps the wound open. Grief lets it close.

Why This Matters:

We're taught to stay strong, keep moving, not dwell. Especially as men. Especially as men of colour. But unprocessed sadness turns into a mask. It resurfaces later as anger, disconnection or silence.

In leadership too, unresolved emotional weight becomes friction, blocking empathy, trust, and genuine connection. Grief isn't weakness. It's maturity. It allows us to close chapters without infecting what comes next. If you don't make peace with what's ended, you'll contaminate what begins.

My Reality:

Some mornings, the sadness arrived before I opened my eyes. Not just about the relationship but about the story I thought we'd live. I wanted to rage. To rationalise. To numb. But my daughter was watching. And I wanted her to see that real strength includes softness. That you can stand tall and still allow yourself to weep for what was lost.

Lived Lesson:

I began naming my grief out loud, not in front of an audience, but in quiet spaces, sometimes on a drive, sometimes late at night in my living room. Saying the words softened their weight. What I had carried silently turned into something acknowledged, something human. And with each naming, I felt a little less bitterness and a little more space for peace.

This taught me a deeper lesson about emotional hygiene, something we don't often talk about in high-performance spaces. But the truth is: soft skills aren't soft. They're survival skills. And grief, when honoured, clears the space for clearer leadership and deeper love.

Make it Real:
Name your grief out loud. To yourself. A friend. A therapist. Name it without apology.

Reflection Prompts:

- What part of my grief have I been silently carrying out of pride or fear?
- What might shift in me, or in my relationships, if I gave that grief the space it deserves.
- Where in my life, home or work, am I leading through a wound that still needs attention?

The Fire Within

You are not broken.
You are rebuilding.

This season is not about shame, it's about responsibility. Quiet, sacred, grown-up responsibility.

To show up even when it hurts.
To let go of what no longer fits.
To stand in the silence and say,
"I'm still here. I'm still choosing. I'm still becoming."

Because wholeness isn't found in perfection.
It's found in the choice to keep loving,
keep learning,
and keep leading, even through the rubble.

PART IV:

BUILDING LEGACY WITHOUT A MAP

13

THE POWER OF A RECLAIMED LIFE

Owning My Past – From Shame to Strength

After the separation, life in Zurich was quieter, quieter than it had ever been. No calls to return. No flights to catch. No partnership to maintain.

The noise I had lived with for so many years, professional urgency, personal tension, was gone.

And in its absence, something unexpected arrived.

Silence.

And in that silence came the one thing I had spent years outpacing: reflection.

At first, it was disorienting. The solitude felt like a spotlight. With nothing to distract me, old questions returned, questions I'd thought I'd buried beneath ambition and achievement.

There are questions that live in your body long before you find the words to ask them.

In the quiet after the separation, when the routines of fatherhood were overlaid with hours of stillness, a different kind of weight began to surface.

Not the pain of what had ended but the deeper, older ache of what had always been missing.

Growing up mixed race in Morley, I had always known I was different but never fully understood what that difference meant. British and Caribbean but with no real connection to the Caribbean side of my identity.

As I moved through boardrooms, business schools and international networks, I began to carry a new kind of awareness. I wasn't just scanning the room for people who looked like me, I was starting to reckon with what it meant when they weren't there.

In the early years, it stung. Not because I lacked pride but because I lacked mirrors. My Jamaican heritage, my working-class Yorkshire roots, my upbringing without a father, all of it felt unspoken in these spaces. And when no one else names your story, you start to wonder if it belongs.

But over time, the pain gave way to clarity. I realised I wasn't alone, I was just one of the quiet ones. In private conversations, I began to hear the echoes: Indian colleagues masking their accent, Eastern Europeans downplaying their upbringing, Middle Eastern peers feeling pressure to downplay their beliefs.

We had walked different roads but the fear was familiar: that where we came from might disqualify us. And for many of us, that quiet fear had become our fuel.

But now, I was beginning to ask a different question: What if our difference isn't a burden to conceal but a foundation to build from?

That question changed everything.

I had spent years navigating rooms without mirrors, learning to belong without a blueprint. And slowly, I began to see that absence didn't mean insignificance. It meant I was walking a path less mapped but no less worthy.

I started to lean into what I *did* know. My Yorkshire roots were firm, practical, structured, no-nonsense. They gave me grit. They gave me form. But my Jamaican side? That was a blank space.

My father had been absent. The stories were absent. The rituals, the language, the anchors that others inherited, I didn't have them. And in that silence, shame found room to grow.

Not shame of who I was. But of what I didn't know.

The missing memories. The cultural compass I never received. The ache of questions left unanswered, passed down like heirlooms.

It wasn't just about my own story anymore.

It was about the stories I had inherited but never been told.

Why was absence so common in families like mine?

Why had I carried such a quiet, corrosive fear of becoming the very thing I swore I wouldn't?

Where did that fear come from and who had taught it to me? For the first time, I wasn't just reflecting on personal choices. I was reckoning with patterns. With history.

I began to dig. Not into my CV or my past achievements but into the past itself.

The systems. The separations. The scars.

I read about the transatlantic slave trade. About how Black families were deliberately fractured. About how absence had been weaponised, used to control, dehumanise and commodify.

And with brutal clarity, I saw it:

This wasn't just my family's pain. It was a pattern. A design.

But then, something shifted.

Maybe it wasn't only pain I had inherited.

Maybe the very fact I was still here, still standing, still striving, was proof of something deeper.

Maybe if I could trace the damage, I could also reclaim the flame.

That's when I took the test.

To answer the question that had haunted me for as long as I could remember:

Where do I come from, really?

Delveland – The Village That Remembered Me

The truth is, the journey didn't begin with a DNA test. It began three years after I met my father, when I flew to Jamaica for the first time in my life.

I was 33.

It was November 2013.

And I wasn't chasing answers, I was searching for a feeling. To listen.

To walk the soil my ancestors had walked.

The first face I saw was his, waiting outside Montego Bay Airport with a quiet pride.

The drive through the hills was long and wild, reggae pouring through the speakers, potholes jolting our bones.

We passed goats, shacks, roadside bars, the island unfiltered and alive.

One track looped in my head for days, Romain Virgo's *Don't You Remember*, a song about love and forgetting.

And somehow, it felt like the island itself was asking me the same thing:

"Don't you remember?"

Then came Delveland, the village where my father was born, tucked in the Parish of Westmoreland, Jamaica, not far from the more famous shores of Negril and its seven-mile beach. Delveland somehow felt like a memory I hadn't lived. Red earth. Breadfruit trees. Laughter that cracked through the air like firewood.

That first night, I met my grandmother, Mrs. Guthrie. Strong and gracious, with hands shaped by hard work and a heart that welcomed me like I had never left. Beside her, Auntie Brenda beamed with joy.

And then came the cousins, forty-five, maybe fifty of them! By the end of the week, it felt like every face I met was family, Shepherds, Lawsons, Fifes, Guthries. I wasn't just meeting relatives. I was meeting reflections.

Each day brought something new. Ackee and plantain in the mornings. Bush tea and dandelion juice with Grandma. Walks through the village with cousins who knew everyone and introduced me to half of them.

One danced like there was no tomorrow and drank like a man with nothing to prove. Another had done 25 years in prison and still greeted me like a nephew. One younger cousin looked so much like me, I could have passed for his father.

I played dominoes by the sea, ate jackfish and jerk chicken straight off the grill, and danced to sound systems that shook zinc rooftops into the night. It was wild, chaotic, beautiful.

But beneath the noise, something ancient stirred. This wasn't just reunion. It was reclamation. I wasn't there to tick a box or take pictures. I was there to remember. Not through fact, but through feeling.

And the feeling was everywhere. In the rhythm of the land. In the rain that fell without apology. In the music that healed and celebrated in the same breath. In the thunder of dominoes on wooden tables. In whispered family names passed from cousin to cousin like sacred history.

That's where the truth began to root itself, not in theory but in lived memory.

There were quiet moments too. Like sitting with my father at sunset, on the terrace of the family home, a bottle of rum between us, Dennis Brown playing through an old speaker. He looked at me and said, "*Every man has fear. The key is knowing how to control yours.*"

He wasn't just talking about courage. He was showing me what it meant to be a man in this lineage. I didn't respond. I didn't need to. Because something in me clicked.

I wasn't just visiting Jamaica. I was claimed by it.

Jamaica didn't explain everything. But it remembered me. And though I didn't yet know the names, I could feel the ancestors moving through that village. Not in history books, but in the dust, the drums, the lilt of laughter beneath breadfruit trees, the echoes of something I had always carried but never known how to name.

Their fire, in my bones.

And in those small, undramatic moments of belonging, something long buried inside me began to rise.

The Bloodline Behind the Silence

Years later, in 2025, I took the DNA test I had been intending to for many years.

Not to trace a family tree. Not to complete some polished narrative of self-discovery.

But to confirm what my spirit already knew, that the pull I'd felt in Jamaica wasn't imagined. It was inherited.

The test itself was simple, a swab, a few forms, a waiting period.

But when the results came back,it wasn't just data on a screen.

It was remembrance made real.

My ancestors were Akan.

They were Igbo.

My bloodline stretched back to Ghana and Nigeria, to tribes and nations whose wisdom predated colonialism and whose resilience was built long before Jamaica even existed.

The Akan, fierce warriors, brilliant strategists, architects of revolt.

The Igbo, poets, philosophers, deeply spiritual people who, when faced with the horror of slavery, often chose death over bondage.

I read about the Igbo Landing, where many took their own lives rather than live in chains.

I felt something ancient and defiant rise within me. A quiet, fierce fire.

The kind you don't learn, you remember.

And I realised: these weren't just stories in a history book. They were mine.

The resilience I had carried through Morley, through rejection, through glass ceilings and broken stereotypes, that was their resilience. Their fire. And it was still burning.

I kept searching.

And one day, years after Jamaica, I stumbled across a name I'd never been taught in school but should have been.

Tacky.

Tacky's Revolt – The Warrior in My DNA

Tacky's Revolt was the largest slave rebellion in 18th-century Jamaica. And where did it take place? Westmoreland. The very same parish my father's family was from. The same red earth I had walked barefoot a decade earlier. The same trees. The same hills.

It sent a jolt through me. Because this land held more than memory, it held resistance.

Tacky, an Akan war captain, enslaved but never defeated, led a revolt that shook the British Empire to its core. Brutality followed, as it always does when power is threatened. But they could not erase his fire. They could not erase his spirit.

And suddenly, everything connected. The blood. The land. The fight.

The Akan in me wasn't just heritage. It was a legacy of resistance. Of refusing to be silenced. Of challenging the structures built to keep us small. Of rising, even when the odds were impossible.

And I saw my own story reflected back. Not with machetes, but with mindset. Not against soldiers, but against systems. Not in shackles, but under pressure.

I had fought to belong in spaces that never expected me. Fought to climb ladders not built for men like me. Fought to stay standing when silence, stereotype and shame tried to knock me down.

This wasn't coincidence. It wasn't just resistance I had inherited. It was identity. A deep, ancestral knowing. Not taught. Not told. But remembered. It was in my DNA.

And when I truly let that truth settle, I thought of him.

A Message to the Boy Who Wondered

And in that moment, I thought of him, that little boy in Morley with skin a shade too dark for the street he lived on, never quite sure where he fit, never fully able to name the ache that set him apart.

The one who smiled through grazes, who kept running with scraped knees and silent questions, all the while just wanting to know where he came from.

I saw him clearly.

And I whispered what he had always longed to hear:

You are not lost. You are not less.

You come from kings and warriors, from visionaries and survivors.

You are not just the echo of endurance, you are the living blueprint of power reclaimed.

He had carried the weight of absence in silence. And now, I could finally lay some of it down. But this journey wasn't only about healing the past. It was also about shaping the future.

A Legacy Reclaimed for Her

And then, I thought of her, my daughter, the one I had promised never to abandon, the one who had brought purpose to my life long before I understood the full depth of where I came from.

When I read the DNA results, when I saw the names Akan and Igbo, I didn't just think about who I was. I thought about who she would get to be.

She wouldn't grow up with the same silence I had. She wouldn't inherit the shame, the confusion, or that quiet fear of not knowing.

Because now I knew and that knowing allowed me to give her something I never had:

A story with roots. Not just a name or a flag, but a flame. A lineage. A legacy.

And in giving her that story, I realised it was more than a gift.

It was a release because in offering her belonging, I found a piece of my own.

No More Shame, Only Strength

For the first time in my life, I let go of the shame.

I no longer saw my story as fragmented or incomplete.

I saw it for what it truly was, a lineage lit from many flames.

British. Jamaican.

Igbo. Akan.

Yorkshire.

Survivor. Fighter. Builder.

Yes, I stood in leadership rooms as an executive, but I stood there carrying centuries of defiance and dignity. I stood on the shoulders of ancestors who had refused to bow their heads, even in the face of chains, injustice and brutality.

And now, at last, I could see it with clarity.

The story of survival wasn't just about getting through Morley, or making it in Paris, or rising in Zurich. It was about honouring everything that had come before me, and using it to light the way for everything that comes next.

Legacy isn't built through perfection.

It's built through truth. Through reclamation. Through remembering.

And in that remembering, I found more than identity.

I found grounding.

A wholeness I never knew was mine to claim not through grand revelations, but through quiet, undramatic moments that whispered, you belong.

In the footsteps I traced through Delveland.

In the sea breeze that touched my face in Negril.

In the sound of my grandmother's laughter, and the rum I shared with my father.

In the thunder of dominoes on wooden tables.

In the names whispered from cousin to cousin like sacred inheritance.

That was where the truth began to root itself not in theory, but in lived memory.

And in those moments, something long buried inside me began to rise.

Not pride, not certainty, but a quieter kind of wholeness the kind that no longer needs to prove itself.

Because now I understood.

You are not weak for wondering where you come from.

You are strong for seeking.

And you are not broken because your story began in silence.

You are whole because you chose to break it.

The Blueprint – Chapter 13: The Strength Beneath the Silence

Key Truth

"Heritage is not just what you remember, it's what remembers you."

Quote

"A people without the knowledge of their past history, origin and culture is like a tree without roots." - Marcus Garvey

---

Theme: Reclaiming Identity Through Ancestral Connection

Sometimes, what we need most isn't more advice or achievement.
It's a story that tells us we're not alone.
That we are not accidents or outliers but living blueprints, sketched by survival, resilience and love passed through generations.
For years, I believed identity had to be earned, through polish, performance, proximity to power.
But the deepest kind of belonging doesn't come from reaching forward.
It comes from reaching back.
Sometimes the silence we carry isn't abstract, it's geographic.
A land we've never stood on. A story we've never heard told in our own voice.

For me, it was Jamaica. And when I finally went, I didn't just connect the dots, I felt them.
In the red earth. The mango trees. The music. The laughter.
That's where the silence first cracked open.

This chapter's Blueprint is for anyone who's felt like they were walking a path no one else could see.
For anyone with gaps in their story.
For anyone born between cultures, names and nations, wondering if silence was all they inherited.
It wasn't.
There is structure in your story.
There is wisdom in your roots.
There is strength beneath the silence.

---

1. Begin where the silence is loudest

Your origins aren't lost, they're waiting.
Silence isn't absence. It's unspoken memory, calling you to listen. What feels like emptiness may actually be sacred space, urging you to ask, feel and remember what was never written down but still lives in your bones.

Why This Matters:
We live in cultures that glorify forward motion but rarely honour what's missing. For those of us with fractured beginnings, due to race, class, migration, or family rupture,

silence can feel like proof we don't belong. But it's also a doorway. Your healing begins where your story once disappeared.

In leadership and life, what you haven't been told is just as important as what you have. Emotional intelligence, identity confidence and deep listening are born when you learn to pay attention to what hasn't been spoken. True belonging often starts with the bravery to ask a question no one else has asked yet.

My Reality:
I avoided the questions for years. Who was my father really? What did it mean to be Jamaican beyond the music and myth? But when I finally stepped into the silence, through Jamaica, through the DNA test, through ancestral study, I began to fill it not with answers but with understanding.

Lived Lesson:
It wasn't the DNA test that cracked something open. It was the sound of dominoes slamming on a table in Delveland. It was my grandmother's hands. It was laughter echoing through mango trees. That was the beginning, not of information but of remembrance. And it taught me something I now carry into leadership: when you make space for what's been silenced, people start to breathe again.

Make it Real:
Write down one question about your origins that you've never dared to ask.

Take one step toward it this month, call a relative, trace a map, cook a traditional dish. Begin. Not with facts. With feeling.

Reflection Prompts:

- What silence are you afraid to break and who taught you it was safer not to ask?
- If your story begins before words, what does your body already know?
- Where in your personal or professional life is silence holding back belonging or growth?

---

2. Investigate the inheritance

You're carrying more than your own story.
To redesign your life, you must first know what you've inherited. From emotional instincts to historical burdens, recognising what was passed down allows you to -transform unconscious repetition into conscious legacy.

Why This Matters:
Marginalised identities are often taught to survive, not to reflect. But unexamined inheritance becomes unconscious

repetition. In both family systems and leadership cultures, we often pass down patterns without naming them.
When you investigate your emotional and ancestral lineage, you unlock not just personal healing but also powerful behavioural insight, why you lead the way you do, where your instincts come from and which inherited traits are worth keeping.

My Reality:
As I read about the transatlantic slave trade, *Tacky's Revolt* and the systematic dismantling of Black families, I began to see the origin of the fear I'd carried my whole life. The silence. The shame. The instinct to hide. It didn't start with me. But neither did the strength. That fire was inherited too and it was time I recognised both.

Lived Lesson:
Learning about Tacky's Revolt, which began in the very same region of Jamaica where my father's family came from. That proximity floored me. These weren't distant ancestors in abstract rebellion. These were my great, great grandfathers and grandmothers, people who almost certainly resisted, fought, refused to be broken. Suddenly, my own instinct to protect dignity, to stand tall in the face of erasure, it didn't feel like defiance. It felt like inheritance. That clarity helps me lead differently now: not from performance, but from legacy.

Make it Real:
List 3 emotional patterns you've inherited around love, trust, masculinity or identity.

Ask: "Is this mine to carry, or someone else's survival?"

Reflection Prompts:

- Whose silence have you unconsciously inherited?
- What buried strength in your lineage are you ready to name?
- What personal or ancestral pattern influences how you lead, connect, or protect today?

---

3. Reframe your definition of heritage

Heritage isn't just about facts or family trees. It's about the deeper imprint, what lives in your instincts, your values, your way of moving through the world. Even if the details are missing, something in you still remembers. Resilience, rhythm, and rituals can carry the wisdom of generations.

Why This Matters:
When your history has been erased, distorted, or ignored, it's easy to feel disconnected from culture. But culture is more than history, it's instinct. Heritage lives in you, not just in facts but in how you nurture, resist, create and connect.

As a leader, this matters too. Knowing where you come from, emotionally and culturally, helps you lead from truth, not mimicry. It builds authentic presence that others can feel, even if they don't know your story.

My Reality:
I didn't grow up with stories of my Jamaican family. But when I landed in Delveland, something clicked. The way I stood. The way I watched. The way I felt seen. It wasn't about facts, it was about fire. I knew I belonged because my body remembered what my mind had forgotten.

Lived Lesson:
Drinking bush tea with my grandmother under the stars, I realised: this was heritage. Not the family tree. But the gaze. The gestures. The grace. The love that didn't ask me to explain. And the same is true in leadership: presence can carry more weight than presentation. Truth resonates without needing to explain.

Make it Real:
List 3 inner strengths that helped you survive. Could these be ancestral? Who else might have lived like this? Name the trait and the ancestor it might come from.

Reflection Prompts:

- Have you mistaken lack of data for lack of belonging?
- What parts of your culture are already alive in you, waiting to be named?
- Where are you overcompensating with performance instead of leading from embodied heritage?

---

4. You don't have to choose between identities

Mixed heritage. Immigrant background. First-generation complexity. For many of us, identity isn't a clear lane, it's a tightrope. But you don't have to choose. The fusion is your power. The convergence is your home.

Why This Matters:
The world often wants you in a box: either/or. But you are both/and. When you stop trying to fit and start standing fully in your blend, you reclaim your agency. You show others that wholeness doesn't need simplification, it needs honour. In life and leadership, integration creates insight. Multicultural, multi-class, and multi-lingual experience is an asset, not an anomaly.

My Reality:
I didn't sound Jamaican. I wasn't fluent in French. I had

Yorkshire grit but moved in elite Swiss rooms. For years, I felt not enough of anything. But when I stopped splitting myself and started integrating, I finally felt at home, in me.

Lived Lesson:

At our St. Moritz wedding: Swiss precision, Caribbean rhythm, Northern warmth. I wasn't torn between worlds. I was the one weaving them. And now, in every room I enter, I bring that fusion. It's not about translation. It's about embodiment. Wholeness is visible when you stop editing yourself.

Make it Real:

Create a Fusion Map, list the cultures, classes and codes you straddle. Write one strength from each. Introduce yourself not as fragmented but as fused.

Reflection Prompts:

- Where have you shrunk or split to fit in?
- What would it feel like to live as someone who belongs everywhere?
- How would your leadership change if you viewed every part of your identity as an advantage?

---

5. Heal the boy / girl who wondered

Your younger self doesn't need you to be perfect. They just needs to know they mattered. When you speak to the child within, with honesty, compassion and presence, you don't rewrite the past but you restore the dignity that silence once erased.

Why This Matters:
Childhood confusion often becomes adult shame. But healing doesn't require a time machine. It requires your voice now. When you speak to the child you once were, with honesty, with pride, you end the silence for good.

My Reality:
I once wondered where I came from. Why no one claimed me. But sitting beside my father in Delveland, holding rum and listening to reggae, I knew: I had always been someone's grandson. Someone's legacy. I had always belonged. If you never received the love, affirmation or recognition you needed as a child, offering it now becomes a powerful act of self-leadership. It also deepens empathy: the more compassion you show to your younger self, the more compassion you offer others, especially those you lead, mentor or raise.

Lived Lesson:
Writing this book became the way I healed him, the boy who wondered if he mattered. Every story I've told, every silence

I've broken, has been a way to reach back through time and say: you were never invisible. You were always part of something bigger. With each word, I've laid down a path, not just for my daughter but for the younger me who once felt unclaimed. This book is his legacy too.

Make it Real:
Honour your younger self this week: write, speak, or share your journey with someone else. Let it remind you: you're not just surviving your past. You're reshaping its meaning.

Reflection Prompts:

- What part of your past still needs to be acknowledged, not to fix it but to honour it?
- What legacy would your younger self be proud you're building?
- In what ways can you model dignity and compassion, for yourself and for others still seeking belonging?

What Jamaica Gave Back to Me:

Legacy isn't just what we build.
It's what we remember.
The names we reclaim.

The silences we speak into.
The children we raise with stories we never had.

To be mixed, to be descended from many worlds,
is not a fracture.
It's a structure.

You are not confusion.
You are continuity.

And when you name your inheritance with pride,
you don't just carry the blueprint,
you become it.
Living, breathing, building.
For those who came before.
For those still to come.
And for the child within who waited so long to feel at home.

14

FROM SHAME TO WHOLENESS

THE SEASON OF BECOMING

After all the chasing, all the striving, all the forward motion, life finally slowed. No flights to catch, no deadlines to dominate, no partner to appease.

Just me, back in Zurich, ten minutes from my daughter.

The silence was deafening at first. Like the aftermath of a storm I hadn't realised had passed.

I wasn't used to the quiet. But in that stillness, I finally heard the truth I'd been outrunning for decades.

I had lived at full tilt, pushing, pleasing, performing.

Now… I had to feel.

And feeling isn't easy when you've spent a lifetime armoured up.

That first year after the separation was one of the hardest of my life. Even though the decision had been made, its echoes reached into everything.

The structure of my days, the rhythm of my emotions, the hollow spaces where laughter used to live.

Yet something else began to stir.

I had already been working with Gary, my psychologist, for a year before the split. At first, I went on the advice of our couples therapist. But I stayed because I realised how much I needed what he offered.

A space to speak freely, to unravel years of silent weight.

Gary wasn't just any therapist.

He was a graduate of the C.G. Jung Institute, trained in Zurich, where he'd lived and practised since 1990.

Fluent in German, fully assimilated, yet unmistakably a New Yorker, with a dry wit, a razor-sharp mind and that unmistakable New World candour.

He was in his sixties but still rode his bike everywhere, swept-back white hair and sharp eyes that carried both wisdom and mischief. There was a twinkle behind the intensity. A man who had lived deeply and read people even deeper. It made perfect sense, in hindsight, that he specialised in the psychology of the father. He never said it outright but I knew he could see straight through my bluster, my social confidence, my armour.

His office was spare but warm, leather chairs, a Persian carpet, walls lined with books.

There were two single windows looking out over the gardens of this residential area of Zurich's Kreis 7 - but most days we didn't need the view.

Because the real scenery was inside me.

And Gary was a guide who never rushed the journey.

Some days, I spoke constantly. Other days, I sat in brief silence while he watched, patiently.

He never pushed. Just waited.

But it was in that quiet, after weeks of circling the same unresolved feelings, that he finally leaned forward, legs crossed, hands steepled and said:

"Ashley, it's not your job to be perfect. It's your job to be whole.

Instead of over-thinking and analysing everything before you respond, learn to listen to your heart and lead with your feelings."

He didn't raise his voice.

But the line landed like thunder.

I tried to shift in my chair, clear my throat, even smiled, as if charm might undo whatever was stirring.

My chest tightened and for a moment I looked away, eyes tracing the spines of his books, searching for something to hold onto.

I felt the heat rise, that old instinct to shut it down, to out-think it.

But this time, I didn't win.

The tears came. Not loud, not dramatic. Just a quiet betrayal, a glint in the eye, a breath held too long.

Enough for Gary to see that the armour had finally cracked.

I didn't break down. But something broke open.

And Gary… he didn't flinch. He just sat there, steady as ever, his face soft but unchanging. Holding the space like a father would.

Not trying to fix it. Just letting me feel it.

It cut through decades of conditioning.

All my life, I'd measured myself against a silent standard, trying to prove I was smart enough, polished enough, acceptable enough.

But in that moment, I realised: I didn't need more polishing. I needed more presence.

I didn't need to be perfect. I needed to be real.

As I stood to leave, Gary looked at me firmly in the eyes,

"That," he said quietly, "was real."

Just three words. But they echoed louder than any praise I'd ever chased.

And for once, I didn't deflect. I didn't perform. I just let them in.

I left the session with my head in a spin, disoriented, exposed, yet somehow lighter.

Something in me had changed.

Changed for the better.

I began letting go of the performance.

Stopped shaping myself to fit the room.

Whether I was walking into meetings or standing at the school gates, I showed up with less armour and more honesty.

And slowly, I started to believe that the man I was, Leeds and Jamaica, executive and council house, disciplined and deeply emotional, was just acceptable.

He was enough.

More than enough.

Together, Gary and I unpacked the old scripts. The quiet contracts I'd signed with the world: The need to overachieve to feel accepted. The belief I had to edit my identity to belong in elite rooms.

I saw it clearly, how often I softened "Leeds" to "Yorkshire," how often i said "the Caribbean" when I meant "Jamaica," just in case the names triggered discomfort or judgement. I hadn't even noticed I was still doing it, still rounding off the edges, still adjusting who I was to stay in the rooms I had fought so hard to enter.

But now, there was nothing left to hide.

It wasn't a dramatic revelation. It came quietly, during one of those sessions.

"*There are seasons in life*," Gary said. Not everything is meant to bloom forever. Some seasons are for building. Some are for breaking. And some, like this one, are for becoming.

It landed softly, but deeply. For so long, I had lived like it was always summer. Always moving forward. Always performing. Always proving.

But now I could see: growth doesn't always roar. Sometimes it's stillness. Sometimes it's unlearning. Sometimes it's the quiet act of no longer running.

This was the season of becoming. Of sitting confidently in myself.

Not because I had all the answers, but because I had stopped asking others to define me.

I no longer felt the need to explain where I was from. I stopped softening the truth. No more swapping Leeds for Yorkshire or hiding Jamaica behind the safer vagueness of "the Caribbean."

I told it straight.

In rooms where I used to perform, I began to speak plainly. "I was raised by a single mother,"

"I come from a working-class town – Morley, near Leeds. We lived in a terrace so tight you could hear the neighbours sneeze."

And the response?

Nothing bad happened.

In fact, the opposite.

People leaned in. They listened. And in that honesty, they recognised something of themselves. My truth gave them permission to share theirs. Because when truth is rooted in love and pride, it becomes more than vulnerability. It becomes power.

For the first time, I wasn't trying to pass. I wasn't trying to impress. I wasn't trying to perform.

I was just being… me.

And in that, I found something I'd been chasing all along: peace.

I thought back to my mum, raising me alone, holding the line with grit and dreams.

I used to think I had to make her proud through achievement.

Climbing. Proving. Winning.

But now I see: becoming whole was the deeper honour.

She never got the chance to rest. Never had the space to unravel, to just be.

But maybe, through me, that cycle ends.

Maybe wholeness is the real legacy I can offer back to the woman who gave me the fire to begin with.

Not just success.

Wholeness.

And so I entered a new season.

Not of proving or performing but of becoming. Becoming myself.

Fully. Quietly. Proudly.

Intentional Fatherhood

This is what fatherhood looks like when it's built on presence, not performance.

The deepest joy, the most transformational light in this season, was my daughter.

In the midst of unravelling one kind of family, we began building another.

Not broken. Just reimagined.

Co-parenting isn't easy, but when it's led with love, it can create something whole in a new way.

That summer, we spent time in the UK, visiting my mum, my sister Maria, my niece, and the Shortes. But this time was different. This time, I saw it all through her eyes.

We started in London. For a child raised between Zurich, St. Moritz, and Dubai, the Underground was a revelation. I held her hand tightly as we boarded the tube at King's Cross, explaining how to mind the gap and stand behind the yellow line. She looked up at me, wide-eyed and curious, as if we were stepping into a different world. And in many ways, we were.

We emerged at Green Park and wandered toward Buckingham Palace. And just as we reached the gates, the sound of drums filled the air. Changing of the Guard. A complete coincidence, or maybe not.

I had never seen it before either. And there we stood, father and daughter, watching the pageantry of Britain unfold just months before the Queen passed away.

It felt symbolic, witnessing history together.

We walked through South Kensington, wandered through Harrods and ended the day at the Natural History Museum.

The moment our daughter saw the towering skeleton of Dippy the Diplodocus, her eyes sparkled with wonder.

She gripped my hand tighter.

And I realised, this was what I had longed for.

To be the kind of father who could show his daughter the world.

To give her a memory that would live forever, not just in photos, but in feeling.

We ended the day in Birmingham, staying in a small hotel, her still buzzing with energy, me quietly reflecting on the gift of the day.

The next morning, I took her on a different kind of tour.

I showed her every flat, every house, every room I had once called home during my years in Birmingham. From the student digs with damp ceilings and dodgy locks, to the slightly nicer flats as life progressed. My daughter processing everything in her wonderfully curious mind.

At first, she was shocked. But then… she smiled. As if she could sense the journey I'd been on.

As if she was walking it with me, step by step.

And then, as if the universe wanted to underline it all, we arrived in Centenary Square.

Jamaica Day.

Unplanned. Unbelievable.

Music thumped through the city centre. Flags waved. Dancers leapt.

On Jamaica's National Day in Centenary Square, we stood in the heart of it all, two generations deep in celebration, in pride, in presence.

My daughter wore her little Commonwealth Games and Jamaican wristbands and clapped along, eyes wide, soaking it all in.

The colours, the rhythm, the warmth of it.

I had tears in my eyes.

Not just for the culture.

But because she was seeing it.

Feeling it.

Knowing it was hers too.

It wasn't a moment I planned.

It was one the universe delivered.

Birmingham, the city where I had once struggled, once hustled to survive. The city where my father arrived from Jamaica as a boy, wide-eyed and hopeful, stepping into a country that didn't always welcome him.

And decades later at university, unknowingly, I had walked his streets, retraced parts of his journey, carried his silence.

And now here I was, with my daughter, on Jamaican Independence Day, standing in a crowd of flags and music and laughter.

Not as a boy trying to find his place.

But as a man offering her one.

That evening, we made our way to Alexander Stadium for the Commonwealth Games. A rebuilt arena not far from Perry Barr, near where I'd once studied and struggled. As we walked up the entrance, the summer light casting long shadows, the roar of 30,000 people thundered around us.

The energy was electric.

And then it happened.

Jamaica's women sprinted to gold.

The crowd erupted.

A wave of sound, of pride, of shared identity.

My daughter turned to me, eyes wide, and said softly,

"Pappy… is this all for Jamaica?"

I didn't know how to answer.

Because in that moment, it felt like it was.

For Jamaica.

For Birmingham.

For my father.

For all we were.

And all she would become.

It wasn't just British pride or Jamaican identity.

It was a convergence.

And through her, it all made sense.

We left Birmingham with full hearts and tired feet, but the journey wasn't over.

We returned to Morley, my hometown, my roots, where life slowed again.

No fanfare. No stadium roars. Just home.

My daughter helped my mum paint the garden fence at the house I'd helped her buy two decades earlier. Brush in hand, laughter in the air, it felt like a quiet kind of legacy.

My sister Maria came over with little Amaya and we all spilled into the garden together. We played catch under Yorkshire skies, my daughter feeding her cousin tea with careful hands, Yorkshire-style, of course.

Then came Stockeld Park in North Yorkshire, full of shrieks and silliness with James and Adam her "uncles." And finally, a visit to "Uncle" Ryan's house, where my daughter tore across the garden in a makeshift race. The same kind of race he, James and I once ran thirty-five years earlier in the yard outside our childhood homes.

It was more than a visit.

It was a homecoming.

A quiet mending of something I hadn't known was still frayed.

Because in those sun-drenched days with my daughter, my mother, my sister, my brothers from another mother…

I felt it.

That deep ache of never having had a "proper" family, not erased, but healed.

Not through performance.

But through presence.

We flew back to Zurich not long after, but something had shifted.

That trip had anchored us both.

My daughter had seen where I came from, walked my streets, met my people, tasted my childhood.

And I had seen what it meant to share it all, not as a story, but as a living experience.

We didn't need luxury or perfection.

We just needed time.

Together.

And back home, it was the quiet moments that carried the deepest magic.

The rituals.

The rhythm of our days.

The kind of ordinary that makes a childhood feel extraordinary.

This is what fatherhood looked like now.

Not grand gestures. Not Instagram-worthy moments.

Just quiet joy. Ordinary magic.

We became detectives, her and I. Solving mysteries around the flat, looking for invisible clues, making up cases that only she could crack. We had official voices and secret handshakes. And somehow, every case ended with a play-fight, then a cuddle.

Bedtime was its own adventure.

She'd leap onto my back as I became the horse, galloping from the living room to her bedroom.

Trotting, neighing, nearly pulling a hamstring, her laughter echoing through the halls.

Then came the wind-down.

She'd snuggle into her bed, her hand still on my arm.

Sometimes she'd ask me to stay a little longer.

Sometimes we'd whisper about the day, or make up dreams for the night ahead.

And sometimes, we'd just sit there in the soft glow of the nightlight, saying nothing.

No deadlines.

No demands.

Just presence.

That was the whole point.

Not just showing up.

But staying.

Being silly.

Being safe.

Being proud.

Being hers.

The Season of Return

Something shifted in that second year. The ache of separation still sat in my chest, but slowly, life began to open in gentler ways. The inner reckoning I had walked through with Gary was only half the story.

The other was this: the quiet power of friendship.

The season of return.

I began travelling back to the UK more often, not for business, not to escape - but to belong. To laugh in that specific way you only can with people who knew you before the striving.

Before the polish.

To speak in a shorthand built over decades, single words that carried whole conversations, memories, meanings.

I spent long, grounding hours with James, my brother in everything but blood. We've walked through every chapter of life side by side, sometimes in sync, sometimes at odds, always with love.

From Leeds to Zurich, from garage sets to funk & soul anthems, from tears of laughter to nights that stitched new memories into old ones, ours is a bond no distance, no mistake, no time could break.

Time with Ryan and Adam too, now fathers, present and proud, filled me with quiet pride.

We came from two terraced houses in a tough working-class area.

No inheritance. No roadmap. Just rhythm, resilience, and each other.

Brothers who were never meant to make it this far, and still somehow, we rose.

And it wasn't just the brothers.

I watched Maria grow stronger as a mother and Amaya blossom into her own joy.

Their presence reminded me of what I had almost lost in the pursuit of more.

Then there was Dan.

Old friend, soul anchor, fellow fool and philosopher. He drove over from the UK, just because he could.

He pulled in behind the wheel of something Bond might drive, I turned up in a machine that growled like it had just left Modena. Two ageing lads in midlife sports cars, convoying our way to Austria like we were filming a forgotten *Top Gear* special. Windows down. Jokes flying. Rhythm returning.

It was our time, just us, catching up on everything and nothing. Talking deeply. Laughing louder.

Rebuilding the rhythm of a friendship that had never really left, just paused.

Twice a year, we met again at Twickenham.

Rituals of rugby, reunion. Mickey, Jonny, Cal, Ben and the barely contained chaos of the full NORS crew.

Old schoolmates turned lifelines.

Beneath the banter and the beer, something sacred held it all together.

A shared history. A shorthand.

A tether to the boy I once was, held by those who had seen it all.

Back in Zurich, there were other anchors.

My daughter's wonderful godparents and their daughter became part of our extended rhythm of family. Afternoons with my wonderful goddaughter, her fun and cheeky little sister and their fantastic parents, filling the room with laughter and life. Cooking lessons with Christian turned my kitchen into a place of patience and presence. Drinks after work with Ben, Chris, Matthias, small moments that built something sturdy and unseen: the feeling of being known.

And then, after more than a decade away, I did something unexpected. I laced up my boots and returned to rugby. Same club: Grasshopper Club Zürich. Same colours. Slightly older knees.

I wasn't exactly first on the team sheet - sometimes I was lucky just to make the bench for the 2nd team -but I loved every second of it. The camaraderie. The chaos. The coach journeys home, where banter flowed and egos were left at the touchline. Our 2nd team would go on to win the league that year, with the occasional cameo from me, usually off the bench and always good for giving away a penalty or a decent pep talk at least!

But it wasn't really about the minutes played. It was about something else entirely. Passing on whatever scraps of wisdom I'd gathered across two decades in the game. Encouraging the next generation. Being part of something bigger than myself again.

Looking back now, with the hindsight this book has gifted me, I can see it clearly: rugby has quietly marked some of the happiest and most grounded seasons of my life. When I've felt most anchored, most connected, most *me* - there's usually been a rugby pitch somewhere nearby.

It's probably no coincidence that one of the people who showed up for me most during this time was also someone who understood that rhythm.

Simon, former Partner at Korn Ferry, mentor, friend, carried that same rugby soul. Fierce in principle, loyal in practice and always ready with a steady word or a sharp insight when it mattered most.

His marriage to Sandy, the warmth of their home, the easy laughter around their dinner table, it all felt like the kind of love that didn't need a spotlight to shine.

Their boys moved through the world with kindness, confidence, and a steady stream of anti-Yorkshire banter. Simon, being from Lancashire (a flaw I've graciously chosen to overlook), kept the Roses rivalry alive, one dry remark at a time.

But beneath the teasing was something rare: quiet strength, sound advice and unwavering belief when it mattered most.

Looking back, I see now what I couldn't name then. That for more than a decade, I had lived at the centre of my own show. Performance masked as leadership.

Presence diluted by pressure. And somewhere along the way, I had mistaken self-sufficiency for strength.

But in this season, something softened. Joy was no longer a solo pursuit. Love, no longer a battlefield.

I stopped trying to earn my place in every room, and started feeling held by the ones I was already in.

Was this healing?

Was it the slow unravelling of my avoidant attachment, the lonely island finally building a bridge?

Maybe.

Or maybe it was simply this: Wholeness doesn't arrive in a blaze of insight. It gathers quietly, in the company of others.

In those ordinary, unremarkable moments, laughter that needs no explanation.

Meals shared without masks.

Friendships that hold through silence.

And family, chosen or given, who show up when your hands are too tired to reach. That's when I finally understood what I had been searching for all along.

Not applause. Not arrival. But the chance to become the kind of man I had needed growing up.

And what I now know, with humbling clarity, is just how close that chance came to slipping away.

My mother had signed the adoption papers. A family had been chosen. And for the first two days of my life, I lay in a different ward, unnamed, untouched and unknowingly awaiting a life that would never come to pass.

But then she held me. And in that quiet, defiant act of love, everything changed.

That moment didn't just alter the course of her life, it created mine.

Legacy, for me, did not begin with inheritance. It began with interruption. Her refusal to let go became the first act of cycle-breaking I would spend a lifetime learning how to honour.

The Role Model I Needed

Legacy is not what you leave behind.

It is who you choose to become.

I once thought being a role model meant achieving more. Winning, breaking barriers, building an empire.

But now I see it differently.

It means becoming someone whole enough that others do not have to fracture to follow.

Not perfect, not polished, just real.

Rooted.

It means turning inward instead of outward, healing old wounds so they are not passed on.

Owning your story, so your child - and the world -can learn what it means to live with truth.

It means taking the pain and shame that once tried to define you, and turning it into something your child can stand on. Breaking cycles without bitterness.

Choosing love over legacy, not the legacy you were given, but the one you are now creating.

It means showing up every day with intention, even when no one is watching.

And then it came to me, the truth had eluded me for most of my life: You cannot give your child what you never had, unless you become it first.

This book, this journey, it's not just for my daughter. It is for Maria too.

My baby sister, now a mother herself, carrying the same weight our mum once shouldered. I see her strength, her joy, her tenderness and I want her to know, it is not too late to choose a different rhythm.

This is not just my story. It is a blueprint, hand-drawn through trial and tenderness, passed gently across the table, from one soul who has walked through the fire, to another, ready to rise.

If you grew up without a father, without a guide, without someone to model strength, softness or presence, you still get to become that person.

Not just for your children, but for your community. For the next generation who needs to see someone like you stand tall, rooted, loving and real.

And that is what I have been learning to do, one quiet evening, one tearful session, one bedtime gallop at a time.

I am not striving anymore. I am living. A life grounded not in perfection, but in presence. And that, I finally realised, is the greatest success of all.

The Blueprint – Chapter 14: From Shame to Wholeness

Key Truth

"Perfection polishes. Wholeness roots."

Quote

"It's not your job to be perfect. It's your job to be whole."
- *Gary* (my therapist!)

Theme: Wholeness Over Perfection

There's a difference between healing and hiding.
For years, I thought I was doing the former, pushing forward, breaking ceilings, staying strong.
But it wasn't healing. It was performing.

It took losing the structure of the life I'd built, marriage, momentum, identity wrapped in success, to even begin the deeper work. In truth, it also took being humbled. Stripped of certainty. Ego softened. Only then could I start rebuilding from the inside out.

Because when the noise fades and the striving stops, you're left with one question:
Who am I when I'm no longer proving myself to the world?

Wholeness isn't about fixing what's broken.
It's about reclaiming every part of yourself, light and shadow, strength and softness, lineage and loss.

This blueprint isn't for the person chasing their next milestone. It's for the one sitting in the stillness, wondering what it means to live without the mask.
It's for you, if you're ready to stop striving and start becoming.

---

1. Choose wholeness over perfection

Perfection polishes. Wholeness roots.
We polish ourselves for applause but roots are what hold us steady when the applause fades. In elite cultures, especially those marked by performance and absence, we learn to lead with image, not intimacy. But presence requires vulnerability and vulnerability is how we finally come home to ourselves.

Why This Matters:
We're conditioned to believe that flawlessness earns acceptance, especially in spaces where we've felt like outsiders. But perfection is a mask; wholeness is a mirror.
In leadership and life, people don't follow polish. They follow truth. Vulnerability, self-awareness and identity confidence build trust in others and strength within ourselves. Wholeness makes room for our full humanity.

My Reality:
For years I performed perfection, editing my roots, softening my story, anticipating judgement. But the more I polished, the more disconnected I became. It wasn't until therapy with Gary

and his words, *"It's not your job to be perfect. It's your job to be whole. Stop thinking. Start to feel."*, that I began to understand who I really was.

Lived Lesson:

The first time I stopped softening "Jamaica" to "the Caribbean" in a corporate room, I held my breath. I expected discomfort. But instead, people leaned in. Not because it was smooth but because it was true. And that moment gave me something I hadn't had before: Proof that my truth belonged in the room. It gave me the confidence to keep showing up fully, not as a version, but as a whole.

Make it Real:

Choose one relationship where you've been performing. This week, share one truth you've been hiding, a background detail, a feeling, a fear. Say it simply. Then stay present.

Reflection Prompts:

- Where in your life are you still rehearsing a role rather than revealing your truth?
- What would it look like to lead not with your strengths but with your story?
- Where in your work or relationships are you polishing instead of grounding?

2. You can't break the cycle until you see it

We don't just inherit bloodlines, we inherit strategies. Performing instead of expressing. Shrinking to be accepted. Changing our tone to avoid discomfort. You can't break what you refuse to see. Naming the cycle is the first act of resistance.

Why This Matters:
Cycles persist in silence. Whether in families, communities or corporate cultures, the patterns we don't name get repeated. Especially in elite or marginalised contexts, code-switching, perfectionism and silence can feel like survival. But over time, they become self-erasure.
Leaders who recognise and interrupt those patterns model something radical: freedom.

My Reality:
I caught myself softening my background without even realising, changing words, shielding others from the sharp edges of my story. But every time I did that, I passed down silence. I taught my daughter that parts of us needed hiding. And that's when I knew: the cycle had to end with me.

Lived Lesson:
At the Birmingham Commonwealth Games, watching my daughter beam with Jamaican pride, I felt the full cost of what I'd once hidden and the full joy of what I was now reclaiming. I had made my past more "palatable," trying to ease

discomfort. But in doing so, I was reinforcing the very shame I wanted to overcome. Watching my daughter celebrate her roots with unfiltered joy made it clear: I couldn't pass down pride until I stopped handing down silence.

Make it Real:

Write down three ways you've made your identity more "acceptable" in elite or unfamiliar spaces. Now write how those same traits are actually sources of power and pride. Practise saying them aloud, unfiltered, unapologetically.

Reflection Prompts:

- What parts of your story have you dulled down to protect others from discomfort?
- What might shift if you let those truths shine?
- What inherited behaviours or strategies have shaped how you lead, love, or belong?

---

3. There are seasons in life, let this one shape you

Stillness is not stagnation. Some seasons don't produce fruit. They prune. They prepare.
And they teach you what growth never could: how to listen to your life.

Why This Matters:

Stillness is not weakness, it's wisdom. But in a world built on motion and metrics, we often confuse reflection with failure. The most transformational leaders know how to pause, reassess, and grow in seasons of pruning, not just performance.

Your quiet seasons may be the ones that shape your integrity, empathy and emotional clarity the most.

My Reality:

The quiet after separation felt empty at first. But in therapy, in co-parenting, in walking slower, I discovered truths I'd spent years outrunning. The version of me that emerged from that stillness wasn't shinier. He was truer.

Lived Lesson:

Sitting in Gary's office, silence hung between us, not empty but alive. It was in those pauses, after he'd asked a question or surfaced a memory, that the real shifts happened. A fragment of a dream. A line from childhood. A buried belief suddenly rising to the surface. Those weren't gaps in the conversation, they were portals. And what emerged from them changed everything.

Leadership is the same, sometimes you hold the space rather than fill it. The version of me that emerged in the stillness wasn't shinier. He was more rooted.

Make it Real:
Identify what season you're in right now, harvest, healing, pruning, planting. Ask: What does this season require of me? More doing, or more listening?

Reflection Prompts:

- Becoming doesn't require blooming. What is this season teaching you… that speed never could?
- How are you letting this season refine you, not just advance you?

---

4. You can become what you never had

Absence shapes us but it doesn't define us. You may not have had a father, mentor or guide. But that gap is not your sentence. It's your invitation. You can become the anchor you once longed for.

Why This Matters:
We say you can't give what you never got. But that's only half true. You can build it. You can live it. You can become it and give it in a form more real than memory.

This is how generational trauma ends: not just through therapy or awareness but through action. And in doing so, we redefine leadership itself, not as status, but as service born from empathy and intention.

My Reality:

I had no blueprint for fatherhood. But galloping like a horse through the hallway, doing voices at bedtime, holding her when she cried, that became the blueprint. I wasn't just giving my daughter the dad I never had. I was becoming him.

Lived Lesson:

There was no manual. Just small moments. My daughter's laughter echoing through Centenary Square, her trust in my arms, those became the blueprint. I wasn't just giving her something new. I was repairing something old. And that's the work of legacy: not perfecting but healing forward.

Make it Real:

Think of one way you wished someone had shown up for you, emotionally, practically, spiritually. Now do that for someone else. This week. Without fanfare. With full heart.

Reflection Prompts:

- What moment this week can you turn into a legacy, not by doing it perfectly but by doing it with love?
- Who are you becoming through your actions today and what blueprint are you leaving behind?

What Wholeness Means:

You don't have to be perfect to be powerful.
You don't need to rewrite your story to inspire others, you just need to own it.
Because when you stop striving and start standing in your truth, you light a path for others to follow.

From shame to strength. From fragments to fullness. From pain to peace.

This is *your* season of becoming.

15

A MESSAGE TO THOSE WHO FEEL DIFFERENT

For a long time, I believed my story was just about me. The battles I fought. The doors I pushed open. The identity I wrestled with.

But now I see, this story isn't mine alone.

It belongs to anyone who has ever felt different. Anyone who's looked around and asked, *Where do I fit in?* Anyone who's carried questions about their past, their identity, their place in the world.

Maybe you've felt like an outsider, because of your race, your background, your family structure, your voice, your name. Maybe the world didn't make room for you.

Different accents. Different surnames. Different reasons.

But the ache is familiar. So is the quiet fire it can spark.

To those who've sat in a meeting and questioned their right to be there.

To those who've looked up in their company and seen no one who looked like them.

To those who've felt like the only one, in the office, on the team, or in the room.

This chapter is yours.

To Those Who Grew Up Without a Father

I know what absence feels like. I know what it's like to carry a hole inside you. To wonder why he left. Whether he thought of you. Whether he cared.

I know the questions that circle in the night: *Did I matter to him? Was I enough?*

But here's what I've learned: You are not broken. You are not defined by someone else's absence. You do not need their presence to become whole. You do not need their approval to succeed. And you do not need their love to be worthy of love.

For thirty years, I believed something vital was missing in me.

But when I finally met my father, I realised: I had already built something solid on my own.

You have too. The absence may have shaped you, but it does not get to define you.

To Those Who Don't Know Their Roots

Not knowing where you come from can leave you adrift. I knew my British side, my Yorkshire upbringing, the working-class pride I came from.

But my Jamaican side? My African ancestry? That part was a mystery. And because I didn't understand it, I felt unanchored.

If you've ever felt like you don't fully belong to your heritage, I see you.

But what I've discovered is this: Your past is already inside you. The blood of your ancestors runs through your veins. Their fire, their resilience, their prayers, their wisdom, They live in you. Even if you've never met them. Even if you've never heard their stories.

You carry a legacy older and deeper than you know. And when you begin to honour that legacy, you'll feel it move through you like a current.

To Those Caught Between Two Worlds

If you've ever felt like you didn't fully belong in one place or another, I understand.

In Morley, I was one of the only kids of colour in a town that wasn't built for difference.

Later, in Paris, in Geneva, in Zurich, I found myself in elite spaces where no one looked like me.

Even in my own family life, I felt the pull of two different worlds.

Maybe you feel it too.

The constant adaptation. The careful translation of who you are. The weight of always standing in between.

Here's what I wish someone had told me earlier: You don't have to pick a side. You are both. You are all of it.

And that isn't a weakness. It's a gift.

You can move between worlds. You carry dual perspective. You bridge cultures.

You don't need to shrink to fit. You expand what's possible.

That is power.

To Those Who Feel Like They Don't Belong

I spent years proving myself, that I was smart enough for grammar school. Tough enough for Morley. Capable enough for Paris, Geneva, Zurich. Worthy enough to sit across from CEOs and multi-millionaires. All while carrying the weight of not belonging.

But here's the truth I now hold: Belonging is not something you wait for. It's something you build.

Sometimes the world won't make space for you. You might have to carve your own.

Bring your own chair. Or build your own table.

But you deserve to be there. You deserve to rise, exactly as you are.

You Are Not Just Your Struggles, You Are Your Strength

You are not just the hard things that happened to you.

You are not just the questions you've carried, or the silence you've endured.

You are the light that kept burning when everything tried to dim it. You are the strength that held steady when the weight was heavy. You are the resilience that turned rejection into resolve. Isolation into insight. Pain into power.

I have questioned myself. I have doubted my place. I have felt the sting of being unseen.

But I also know this: Your story matters. And you are not alone.

Even the fact that you are reading this now, is proof that you are already on your way.

So take up space. Boldly. Own your identity. Fully. Carry your history. Proudly. And shape a legacy that no one else could ever write.

The World Is Watching and It Needs You

In 2020, the murder of George Floyd shook the world.

It shook me.

It wasn't new, but it shattered the illusion that silence was safe. It exposed how fragile dignity can be when it's not protected by power. And it ignited a global reckoning about race, belonging and breath itself.

In the weeks that followed, I wept. Not just for George Floyd. But for all of us.

For every person who's had to walk a little straighter, speak a little softer, shrink themselves a little smaller just to stay safe.

That moment reminded me: Being seen isn't a privilege. It's a necessity.

And those of us who've made it through the fire, who have a voice, a platform, a story, have a duty to use it.

The world doesn't just need your success. It needs your truth.

Building Without a Blueprint

- Even without a map, you've found your direction.
- Even without a blueprint, you've built something lasting.
- Your voice has weight. Speak it.
- Your presence changes rooms. Own it.
- Your future is yours to design.

Wherever you are, know this:

You belong. Not because the world paved a path for you, but because you paved your own. You filled the gaps. You rose from the silence. You became the structure you never had. You are not the exception. You are part of a lineage of builders, dreamers and defiers, people who shaped a life without ever being shown how.

And now…

It's your turn to lay the blueprint for others.

The Blueprint Toolkit – A Legacy of Lessons

This section is your companion for the road ahead.

These aren't just reflections, they're hard-won truths, tested in the silence, the struggle and the search for identity. Whether you've grown up without a guide, battled imposter syndrome, crossed class lines, or carried untold stories, each Blueprint captures a foundational lesson from a life built without instructions.

You may not have been handed a plan.
But you've still built something powerful.
And this toolkit?
It's your inheritance, distilled, strengthened and ready for the journey ahead.

---

1. Survival Without a Guide

Core Truth: You don't need a map when you become your own compass.
Leadership Insight: True leaders emerge not from perfect examples but from lived instinct.
Legacy Reminder: Your courage to chart your own path becomes a lighthouse for someone else.

---

2. Role Models in Imperfect Places

Core Truth: Even broken beginnings can produce powerful anchors.
Leadership Insight: Guidance doesn't always come from above. It often rises beside us.
Legacy Reminder: Your story proves that strength can come from the most unexpected sources.

---

3. Belonging Without Losing Yourself

Core Truth: You don't need to trade your roots to walk in elite rooms.
Leadership Insight: Presence with integrity transforms rooms more than performance ever could.
Legacy Reminder: Every time you show up as your full self, you widen the doorway for others.

---

4. Grit and Growth in the Wilderness Years

Core Truth: Hustle is a classroom. Struggle is curriculum.
Leadership Insight: The years that test you often teach the most about adaptability and grit.
Legacy Reminder: You don't just survive hard seasons, you translate them into strength for others.

---

5. Resilience in Ruthless Environments

Core Truth: You can be humble without being defeated.
Leadership Insight: Strategic composure isn't silence, it's power in restraint.
Legacy Reminder: You carried dignity where others expected collapse. That is its own inheritance.

---

6. Navigating Privilege Without Losing Identity

Core Truth: Adaptation isn't erasure, it's evolution.
Leadership Insight: Inclusive leadership means knowing your worth doesn't require assimilation.
Legacy Reminder: Every room you enter with truth makes it easier for others to do the same.

---

7. Healing the Father Wound & Reclaiming Identity

Core Truth: The search for what's missing becomes the journey to wholeness.
Leadership Insight: When you do the work to confront absence, you become someone else's presence.
Legacy Reminder: Healing begins when silence ends and you ended it.

---

8. Balancing Assimilation with Authenticity

Core Truth: You can hold your ground without raising your voice.
Leadership Insight: The quiet strength of rooted identity is more powerful than mimicry.
Legacy Reminder: You didn't just succeed, you did it without shrinking.

---

9. Breaking Generational Patterns Through Fatherhood

Core Truth: You can become what you never had.
Leadership Insight: Love leads louder than legacy.
Legacy Reminder: Your child will never wonder if they mattered. They will know.

---

10. Thriving in Abundance Without Losing Your Centre

Core Truth: External success reveals internal truths.
Leadership Insight: Stillness amid success is where real clarity - and compassion - are born.
Legacy Reminder: You showed that excellence without grounding is just decoration.

---

11. Identity, Growth & the Cost of Excellence

Core Truth: Growth is a mirror, not a trophy.
Leadership Insight: Transformation demands reflection, not just ambition.
Legacy Reminder: You turned imposter syndrome into insight. That is a roadmap for others.

---

12. Reclaiming Identity Through Ancestral Connection

Core Truth: The silence around your story was never empty, it was waiting.
Leadership Insight: Cultural attunement isn't about performance. It's about honour.
Legacy Reminder: You didn't just reconnect, you remembered aloud, so others could follow.

---

13. Wholeness Over Perfection

Core Truth: Healing is not performance. It's presence.
Leadership Insight: Wholeness invites others to stop hiding and start leading with truth.
Legacy Reminder: You stopped striving to impress and started standing to impact.

---

14. Becoming the Fire for Others

Core Truth: At some point, healing becomes leadership.
Leadership Insight: Once you reclaim your voice, your story becomes someone else's permission slip.
Legacy Reminder: You didn't just break cycles. You built blueprints.

EPILOGUE – BUILT WITHOUT A BLUEPRINT

Looking back, it all feels like a blur and yet more vivid than ever.

The streets of Morley. The classrooms of QEGS. The chaos of Birmingham. The sharp edges of London. The elegance of Paris. The precision of Switzerland. The opulence of Dubai.

Each place shaped me.

A different lesson. A different scar. A different strength.

But as I stand here now, with the battle wounds, the wisdom and the will to keep going, I know this story was never just about survival or success.

It was about becoming whole. About shedding the shame. Reclaiming the roots. And building a life not from a perfect plan but from raw truth, from fire, from love.

I no longer soften the edges of who I am. I don't flinch at my story. I don't round off the truth to make it easier to swallow.

I say it with pride: I am the son of a single mother. I was raised in a town that tried to reject me. I carry the blood of Jamaican rebels and Yorkshire grafters. I have walked through elite spaces that weren't built for people like me and I held my ground.

But the greatest victory?

It wasn't the titles. It wasn't the travel. It wasn't the suits or the skyline views.

It was becoming the father I never had.

It was standing tall in front of my daughter and showing her: We come from survivors. We come from builders. We come from warriors. And we dare to dream beyond what we were given.

This book isn't just a reflection. It's a blueprint, drawn not from certainty but from courage. From every ancestor who refused to bow. Every mentor who showed up. Every friend who held space. Every child who needs to know that difference is not a deficit. It's a gift.

The next chapter is no longer just mine to write. It belongs to those walking behind me. Those still searching. Still healing. Still building without a blueprint.

To them I say: Your pain is not the end of your story. It's the beginning of your power.

So take your tools. Take your truth. Build boldly. And when it's your turn to lead, leave the light on.

Because someone else is finding their way.

And quietly, in the midst of healing and rebuilding, I've begun to open my heart again. Not to fill a gap but to share the fullness I've worked so hard to reclaim.

In this season, I've been reminded, *life is not a bed of roses.* But even among the thorns, there is tenderness.

Lessons tucked inside the struggle. Beauty that blooms through the cracks.

Love, I've come to learn, is not a finish line. It's a gentle invitation, to be seen, to be known, to walk forward not as a perfect man, but as a whole one.

And wherever that path may lead, I now have the courage to walk it, truthfully, tenderly and with hope.

A Personal Note: To My Sister and My Daughter

To my sister, Maria:

We were shaped in the same storms.
Your laughter, your resilience, your quiet strength,
these are stories still unfolding but powerful already.
You've faced the world with courage, just like our mum did.
And though our paths were different,
I see the same spark in you that once saved me.
You've reminded me that wholeness isn't just a man's story.
It's a human one.
A legacy not of perfection but of progress.

This book isn't just my reckoning.
It's a gift I wish I could have handed you sooner,
A blueprint, built from all the lessons I had to learn the hard way.

So take what serves you.
Discard what doesn't.
And know this:
You're not just part of the legacy.
You are its next chapter.

To my daughter:
Your arrival changed everything.
You gave me a reason to rewire what I thought fatherhood could be.
I wrote this, in part, so that one day you'd know exactly where you come from,
Not just the places and people but the battles fought in silence, and the lessons carved out of struggle.
You are the brightest part of my legacy.
Through you, I discovered what unconditional love truly means, not as an idea but as a presence, a promise, a way of being.
I love you more than words will ever fully hold.
And I will always, always be there for you.
In every season.
In every chapter.
For as long as I live - and beyond.

With love and gratitude,
Ashley, Papa, Big Bro.

XXX

WHERE NEXT?

This book may have come to an end, but your journey hasn't.

If something stirred in you as you read a memory, a moment, a question you've carried quietly for years, you are not alone.

Whether you're navigating life without a blueprint, leading others while healing yourself, or simply searching for deeper truth and belonging, there are paths forward.

Here are some ways to keep walking:

Find Support or Community

Transformation doesn't happen alone. If you're processing the themes in this book and need a next step, here are some trusted spaces to explore:

- **Therapy and Mental Health Support**
  - Mind (UK)
  - Shout (24/7 text line)
  - Rethink Mental Illness
  - Mental Health UK
  - Hub of Hope
  - United for Global Mental Health

- **Mentorship & Role Model Networks**
  - Cross-Organisational Mentoring Circles
  - We Rise In
  - B-MEntor Mentoring Programme
  - The Black Heart Foundation

Stay Connected

I share monthly reflections on identity, resilience, and leadership for anyone building without a map.

Join the newsletter:

www.builtwithoutablueprint.com

Ashley Mills

Instagram: @AshleyMillsBlueprint

LinkedIn: https://www.linkedin.com/in/mrashleymills/

X: @ashleypmills

Printed in Dunstable, United Kingdom

72664673R00248